The Censor's Hand

Basic Bioethics

Arthur Caplan, editor

A complete list of the books in the Basic Bioethics series appears at the back of this book.

The Censor's Hand

The Misregulation of Human-Subject Research

Carl E. Schneider

The MIT Press
Cambridge, Massachusetts
London, England

MIT Press books may be purchased at special quantity discounts for business or sales promotional use. For information, please email special_sales@mitpress.mit.edu.

This book was set in Sabon by the MIT Press. Printed and bound in the United States of America.

Library of Congress Cataloging-in-Publication Data
Schneider, Carl E., 1948– , author.
The censor's hand : the misregulation of human-subject research / Carl E. Schneider.
    p. ; cm. — (Basic bioethics)
Includes bibliographical references and index.
ISBN 978-0-262-02891-2 (hardcover : alk. paper)
I. Title. II. Series: Basic bioethics.
[DNLM: 1. Human Experimentation—ethics. 2. Bioethical Issues. 3. Ethics, Research. 4. Research Subjects. W 20.55.H9]
R853.H8
174.2'8—dc23

2014034246

10 9 8 7 6 5 4 3 2 1

TO JOAN

κλαῖε δ᾽ ἔχων ἄλοχον θυμαρέα, κεδνὰ ἰδυῖαν.

Contents

Series Foreword

Glenn McGee and I developed the Basic Bioethics series and collaborated as series coeditors from 1998 to 2008. In fall 2008 and spring 2009, the series was reconstituted, with a new editorial board, under my sole editorship. I am pleased to present the forty-fourth book in the series.

The Basic Bioethics series makes innovative works in bioethics available to a broad audience and introduces seminal scholarly manuscripts, state-of-the-art reference works, and textbooks. Topics engaged include the philosophy of medicine, advancing genetics and biotechnology, end-of-life care, health and social policy, and the empirical study of biomedical life. Interdisciplinary work is encouraged.

Arthur Caplan

Basic Bioethics Series Editorial Board
Joseph J. Fins
Rosamond Rhodes
Nadia N. Sawicki
Jan Helge Solbakk

Preface

CITATION PRACTICES

Convention requires "et al." or another graceless locution in text for multi-author works. For euphony, I name both authors of a two-author article but only the first author of several-author articles, leaving the full citation to the footnote.

I use lawyers' citation forms because I use legal sources ill-cited otherwise. In lawyers' style, the volume number of a journal precedes the name of the journal, the page number on which the article begins follows the name of the journal, the page on which a quotation appears follows the initial page, and the date concludes the series. Thus 92 Annals of Internal Medicine 832, 834 (1980), cites a quotation on page 834 of an article published in 1980 that starts on page 832 of volume 92 of the Annals of Internal Medicine. I vary from lawyers' practice in one way—I do not cite pages of quotations from very short articles. And I have almost avoided textual footnotes.

ACRONYMS (ORGANIZATIONS)

AAUP is the American Association of University Professors
FDA is the Food and Drug Administration
HHS is the U.S. Department of Health and Human Services
IOM is the Institute of Medicine
The National Commission is the National Commission for the Protection of Human Subjects of Biomedical and Behavioral Research
NBAC is the National Bioethics Advisory Commission

NRC is the National Research Council

OHRP is the Office for Human Research Protections

The President's Commission is the President's Commission for the Study of Ethical Problems in Medicine and Biomedical and Behavioral Research

ACRONYMS (TERMS)

ELBW is "extremely low birth weight" babies (who weigh 14–35 ounces)

ICU is intensive care unit

NICU is neonatal intensive care unit

ABBREVIATED JOURNAL NAMES

AEM is Academic Emergency Medicine

AJOB is the American Journal of Bioethics

AM is Academic Medicine

AnIM is the Annals of Internal Medicine

ArIM is the Archives of Internal Medicine

BMJ is the British Medical Journal

HCR is the Hastings Center Report

IRB is IRB: Ethics & Human Research

J is Journal or Journal of

JAMA is the Journal of the American Medical Association

JERHRE is the Journal of Empirical Research on Human Research Ethics

JLME is the Journal of Law, Medicine & Ethics

L Rev is Law Review

NAP is the National Academies Press

NEJM is the New England Journal of Medicine

NwS is the IRB Symposium at 101 Northwestern University Law Review 399 (2007)

SSM is Social Science and Medicine

SHORT TERMS FOR IRB MANUALS

Amdur, *Handbook* is Robert J. Amdur, The Institutional Review Board Member Handbook (Jones & Bartlett, 2002)

Bankert & Amdur is Elizabeth A. Bankert & Robert J. Amdur, Institutional Review Board: Management and Function (Jones & Bartlett, 2006) (2nd ed.)

Mazur, *Guide* is Dennis J. Mazur, Evaluating the Science and Ethics of Research on Humans: A Guide for IRB Members (Johns Hopkins University Press, 2007)

OHRP *Guidebook* is the OHRP *IRB Guidebook*, http://www.hhs.gov/ohrp/archive/irb/irb_guidebook.htm

OHRP DIRECTORS

Jerry Menikoff	2008–
Ivor Pritchard	2007–2008
Bernard A. Schwetz	2003–2007
Greg Koski	2000–2002

Acknowledgments

This book had its start in plans Simon N. Whitney, M.D., J.D., and I had to write an article criticizing the IRB system. It soon became plain a book was necessary. That book took shape during many long discussions we had about law, medicine, research, rhetoric, and persuasion. It benefitted richly from Simon's broad knowledge of medicine, his acute understanding of law, his research into and writing about many aspects of IRB activities, and his frequent reading of manuscripts.

Because information about how IRBs work is so scattered, this has been a laborious project. My labors would have been wretchedly long but for an exceptional secretary, Shelley Anzalone, whose fine work with both my sources and my drafts has been indispensable. My labors were also sustained by the University of Michigan Law School's Cook, Wolfson, and Elkes funds and the Homeland Foundation's gift of my chair. The *good* men do can live after them.

I joyfully thank many colleagues for much help. From the start two remarkable people—Paula Knudson and Jon Tyson—offered aid and inspiration. Omri Ben-Shahar, Philip Hamburger, and Charles T. Myers offered sage guidance. Nicholas Bagley, Omri Ben-Shahar, Mark Hall, Sydney Halpern, Philip Hamburger, Carol Heimer, Don Herzog, David Hyman, James Lindgren, Carl J. Schneider, Dorothy Schneider, Joan Schneider, Zachary Schrag, Jon Tyson, and Susan Wootton all nobly read and instructively criticized entire drafts. Many colleagues both at Michigan and around the country gave generously of wise counsel when I most needed it. Among these valued friends I owe a special debt to Marie Deveney and Martin Pernick. Finally, Joan Schneider contributed magnificently to this book in every way that I can imagine. *Amicus certus in re incerta cernitur.*

Finally, while writing this book I have become ever more aware of how much I, my family, and the world are indebted to the people who participate in human-subject research, both as researchers and subjects. If this book helps liberate them from the irrational ways the IRB system interferes with the good they do, I will only have begun to repay my debt.

[If the] censor's hand [must] be his bail and surety that he is no idiot or seducer, it cannot be but a dishonour and derogation to the author, to the book, to the privilege and dignity of learning.

—John Milton, *Areopagitica*

Introduction

The science of constructing a commonwealth, or renovating it, or reforming it, is, like every other experimental science, not to be taught a priori. ... [V]ery plausible schemes, with very pleasing commencements, have often shameful and lamentable conclusions.

—Edmund Burke, *Reflections on the Revolution in France*

No research using "human subjects" may be done in an institution receiving federal research funds unless an "Institutional Review Board" licenses and monitors it. Not just federally funded research, but all research, however funded. Not just biomedical, but social-science research. Not just faculty research, but students' and staff's. IRBs are appointed by researchers' institutions, but they are required and overseen by the federal Office for Human Research Protections.

The ideals underlying the IRB system—that research subjects' informed consent should be obtained and that they should be protected from harm—have "long been at the center of scientists' moral traditions."[1] Nor is ethical review of research new. But the IRB system's proximate cause was the revelation of the Public Health Services' Tuskegee study of untreated syphilis among poor blacks, a revelation that reanimated memories of the Nazi atrocities that inspired the Nuremberg Code. The National Research Act (1974) obliged HHS to oblige institutions seeking research funds (principally universities and hospitals) to have IRBs.[2] HHS created what is now OHRP to supervise IRBs.[3] The act also mandated a National Commission for the Protection of Human Subjects of Biomedical and Behavioral Research, whose Belmont Report stated the IRB system's foundational guidelines.

Halpern divides the system's history into four phases. In its "formative period" (through the early 1980s), its core features were established, but its yoke was easy. During a consolidation period (through the early 1990s), oversight expanded. In the enforcement period (through the late 1990s) "federal policy makers depicted IRBs as overtaxed and inadequately supported by sponsoring institutions," and HHS expanded its purview, abandoned "its largely educative stance," grew "unprecedentedly rigid," and launched "compliance action that suspended IRB operations at major universities." Thus research institutions became "highly risk averse." Finally, starting in the late 1990s, a reprivatization period moved toward accreditation of institutions' regulation of research.[4]

Each institution appoints its own IRBs, predominantly from its own faculty, physicians, and staff. IRBs must have more than four members. At least one cannot be an employee, at least one's primary concerns must be scientific, and at least one's primary concerns must be nonscientific. Members should be expert, experienced, and diverse enough to command respect.

IRBs have imposing authority. First, the federal regulations' definitions are broad and loose: Research is "a systematic investigation, including research development, testing and evaluation, designed to develop or contribute to generalizable knowledge."[5] A human subject is a living person about whom a researcher "obtains (1) [d]ata through intervention or interaction with the individual, or (2) [i]dentifiable private information."[6] IRBs thus regulate not just cancer trials but studies of violin lessons. IRBs must require that risks be "minimized"; that they be "reasonable in relation to anticipated benefits"; that subjects be selected equitably; that consent be (elaborately) obtained; that data be (elaborately) monitored; that privacy be (elaborately) guarded; and that "additional safeguards" protect "vulnerable" subjects.[7]

IRBs interpret these broad and loose regulations broadly and loosely. Even "exempt" research is reviewed to make sure it is exempt. IRBs increasingly define quality-improvement programs as research. And OHRP, IRBs, and the literature treat regulations as a floor for, not the ceiling of, IRB authority. IRBs view their mission broadly and loosely. They do not just protect subjects; they ask if research is "ethical." They evaluate not just ethics, but methodology and scholarship. They increasingly monitor research while it is conducted and while its results are analyzed and published. Many IRBs enforce conflict-of-interest rules and HIPAA confidentiality regulations. IRBs are building "mechanisms to ensure that institutions, IRBs, and investigators are following regulations and guidance."[8] IRBs teach researchers ethics and test their learning.

IRBs are increasingly exigent. They regulate slighter chances of slighter harms (psychological, social, economic, legal, and dignitary). IRBs may shelter subjects from "depression, altered self-concept, increased anxiety, decreased confidence in others, guilt, shame, fear, embarrassment, boredom, frustration, receiving information about oneself that is unpleasant, and inconvenience."[9]

All this understates IRB authority, for researchers cannot effectively appeal IRB decisions within their institution, to OHRP, or to a court. IRBs may operate as secretly as they wish and need explain decisions only when flatly forbidding research. Thus IRBs not only have virtually plenary discretion, their decisions are procedurally insulated from challenge.

The breadth and detail of IRB review are suggested by the University of Michigan Medical School's IRB application form. It contains 993 questions, many directed to particular areas, but many requiring complex answers or documentation. The form asks about a project's personnel and their ethics training, sponsors and funding, consent, consent-form templates, the research's significance and benefits, risks to the subjects, recruitment of subjects, financial documents, special considerations and vulnerable subjects, payments, confidentiality, and more. Or consider the breadth and detail of IRB review in a garden-variety study:

CASE STUDY: FREE PARKING

Extremely low birth weight infants weigh from about 14 to 35 ounces. They are usually 3 months premature. Many die; all must fight for life. Those who live stay in the neonatal intensive care unit as they are stabilized and coaxed to grow. On average, they are hospitalized almost 100 days at $3,035 per day. Parental involvement shortens hospital stays, teaches parents to care for the child, and encourages follow-up care and evaluation. And it helps the infants. Parents have more time to feed a child than a nurse. Babies whose parents change, feed, console, and bathe them get fewer infections (since fewer people touch them). Mothers can feed children fresh breast milk, which reduces the risk of visual problems and of major infections that can prolong NICU stays and impair mental development.

Patricia Evans was a NICU attending physician who wanted to improve care. Research had suggested that the cost of parking discouraged parents from visiting. It costs $10 to park for 3 hours, so a family might pay $1,000 during a hospitalization. Mothers of ELBW babies are often single and poor, NICU bills are enormous, and children need months or even years of costly care and attention. Evans and her colleagues hypothesized that free parking would help bring parents to the NICU and lower its costs. The hospital wanted proof, so she proposed giving a random half of the parents free parking—a simple, harmless, beneficial study. It would leave half the parents where they were and give the others perhaps $1,000 in parking.

Had the hospital wished, it could simply have given parents free parking. But this was "research," so it needed IRB permission. Evans' IRB application detailed her plan. The IRB was free to examine any aspect of her research in any way. It required, for example, informed consent; that is, Evans had to warn parents of the risk of offering them a 50-50 chance of a $1,000 voucher and of asking them a few questions. Originally, consent had to be in writing and include a HIPAA (privacy) release. The IRB required a data and safety monitoring plan. The IRB required that the research data be stored in a locked file in an office on a secure floor.

Even after the IRB approved the research, it supervised it, as Evans' log of interactions with the IRB shows. It began on June 21, 2007, with the application. Even before the analysis was complete, the log included the entries shown in table I.1.

Why so many entries? Some reflect annual IRB review, some a requirement that everybody involved annually submit a CV and proof of completion of ethics training. Some are requests for and grants of IRB approval of changes in research personnel. Some report protocol violations. (At one point, the researchers found that one person's consent and HIPAA forms were missing and that another's HIPAA form was unsigned. As the IRB later put it, "[t]hese deviations were reported on one Protocol Deviation form.")

The breadth and detail of IRB authority increase rapidly. The number of IRBs, members, and applications have grown, and "the number of IRB professionals has grown especially dramatically." The IRB movement comprises not only IRBs and their staff but organizations like PRIM&R

Table I.1
Evans' Log of Interactions with the IRB

Initial application submission	Continuing review submitted	Continuing review submitted
Pre-review corrections requested	Assigned for expedited review	Review and notification sign-off
Pre-review corrections submitted	Approval of continuing review	Review and notification sign-off
Pre-review corrections requested	Personnel change request submitted	Change request submitted
Review process for MHH initiated	Change request submitted	Pre-review corrections requested
Pre-review corrections requested	Approval of removal of W. from team	Change request submitted
Sign-off removal	Approval of Spanish surveys	Pre-review corrections requested
Sign-off reminder	Change request submitted	Protocol reviewed and approved pending
Assigned for expedited review	Pre-review corrections requested	Change request submitted
Protocol reviewed and approved pending	Change request submitted	Notice of assignment for expedited review
Pre-review corrections requested	Pre-review corrections requested	Approval—Spanish letter of information
Assigned for expedited review	Approval of addition of L. to team	Notice of assignment for expedited review
Approval to begin research by expedited review and approval	Change request submitted	Notice of continuing review approval
Change request submitted—protocol	Pre-review corrections requested	E-mail to staff
Assigned for review by SAC 08/30/07	Approval of addition of R. to team	Approval—waiver of signed HIPAA form
Pre-review corrections requested	Approval to remove B. and add K. to team	Submitted personnel change request
Assigned for expedited review	First notice of continuing review	Pre-review corrections needed
Approval to implement requested changes	Change request submitted	Submitted pre-review corrections
Change request submitted	Second notice of continuing review	Pre-review corrections needed
Change request submitted	Pre-review corrections requested	Submitted pre-review corrections
Approval of activity log	Pre-review corrections requested	Approval—change of personnel
Pre-review corrections requested	Correction submitted	Additional information required
Assigned for expedited review	Assigned for expedited review	Principal investigator sign-off notification
Approval of data forms	Change request submitted	Require stamped copy, Spanish information sheet
Change request submitted	Pre-review corrections requested	Notification of subject death
Assigned for expedited review	Final notification of continuing review	Subject death notification not required
Assigned for expedited review	Approval—waiver of informed consent	
	Letter from K. to G.	

Table I.1 (cont.)

Decision to defer request response submitted	Impending termination of continuing review	Notice of assignment for expedited review
Assigned for expedited review	Review and notification sign-off	CPHS monitoring visit required
Approval of revised ICF	Review and notification sign-off reminder	Human subjects education certification expired
Submission of misc. study documents	Review and notification sign-off	Protocol deviation received and reviewed
Approval of map, welcome letter, booklet	Review and notification sign-off reminder	Approved by expedited review
Submission of misc. study documents	Continuing review submitted	CPHS oversight monitoring report
Approval of Spanish ICF	Assigned for expedited review	1st notification of continuing review
Submission of misc. study documents	Approval of continuing review	2nd notification of continuing review
Approval of Spanish weekly log	Correction submitted	Final notification of continuing review
Change request submitted	Approval of addition of N. to team	Impending termination of continuing review
Approval of changes to satisfaction survey	First notification of continuing review	Notice of assignment for expedited review
First notice of continuing review	Change request submitted	Study closure confirmation
Change request submitted	Review and notification sign-off	Principal investigator sign-off notification
Assigned for expedited review	Review and notification sign-off	Review and notification sign-off
Approval of updated PKSA	Approval—updated information sheet	Notice of approval to implement requested changes
Second notice of continuing review	Second notification of continuing review	Notice of assignment for expedited review
	Final notification of continuing review	Notice of approval to implement changes

(Public Responsibility in Medicine and Research), CITI (the Collaborative Institutional Training Initiative), and AAHRPP (the Association for the Accreditation of Human Research Protection Programs). It includes people who study, write about, or teach research ethics. The movement wants professional status and advocates standards, certification, and continuing education.[10] There are "certified ethicists, ethics conferences, training workshops, professional literature, scholarly journals, research programs, local networks, and national and international associations focused on research ethics."[11]

The IRB movement finds unity in its creed. As van den Hoonaard found at national meetings in America and Canada, "there were no critical challenges posed about the ethics-review system itself. No critical self-reflection about the work and nature of ethics committees. Participants of both conferences lived in a bubble of compliance. Unlike academic conferences, there were no voices of dissent, nor were any expected."[12] Thought in this bubble is articulated in OHRP's pronouncements, government and elite committees' reports, manuals instructing IRB members,[13] and journal articles.

OHRP's first director—Greg Koski—limns the creed. Research uses people as an end, which appears "to violate the fundamental ethical principle of respect for persons." Such "exploitation" is tolerable only if research is done "responsibly within an established framework of ethical principles." But research scientists' abuses "fostered a regulatory approach" to research. Biomedicine's "noble reputation" was "severely compromised" by the crimes of German and Japanese doctors and scientists during World War II. "The extreme nature of these atrocities may have allowed American scientists" to disregard them—until Tuskegee and other scandals, many described in Henry Beecher's influential 1966 article.[14]

After Tuskegee, Congress wanted clearer research ethics and "a regulatory framework" to "ensure" that publicly funded research was ethical. "Having already decided that the competing interests of scientists precluded their ability to independently govern their own conduct, a system of peer oversight" was adopted. "Regrettably, from the outset neither" principles nor regulations "were enthusiastically embraced by the research community." Only when researchers had to have "some training in research ethics" did they even begin to read OHRP's principles.[15] Because researchers' scientific zeal may blind them to ethical problems, IRBs with wide authority and discretion must license and supervise each research project.

I need a term for people who generally support the IRB project. "Regulationist" seems neutral and workable. It is a generalization, like, say, "environmentalist." Like "environmentalist," it is imprecise: everybody wants research regulated in some fashion (as I do). Like "environmentalist," the term encompasses a range of opinion. Among regulationists are true believers in the present system, purifiers who think it rightly conceived but poorly run, reformers who favor licensing research but with significant changes, and exemptionists who would exclude some kinds of research from scrutiny.[16]

For example, in 2011 OHRP's "advanced notice of proposed rulemaking"[17] (ANPRM) acknowledged serious problems in the IRB system, including mismatching the severity of review with the severity of the risk, multiple reviews of single studies, and obscure guidance. Yet the ANPRM suggested no doubts about the system's basic structure and assumptions, and while some of its proposals might moderate the system's inefficiency, others would expand its reach and intensify its scrutiny.

IRBs are agencies established by government and wielding government power. They do not just debate ethics; they make and enforce decisions. Measured by their growth and power, they are successful agencies. But the measure of regulatory success is not an agency's size or strength but whether it does—or can do—more good than harm. Each regulatory problem presents its own issues and solutions. Yet the IRB system is so anomalous, so flouts core regulatory principles, that it demands scrutiny. IRBs are anomalous because virtually identical but far riskier activities are regulated far less severely. "IRBs' review of research projects is both more frequent (annual review of every project) and more intense (requiring human subjects training, registration of staff, adoption of very specific routines, e.g., for informed consent and for data storage) than is oversight of most professional workers."[18] More specifically, doctors must daily use unproved treatments, and patients often face choices much more numerous and dangerous than most research subjects. Doctors cause over 50,000 unnecessary deaths annually—incalculably more than research misconduct in all its history. Yet doctors are regulated by licenses and tort liability, not a Treatment Review Board. Journalists routinely expose people to many and harsh risks and sometimes try to expose and even ruin them (for idle or lofty reasons). Yet journalists rarely need fear litigation, much less a Press Review Board.

IRBs have anomalously unfettered discretion. What agency is so little constrained by law or accountability? Courts and agencies must explain their actions publicly; IRBs need not explain decisions even to themselves and may operate in secret. Agencies' decisions can be appealed; IRBs' decisions cannot be. Agencies report to bureaucratic superiors; OHRP's small staff could not supervise the flood of IRB decisions even if it wanted to.

IRBs are anomalous because they are censors, an enterprise virtually driven out of American law. And IRBs censor in universities, where freedom of inquiry and expression are vital.

But are IRBs desirable even if anomalous? The conventional answer is Koski's: that only they can protect subjects. Regulation is one of the balkier human enterprises, however, and anyone recruiting the state's co-ercive power to restrict citizens' freedom and expend their resources owes them well-founded reasons. Yet neither at the IRB system's inception, nor during its rise, nor in its present triumph have such reasons been given. Despite pleas "for measures of IRB quality and effectiveness," Abbott and Grady "could not identify one study that evaluated the effect that IRB review has on the protection of human subjects."[19] And "few studies" have investigated how the system works.[20] For all anyone knows, IRBs chronically approve bad but impede good research.

So does the IRB system meet the fundamental regulatory criterion—that it do more good than harm? Can it? Part I begins to answer these questions by examining the extent of and reasons for the system's costs and benefits. Because so little is known about IRBs' efficacy, chapter 1 principally asks how much good IRBs can do. Surprisingly, research is not especially dangerous. Some biomedical research *can* be risky, but much of it requires no physical contact with patients, and most contact cannot cause serious injury. Ill patients are, if anything, safer in than out of research. Social-science research cannot injure people physically, and its risks are trivial compared with daily risks like going online or on a date. Research, Hamburger concludes, has been far less risky "than many entirely ordinary activities" like walking.[21] No doubt IRBs sometimes make research safer and better. But they have less scope to do good than their harshness suggests because research is safer than their rhetoric of scandal implies.

Chapter 2 argues that regulatory choices drive the IRB system's costs abnormally high. The IRB system might, for example, make researchers partners in writing and enforcing research ethics. Or it might punish and exact restitution from erring researchers. Crucially, however, it instead uses an extravagant version—"event licensing"—of a costly regulatory form—"command and control." Event licensing requires IRBs to examine every study in advance. Event licensing makes sense only if activities are exceptionally dangerous or actors are exceptionally unscrupulous, other-wise mountains of innocuous projects must be reviewed to find molehills of baneful ones. Event licensing's costs are raised by the crescendoing intensity of review, which is driven by the distrust, even demonization, of researchers that animates the IRB ethos.

Furthermore, intensively reviewing so many protocols promotes another structural feature of IRBs—bureaucratization. Bureaucratized event licensing requires thousands of IRB members (often expensive people, like doctors) and burgeoning staffs. Researchers must devote scarce resources to dealing with IRBs (in some multisite studies, 15% of the research budget). IRBs, chapter 2 finds, delay, distort, stop, and deter research; impede training in research; and drive researchers from fields IRBs regulate. "Because research on human subjects is how we produce the innovations that improve health, reduce morbidity or mortality, and alleviate human suffering, preventing or delaying research results in vastly more suffering and death than occurs from researchers' ethical lapses."[22]

Part I, then, contends that IRBs have modest scope to do good because they regulate so much research that is so little risky and that IRBs are inescapably costly in dollars, lives, health, and welfare. In short, the system can hardly help doing more harm than good.

IRBs' costs and benefits both depend on how well IRBs make decisions. Part II argues that IRBs' structure, incentives, and ethos all impair IRBs' decisions. Chapter 3 finds much evidence that IRBs make decisions poorly. For example, it describes multisite research in which IRBs treat identical protocols so variously that one study concluded that decisions "defied any pattern" except "that IRBs approve inappropriate investigations and inhibit appropriate investigations."[23] Chapter 3 finds that bureaucratized event licensing so overtaxes IRBs that informed and thoughtful decisions are discouraged, especially when IRBs regulate so many specialized fields that tyros must routinely make expert judgments. IRB incentives also distort decisions. Unlike the FDA, which weighs a drug's benefits against its costs, IRBs are told to protect research subjects without considering protection's costs. Also, if IRBs say no to research, they are safe; if they say yes, they risk institutional disgrace, lawsuits, and federal sanctions that have included (briefly but unforgettably) closing down research at major universities.

Reviewing consent documents preoccupies IRBs, yet much research shows that people understand little that those documents say, even in optimal circumstances.[24] "Consenting" chronically falls between two stools: complete information and comprehensible information. Bureaucratization, distrust of researchers, and fear of liability push IRBs to prefer completeness to comprehension and to make forms grow longer, denser, and deadlier. Research ethics thus comes to mean having subjects sign "documents that conform to the increasingly rigid specifications of OHRP,"[25] while protecting IRBs and their institutions can edge out protecting subjects.

Bureaucrats need good guidance to make good decisions, so IRBs thus need a coherent and legible ethics. Instead, chapter 4 finds, they get the Belmont Report's principles—respect for persons, justice, and beneficence. But as Holmes said, "General propositions do not decide concrete cases." In addition, a "bureaucratized research ethics is essentially an ethics of documentation."[26] Yet how could anyone write a coherent and legible ethics when so many disciplines with so many complex ethical problems must be managed, and researchers (who best know their disciplines' problems) are largely excluded from the task? Finally, IRB ethics privilege autonomy, but IRBs are "deeply and pervasively paternalistic,"[27] for they tell people whether and how they may participate in research, even though research subjects as a class are no less competent to evaluate risks than, say, patients contemplating surgery or homeowners choosing a mortgage. The IRB ethos aggravates IRB paternalism by treating research subjects as manipulable victims while anathematizing researchers.

Even if IRBs lacked an adequate ethics, they could have effective rules, but chapter 5 finds that IRB regulations are so vague and crude that subjectivity reigns. As one IRB manual says, "Each member will have a different threshold for when he or she becomes concerned about a scientific protocol or informed consent form."[28] To make good decisions, agencies also need good procedures—in lawyers' terms, due process. IRBs, however, need respect *none* of due process's basic elements. Finally, while bureaucratic decisions benefit from accountability, IRBs essentially need not explain their decisions to researchers, an appeals board, or a court. In short, IRBs make poor decisions because they are essentially lawless and unaccountable.

IRBs' decisions are also warped by their role as censors: IRBs tell researchers what they may study, how they may conduct research, what they may say to subjects, and how they may report results. Chapter 6 consults first-amendment jurisprudence to see how IRBs' censorship duties lead them to underweight interests in free inquiry and speech. For example, censors ordinarily prefer orthodoxy to heterodoxy, and chapter 6 reviews evidence that IRBs tend toward orthodoxy in both scholarship and ideology.

In sum, the IRB system has proved a poor tool because it is compounded of ill-judged regulatory choices. It was born out of scandal, not study of the extent and nature of ethical problems and of possible solutions to them. Its framers were too inexpert in regulation to appreciate the costs of event licensing. Its design invites IRB imperialism, and it has invaded new areas (like social-science research) and seized new powers (like reviewing the substance and methods of research). What Becker called moral entrepreneurship leads the movement always to see new evils to suppress, and IRBs have reasons to regulate more research ever more strictly. The system today is so distant from its origins that Zywicki thinks that IRBs' "defining feature" may be a "tendency to expand well beyond their originally designed scope and purpose."[29]

To find the IRB system fundamentally misconceived is *not* to oppose regulating research. The problem is not regulation, but bad regulation. Were IRBs abolished today, research would still be regulated: Funders often review research ethics. Injured subjects may sue researchers for damages, as injured patients may sue doctors. Unethical researchers risk formal and informal professional sanctions, including loss of standing, funding, publication, and jobs. Those sanctions can be much increased, even through criminal penalties. I object not to severity, but to severity that does more harm than good. Furthermore, the modern view is that regulation is most effective not when it is severe but when people regulated believe its source is legitimate, its procedures just, and its principles wise. I object not to regulation, but to regulation based on a misunderstanding of what subjects need, researchers think, and regulation achieves.

It is right to be angry at unethical researchers, but it is foolish to regulate them destructively. We need a wise ethics of research, but the system promotes a puerile one. We need to discourage bad research, but amateurs are unsuited to do so. We should cherish research subjects, but IRBs protect them erratically and perversely. Researchers must be law-abiding and accountable, but lawless and unaccountable regulation is a feckless means to that goal. In short, the IRB system was perhaps a plausible scheme. Perhaps it had a pleasing commencement. But it is demonstrably having shameful and lamentable conclusions. If its deficiencies could be repaired, reform would be the answer. But because the system is fundamentally misconceived, it should be abolished and replaced by regulation that does more good than harm.

Part I
More Good than Harm

Some research can harm subjects. Some researchers have behaved, are behaving, and will behave badly. But the regulatory issue is not whether bad things happen, it is what regulation—if any—can do more good than harm.

Part I begins to answer that question by comparing the IRB system's potential benefits with its actual costs. IRBs aspire to protect research subjects, so their benefit depends first on (1) the risk subjects run and (2) how well IRBs manage that risk. Chapter 1 assesses the risks of the categories of research IRBs regulate. It asks four questions: First, how do regulationists assess that risk? Second, what is the risk? Third, does researchers' untrustworthiness heighten risks? Fourth, by what standards should risk be evaluated?

Research is safer than regulationist rhetoric implies. Social-science research and much biomedical research cannot harm subjects physically. Most other research involves little opportunity for physical harm, serious physical harm is improbable in most of the remaining kinds, and many serious risks are diminished by the structure of research. And while all research can inflict social, psychological, and dignitary harm, it happens little and is rarely grave.

Chapter 2 assesses the system's costs. When it—and thus part I—are finished, we will find the modest good IRBs can do outweighed by the costs they exact. Part II suggests that IRBs do less good in practice than they might in theory. Chapter 3 concludes that IRBs make decisions so badly that they cannot reliably assess or reduce risks. Chapters 4 and 5 suggest that IRBs err because they lack the guidance—in ethics, regulations, and procedures—agencies need to work well. Chapter 6 describes another reason IRBs err: their task of censorship is basically incompatible with a free society. Finally, the IRB system's unsatisfactory ethics, unfair procedures, and erratic decisions hardly seem calculated to win researchers' respect and collaboration. In sum, IRBs cannot accomplish even the modest good part I describes.

1

Research Risk and Regulationist Stereotypes

There is no empirical evidence that IRBs have any benefit whatsoever.
—David Hyman, *IRBs: Is This the Least Worst We Can Do?*

A. INTRODUCTION: "THAT'S NOT LIKELY, BUT IT'S POSSIBLE"

[Subjecting] animal experimenters to special supervision and legislation … involves the revival of that animosity to discovery and to the application to life of the fruits of discovery which, upon the whole, has been the chief foe of human progress.
—John Dewey, *The Ethics of Animal Experimentation*

I begin with an example of what researchers do and IRBs regulate:

CASE STUDY: KEYSTONE[1]

Intensive care units try to keep desperately ill people alive long enough for their systems to recover. Crucial to an ICU's technology is the plastic tube threaded through a major vein into the central circulatory system. This "central line" lets doctors give drugs and fluids more quickly and precisely and track the patient's fluid status better.

Every tool has drawbacks. An infected IV in your arm is a nuisance, but the tip of a central line floats near your heart and can spread bacteria throughout your body. When antibiotics fail to stop these infections, patients die. Because there is one central-line infection for every 100 or 200 patient-days, a hospital like St. Luke's in Houston, with about 100 ICU beds, will have a central-line infection every day or two. There are perhaps 10,000 or 20,000 central-line fatalities annually, and a 2004 study estimated 28,000.

There is a well-known sequence of steps to follow to reduce these infections: (1) wash your hands, (2) don cap, mask, and gown, (3) swab the site with antibiotic, (4) use a sterile full-length drape, and (5) dab on antibiotic ointment when the line is in. Simple enough. But doctors in one study took all five steps only 62% of the time. No surprise. Doctors might forget to wash their hands. Or use an inferior alternative if the right drape or ointment is missing.

Peter Pronovost is a Johns Hopkins anesthesiologist and intensivist who proposed three changes. First, have a nurse with a checklist watching. If the doctor forgets to wash his hands, the nurse says, "Excuse me, Doctor McCoy, did you remember to wash your hands?" Second, tell the doctor to accept the nurse's reminder—to swallow hard and say, "I know I'm not perfect. I'll do it right." Third, have ICUs stock carts with everything needed for central lines.

It worked. Central-line infections at Johns Hopkins fell from 11 to about zero per thousand patient-days. This probably prevented 43 infections and 8 deaths and saved $2 million. In medical research, reducing a problem by 10% is ordinarily a triumph. Pronovost almost eliminated central-line infections. But would it work in other kinds of hospitals? Pronovost enlisted the Michigan Hospital Association in the Keystone Project. They tried the checklist in hospitals big and small, rich and poor. It worked again and probably saved 1,900 lives.

Then somebody complained to OHRP that Keystone was human-subject research conducted without informed consent. OHRP sent a harsh letter ordering Pronovost and the MHA to stop collecting data. OHRP did not say they had to stop trying to reduce infections with checklists; hospitals could use checklists to improve quality. But tracking and reporting the data was research and required the patients', doctors', and nurses' consent. And what research risks did OHRP identify? Ivor Pritchard, OHRP's Acting Director, argued that

"the quality of care could go down," and that an IRB review makes sure such risks are minimized. For instance, in the case of Pronovost's study, using the checklist could slow down care, or having nurses challenge physicians who were not following the checklist could stir animosity that interferes with care. "That's not likely, but it's possible," he said.

B. THE REGULATIONIST STEREOTYPE OF RESEARCH RISK

The history of bioethics follows a pattern . ... Some catastrophe happens, then people look for some rule that would have prevented the catastrophe. ... [T]hey do not think much about whether the rule may also prevent other things that would not be so bad in its absence, or whether the rule will prevent the next catastrophe.

—Jonathan Baron, *Against Bioethics*

Regulationists know little about research risks but treat them as dangerous. NBAC said that whether subjects in unregulated research are harmed more than those in regulated research "is not and cannot be known" but that "protecting the rights and welfare of all participants is necessary."[2] The IOM said that "until evidence is available" we must "pursue every promising mechanism to maximize" subjects' protection.[3] Robert Levine—a father of the IRB system and author of its bible[4]—advocates deference to "the reasoning and recommendations" of "deliberative bodies" like the [National] Commission and the President's Commission," whose membership, resources, and "circumstances" place on the rest of us a "weighty burden of proof."[5]

Instead of evidence and argument, regulationists use "justification by scandal." They invoke a few emblematic disgraces to show that research subjects are abused. Even as the principal scandals of their rhetoric recede into the past, even as their system moves into scandal-free areas of research, regulationists recite the litany of shame. As an OHRP director (Koski) wrote,

The noble reputation of biomedical science was severely compromised by revelations of atrocities and crimes ... by Nazi physicians in European concentration camps. ... The germ warfare experiments conducted by Japanese scientists ... are no less horrific. The extreme nature of these atrocities may have allowed American scientists to disavow their relevance, at least until revelation of the US Public Health Service [Tuskegee] Syphilis Study in 1972.

Thus "abuses" have "fostered a regulatory approach to oversight of human research."[6]

Justification by scandal is a bad way to make public policy. A scandal is not an argument; it is an event to be interpreted. This regulationists do not do. Consider Koski's linking of Nazi and American doctors. His logic is apparently that Nazi doctors did research and brutalized their victims.

American doctors do research. Therefore (?) American doctors brutal-
ize research subjects. Therefore (?) American doctors must be restrained.
Therefore (?) all human-subject research (including research where physical harm is impossible) must be regulated by something like the IRB system. This is not an argument but a series of dubious and dubiously related
assertions.

If Koski has an argument, it proves too much. The Nazis debased all
they touched, especially regulation and bureaucracy. If Nazi Germany has
lessons for today, they concern the danger of government, not citizens.
The last thing Nazi tyranny justifies is an unaccountable agency with unconstrained power. Furthermore, Nazi doctors doing research killed hundreds of prisoners; Nazi doctors practicing medicine killed thousands of
"defectives." By regulationist logic, doctors, more than researchers, need
government permission for every decision.

Worse, "the historical record has been mischaracterized. Harms to research subjects were (and are) rare and typically modest; harms attribut-
able to researcher misconduct were (and are) even rarer. The moral and
regulatory traditions of clinical researchers were often quite robust" and
long-standing. "And some research projects characterized in hindsight as
abusive did not seem morally wrong to either researchers or research subjects at the time." Furthermore, Nazi atrocities "occurred despite pre-war
German regulations, which were 'as strict and comprehensive as the post-
war Nuremberg Codes.'"[7]

In short, the IRB system received its impetus from and invokes a stereotype—unscrupulous researchers restrained only by the leash and muz-
zle of the IRB system. How accurate is that stereotype?

C. THE PHYSICAL RISKS OF HUMAN-SUBJECT RESEARCH

Researchers know that it is often inappropriate to rely primarily on anecdotal evi-
dence, on the isolated results of what happened in only one or another instance.
… Or, in shorthand terms: garbage in, garbage out.
—Jerry Menikoff (Director, OHRP), *Where's the Law?*

The regulationist stereotype is that subjects routinely risk serious physical injury. As Levine said, much regulationist literature assumes that being a subject "is a highly perilous business." But as Levine warned, that
is not true.[8]

1. AN OVERVIEW OF THE EVIDENCE

What, frighted with false fires?
—William Shakespeare, *Hamlet*

First, general evaluations of research risks have long found little to measure. In 1977—well before IRBs proliferated—2,000 researchers, 800 IRB members, and 1,000 subjects were asked about harmful effects from research not predictable "as integral to the procedure." The vast majority of projects had no such effects. Three percent of projects experienced harms (to an average of two subjects), generally trivial or temporary. The three projects with fatalities involved cancer research, and in two at least some subjects were already terminally ill.[9] Similarly, Levine reported that three large institutions studied "reported a very low incidence of injury to research subjects and an extremely low rate of injuries that could be attributed directly to the performance of research." In both 1981 and 1988, Levine concluded: "On the basis of all the empirical evidence" he knew, "the role of research subject is not particularly hazardous. ... [A]ttempts to portray it as such and arguments for policies designed to restrict research generally because it is hazardous are without warrant."[10] Recent literature reviews concur. Burris and Moss report that harm from research misconduct is "apparently very rare."[11] Saver says "the Advisory Committee on Human Radiation Experiments' comprehensive review of federally funded research ... determined that most studies posed only minimal risks of harm."[12]

Revealingly, OHRP compliance audits are *not* about death and disaster. Most commonly, they are about following and documenting "required procedures," about "poorly kept minutes, inappropriate use of expedited review, failure to make or document the required special findings for research involving children, lack of required diversity on the IRB, and poor management of continuing review." The "vast majority" of letters showed no harmed subjects, or undue risks, or even that "a substantive violation of the regulations (as opposed to a failure to document compliance) had occurred."[13]

Finally, if research is perilous, there should be a "trial effect" of research subjects faring worse than ordinary patients. But literature reviews repeatedly find none. In 1998, Edwards examined fifteen studies going back to 1971 (before IRBs' heyday) of physical harm from trial participation. Two studies found no difference, three a statistically non-significant trend toward *better* survival in trials. Seven found a statistically significant *higher* survival rate among subjects in trials.[14] Edwards' review offered "some support for the plausible belief that well-researched treatment protocols" help patients.[15] In 2001, Braunholtz (reviewing 21 trials, most of cancer treatments) found the evidence "not conclusive" but thought it likelier that clinical trials' effect is positive.[16] In 2004, Peppercorn reviewed 24 articles comparing cancer patients in and out of trials and discarded poor studies. Trial patients did better in seven of 17 comparisons. In four, trial patients in some subgroups did better, and in one trial patients had better endpoints by some measures. No studies found patients in trials doing worse.[17] Finally, in 2008 Vist's ambitious Cochrane review found no strong evidence of a trial effect of either kind.[18]

In sum, three kinds of evidence confirm Levine's view that being a subject "is not particularly hazardous."[19] First, surveys both before and after the rise of the IRB system found few examples of serious risk. Second, people and institutions with incentives to discover and publicize risk locate little. Third, studies repeatedly find that patients are not hurt and might be helped by being research subjects.

2.   WHY THE REGULATIONIST STEREOTYPE ERRS

This empirical evidence is confirmed by the strength of the explanations for it: The category of "human-subject research" cannot be as risky as the regulationist stereotype: First, most inquiries offer modest scope for harm. Second, research is constructed to minimize risks. Third, regulationists overestimate some kinds of serious risks.

First, research is safer than the regulationist stereotype because so much of it cannot cause physical harm, so little can cause serious physical harm, and serious risks often are not increased by research. Most damningly, the stereotype ignores social-science research, although it is a large part of IRBs' jurisdiction. Large categories of biomedical research are physically riskless: some need no encounter with patients; some use data already collected; some consult patients' charts; some use stored body parts and products. Some research is just observational. Much research (like "Free Parking") involves interaction but no physical contact: Researchers ask doctors to define brain death, or patients about taking prescriptions, or families about how asthma patients died.

Another hefty category of biomedical research involves physical contact without physical risks, like lung-function tests, ultrasounds, retinal photography, functional MRI of the brain to identify areas activated by performing work, photography to study light-sensitive retinal tissue, neurological examinations to track disease progression, tests of blood gases in mountain climbers at altitude, measurement of bladder pressure in incontinent patients, using contact lenses to monitor which visual cues are watched, testing saliva for HIV/AIDS infection, clipping toenails to study fungal infections, Pap smears to evaluate viral infections that precede cervical cancer, Doppler evaluation of blood flow in carotid arteries to assess cholesterol treatments, cheek swabs of superficial cells for DNA analysis, cutting hair for heavy metal analysis, and hearing tests of rock bands.

Some research involves physical contact in which nontrivial harm is nontrivially possible. Even it fits the regulationist stereotype badly. The issue is not whether patients may suffer harm during research; it is how much harm they risk *because they participate in research*. In most riskier research, patients are ill. Once you've made the mistake of becoming sick, both the illness and the treatment pose risks. The issue is how research increases them.

The baseline, then, is sickness and ordinary medical care. Crucially, much that the IRB system regulates because it is "research" is just ordinary medical care provided in a structured way. For example, there are often two standard treatments but doubt about which is better. Each has risks, but nobody knows which has fewer. In clinical medicine, patients routinely make such choices without government supervision. But when the choices are studied, treatment becomes research vulnerable to the severities of IRB review. This is exemplified by our next case study.

CASE STUDY: THE LOST CORD[20]

Very premature infants suffer serious complications and often die. When they are born, the obstetrician can either clamp and cut the umbilical cord immediately or wait until it stops pulsating. There are good arguments for both methods: The pulsations provide additional blood and reduce the risk of anemia. But the additional blood may overtax the infant's frail circulatory system and eventually cause respiratory distress and heart failure. No obstetrician consults any patient about when to clamp.

A fine study of clamping could easily be designed. Women in premature labor could be assigned randomly to early or late clamping, and each infant's progress could be tabulated. (Randomization is essential. If we simply compare the differences between children delivered by early and later clampers, we wouldn't know if the differences were caused by the time of clamping or by some other systematic characteristic of early or late clampers.) Hundreds of infants would have to be followed, but apart from the costs of coordinating the study and analyzing the data, the study would not be expensive and could be done in a reasonable time if several hospitals participated.

However, the neonatologists who believe this study is necessary also believe that IRBs would require consent from the women in labor, requiring a research nurse on duty all day every day at several centers for several years. The cost is prohibitive; the study impossible. So one of the cord-clamping practices is probably increasing the risk that very premature infants will suffer and die. We could easily find out. But the neonatologists who considered the study rejected it because their IRBs seemed too likely to prohibit the research.

Is the IRB system protecting mothers and infants? No. Every day doctors decide when to clamp cords. Either practice is proper in the present state of knowledge. No doctor asks for consent to early or late clamping. Research adds no risk. It simply makes the choice of treatment systematically, rather than haphazardly, random.

As this case suggests, much research does not increase risk because patients get what they would have gotten anyway—a standard treatment where no alternative is demonstrably superior. This is unpleasantly ordinary because, as Tyson writes, "many, if not most, therapies have unproven value," and "informal experimentation is commonplace in clinical practice."[21]

At the riskiest end of the research continuum, regulationists generally put Phase 1 trials. Horng writes that "the prospect of direct clinical benefit in them "may be extremely low, whereas the risks may be substantial and the possible harms severe."[22] Yet what is the risk of death? In this riskiest of trials with fatally ill patients whose disease resists all other treatments? Over the years, about 0.5% of Phase 1 trials include a bedeviling blend of suffering and hope. The average subject can expect, at most, slight benefit. Toxicity from new medications is a significant risk, and there is a small but unavoidable risk of death. But while one out of 200 subjects in a Phase 1 cancer trial dies from the treatment, the remaining 199 die from the cancer.

Second, research is safer than the regulationist stereotype because it is generally structured to minimize risk. Researchers consider subjects' welfare in planning research, and research is cautiously incremental. Consider Phase 1 studies of cancer medications. New treatments are not haphazard; they grow out of knowledge about the body, the disease, and current treatments. Progress is generally by slow steps. For instance: Estrogen stimulates some breast tumors by binding to receptors on cancer cells. Using what is known about estrogen and the receptors, biochemists can custom-make compounds to block estrogen-receptor interaction. Prospective therapies are then tested for safety and (where possible) efficacy in animals. Next, the medication is tried in a Phase 1 trial in a few (from 20 to 80) humans. The first patients receive a low dose, which is increased cautiously until the maximum tolerated dose is reached.

The first humans to receive cancer drugs have cancer unresponsive to standard therapy. If there is no evidence of effectiveness, or if toxicity is excessive, the test is ended. Phase 1 trials are designed to give patients enough of the drug to assess efficacy while minimizing toxicity. Phase 2 trials involve more subjects (100–300) and test effectiveness as well as safety. Phase 3 trials give the medication to many subjects (often 1,000–3,000) to confirm its effectiveness and compare it with standard treatment. For every drug approved, 5,000 to 10,000 enter preclinical testing. From preclinical testing to completion of clinical testing (including any postapproval) takes 8 to 12 years.[23] None of this makes research riskless, but it does reduce risk.

Third, the regulationist stereotype exaggerates clinical trials' risks. OHRP Director Menikoff's book[24] virtually caricatures those exaggerations, so consider the careful work of Charles Lidz. He describes four standard concerns: randomization, placebos, double-blind designs, and restrictive protocols.[25] As to the first of these (randomization), Lidz says that while "there may be no evidence that any one treatment is better than another," that "may not be true for the individual."[26] But trials are typically conducted when the better treatment is uncertain. If special circumstances make one treatment preferable, the patient is an inappropriate subject.

It is easy to suppose standard is safer than innovative care. But both may present problems of efficacy, side effects, costs, and convenience. Nobody knows *a priori* which is best. It is unnerving to think that there may be no convincing evidence of the superiority of a standard treatment, but it is a truism of sophisticated medicine that many decisions must be made without reliable information. Uncertainty "is clinically commonplace."[27] Medicine "is engulfed and infiltrated by uncertainty"[28] and practiced "in a sea of doubt and uncertainty,"[29] so that doctors must rely on "personal experience of past cases; the comparison of the present size, sound or feel of something with what is remembered; and on what a clinician believes to be the problem, based sometimes on very scanty evidence."[30] So in a sense "'every clinical act is an investigation.'"[31]

Second, Lidz fears that in research but not clinical medicine, subjects "may receive placebos for reasons unrelated to improving their condition."[32] But this is a special case of "treatments assigned at random." Even the best standard treatments can harm or fail some patients. Some treatments are worse than no treatment. For example, surgeons used to remove scar tissue from the abdomen to reduce "chronic abdominal pain—until researchers faked the procedure in controlled studies and patients reported equal relief." And when doctors tested the efficacy of surgery for Parkinsonism by drilling holes in the skull without doing the full procedure, the sham surgery patients did as well as the patients receiving the conventional treatment.[33]

In a review of 147 studies, Willcox found that antioxidants "delay or prevent oxidative stress" (although she advocated "controlled studies").[34] Yet a review of 68 randomized trials of antioxidants with 232,606 participants found the placebo arm the place to be, since antioxidants "significantly *increased* mortality."[35]

The Cardiac Arrhythmia Suppression Trial classically showed how research can unmask harmful treatments. In the 1980s, heart-attack patients who developed a dangerous arrhythmia were given an electric shock to convert them out of it. Patients with milder and asymptomatic arrhythmias received medication intended to keep mild arrhythmias from progressing to worse ones. Plausible enough, but when cardiologists conducted a study withholding three popular antiarrhythmics, the death rate was higher in patients given an antiarrhythmic than in those receiving a placebo.[36]

Third, Lidz writes that research (but not clinical medicine) may be double-blind, with neither doctors nor patients knowing which treatment a patient receives. Lidz fears that "clinicians' and subjects' abilities to recognize physical and mental symptoms as related to the intervention they are experiencing may be impaired by their ignorance," despite protocols designed to protect patients from such problems. Studies are double-blinded because patients' and doctors' perceptions may change if they know what medication the patient is getting. Lidz contends that researchers are "often hesitant" to break the blind in an emergency, but he provides no evidence.[37] Nor do the trial-effect data confirm his concerns.

Fourth, Lidz writes that in research, protocols and not patients' responses often determine dosages and management of side effects. As Fried put it, subjects in randomized trials lose the "good of personal care."[38] And a 1998 review showed 10 articles arguing that randomized trials "necessarily violate patient rights to the best treatment available" and oblige patients to sacrifice themselves to help future patients.[39]

There are three problems with this argument. First, sometimes the only controlled element is the treatment itself. Second, following restrictive protocols can be a road to better care, not disaster. Algorithmic care is increasingly favored because studies recurrently show its superiority over clinical judgment. About 60% of some 200 studies comparing clinical and statistical predictions found algorithms significantly better, while in the rest algorithms were no worse than clinical predictions.[40] Meehl argued long ago that judgment is rarely superior to formulas.[41] One reason is that people "are incorrigibly inconsistent in making summary judgments of complex information. When asked to evaluate the same information twice, they frequently give different answers." Even experienced radiologists given the same chest X-ray on different occasions "contradict themselves 20% of the time."[42] Third, the argument that protocols injure subjects lacks good evidence and is contradicted by the trial-effect findings.

More specifically, OHRP director Menikoff says that strict protocols "may to some extent intentionally be subordinating" subjects' well-being to "better research results."[43] His evidence is a footnote that says only "[for] a discussion of some empirical evidence that being denied the individual care of a doctor and instead having care determined by a protocol may be better for some patients, see S.J.L. Edwards et al."[44] But Edwards found no evidence that research harms patients and some that it benefits them.

Regulationists, then, say things like: "Randomized trials often place physicians in the ethically intolerable position of choosing between the good of the patient and that of society."[45] Lawrence studied the issue and concluded that "researchers were strongly oriented toward protecting individual subjects' best interests. If a participant needed a treatment not permitted by protocol or if the patient were at risk for doing poorly in the study, researchers preferred to remove the subject or to defer enrollment, rather than place the subject at risk or violate the protocol."[46] Nor is it clear that IRBs improve the situation. Interpreting protocols requires judgment. But the literature is "clear that protocol deviations need to be IRB-approved" and that approval takes "time and energy," since deviations are suspect. How often does the burden IRBs thus place on researchers' judgment help either patients or science?[47]

3. CONCLUSION

The regulationist stereotype emphasizes research's physical risks. Research *can* kill and injure people. But research is so unlikely to produce death and disaster that IRBs have limited room to reduce physical risks to subjects. I have emphasized three reasons. First, the regulationist stereotype treats the riskiest segment of research as typical of the whole (which includes social-science research). Second, the stereotype ignores ways good research practices reduce risks. Third, the stereotype exaggerates the disadvantages of the four most prominent problems with the riskier kinds of research.

D. THE NONPHYSICAL RISKS OF HUMAN-SUBJECT RESEARCH

A very large proportion of the matters upon which people wish to interfere with their neighbours are trumpery little things which are of no real importance at all. The busybody and world-betterer who will never let things alone, or trust people to take care of themselves, is a common and a contemptible character.

—James Fitzjames Stephen, *Liberty, Equality, Fraternity*

Human-subject research, then, poses much smaller risks of *physical* harm than the regulationist stereotype implies. What of the nonphysical harms regulationists increasingly invoke? They are generally the kind that people daily manage. IRBs routinely see harms where there are none and overestimate the likelihood of real harm.

1. INTRODUCTION

My life has been full of terrible misfortunes most of which never happened.
—Michel de Montaigne

Regulationists emphasize three nonphysical harms. First, social harm, like "embarrassment within one's business or social group, loss of employment, or criminal prosecution." Second, psychological harm, like "undesired changes in thought processes and emotion," including "feelings of stress, guilt, and loss of self-esteem."[48] Third, dignitary harm, which is suffered when people are treated as "mere means" rather than "as persons with their own values, performances, and commitments."[49]

2. THE REGULATIONIST STEREOTYPE AND THE EVIDENCE

[I]n all the years I was responsible for human-subjects issues at NSF, I never learned of one case in which a respondent was actually harmed from participation in anthropological research. So, although the possibility of harm to participants in ethnographic research is real, the probability of harm is very low.
—Stuart Plattner, Comment on IRB Regulation of Ethnographic Research

With mounting zeal but minimal evidence, regulationists treat nonphysical harm as both serious and probable. Elite commissions emphasize it. NBAC lamented that "the possibility of such harms is not widely appreciated" and wanted "to ensure that IRBs are sensitive to such risks."[50] Officialdom concurs. An NIH director once said it's "not the scientist who puts a needle in the bloodstream who causes the trouble. It's the behavioral scientist who probes into the sex life of an insecure person who really raises hell."[51] OHRP director Schwetz "dismissed the notion that most nonmedical research carries few dangers. 'Obviously the balance is very subtle,' he said. 'I think it's naïve to say there isn't any risk.'"[52] IRB manuals join in: surveys' risks "may be every bit as serious as the physical risks associated with an investigational drug." Like "harm or loss (e.g., disclosure of private medical problems or sexual preference), inconvenience (e.g., boredom, frustration), psychological risk (e.g., insult, trauma), and legal (e.g., subpoena, fine) risk."[53]

Commentators agree. Saver concedes that many subjects probably are as well or better off therapeutically than patients getting medical care,[54] but they face "a range of serious potential hazards," including "lost opportunity costs, destruction of trust and confidence in the research process, ... breach of confidentiality, invasion of privacy, loss of meaningful choice about use of one's body as an experimental object, [and] participation in a study that fails to disseminate trial data. ..."[55] De Wet claims that "any research" can be harmful and that "[p]sychological harm, unfulfilled expectations, deception, unexpected or erroneous representations and different interpretations" exemplify risks of nonmedical research.[56] The "preconceived idea that social science does not need ethical clearance" because it is harmless "points to a generalized ignorance and unconcerned attitude."[57]

The apotheosis of such risks is the following

CASE STUDY: THE NIGHTMARE[58]

Hadjistavropoulos and Smythe discern "important elements of risk in qualitative research" that researchers and IRBs "often" disregard. Its "main ethical problems" arise from "its open-ended methodology and the nature of the questions posed." Interviews "may touch on issues that neither the researcher nor the participant was prepared to discuss," leading "participants to disclose sensitive psychological themes and information about third parties that can be problematic." Hadjistavropoulos and Smythe fear "'the subtle and often unforeseeable consequences of writing about people's lives' and, in particular, 'the emotional impact of having one's story reinterpreted and filtered through the lenses of social scientific categories.'" The "researcher's status as a duly constituted 'expert' interpreter of social and psychological phenomena can seriously undermine an individual's inherent authority to interpret his or her experience. ..." Nor is it hard to imagine a participant who "suffers from major depression and participates in a study that involves a narrative about his or her life's experiences." And in interviews, "a negative social experience could exacerbate the negative mood state of the already depressed participant."

Furthermore, interviews could harm third parties "who never consented to participate in the research." They might become angry at the interviewees and "could sue them for defamation and perhaps even violation of privacy." Finally, interviewees are often quoted "in publicly accessible documents such as theses, dissertations, and published articles," creating "the possibility of identifying the participants as well as third parties mentioned in narratives."

This is Pritchard's wondrous world of "not likely, but possible." As one manual says, since "IRBs know very little about such risks" they "must speculate and make decisions on the basis of worst-case scenarios. The word *must* is important because … the absence of data on risks and wrongs in social scientific research does not prove that subjects go unscathed."[59]

In this world where scandals are evidence that risks run high and where the absence of evidence justifies regulation, social, psychological, and dignitary harms seem omnipresent. For IRBs, for example, breaches of confidentiality are principal social harms, and many IRBs enforce HIPAA (elaborate regulations of confidentiality in clinical medicine and research). Yet, who cannot imagine *some* way *some* information about *some* person might *somehow* reach *some* person who for some reason uses it in *some* damaging way? Imagination is inflamed by "risk-averse administrators" interpreting regulations "very broadly" to protect subjects "at risk of any dismay at all."[60] But long before HIPAA, a survey found that in over 2,000 projects, three had a confidentiality breach "that had harmed or embarrassed a subject. And of 729 behavioral projects, only four reported 'harmful effects.'"[61] More recently, Campbell could find "very few" violations of confidentiality.[62] Green knows of "no instances of harm from unauthorized disclosures" in observational health-services research. Nor has Georgetown's Health Privacy Project documented any.[63] An HHS advisory committee found no confidentiality breaches in researchers' use of records (though HHS still subjected research to HIPAA).[64]

Harms are rare because risks are low. First, confidentiality is an old principle. As an AAUP subcommittee says, concerns are "entirely met by long-standing departmental and disciplinary practice."[65] Second, confidentiality is a legal duty. Thus the Association of Academic Health Centers argues that HIPAA may offer no "greater protection than current long-standing effective regulation,"[66] like FDA and NIH rules and state privacy law.[67] Thus before HIPAA there had been no "explosion of improper disclosures" or any "systematic unwillingness to deal with the problems that do arise."[68] HHS's rationale for HIPAA centrally relied on nine anecdotes, like health insurance claims forms blowing out of a truck or a health department employee stealing a computer disk. Unfortunate, but no law can keep winds from blowing or employees from stealing, and state law already penalizes negligence and theft.

Third, as the (British) Academy of Medical Sciences concluded, in most research "the risk of inadvertent or damaging disclosure of sensitive information is extremely low."[69] Harm hangs on a long chain of events: Information the subject wants kept secret must be collected. Most research does not do so. That information must leave the researcher's custody. Researchers have few incentives to release and many incentives not to. That information must reach someone able and willing to misuse it. But to whom is that information useful? Consider the modal regulationist fear—insurance companies getting genetic information and denying coverage because of it. Hall and Rich report that there has not been and is unlikely to be "serious adverse selection."[70] Furthermore, "[m]ultiple, independent sources refuted" or could not "document, any substantial level of genetic discrimination."[71] Another study found no evidence of insurers canceling such policies.[72]

IRB fears of social harms stretch beyond confidentiality. Recall, for example, our case study's nightmare that interviewees might defame someone. Anybody *can* sue anybody for anything, but only a chain of gossamer links could make this nightmare real. An interviewee would have to say something defamatory *and false*. The defamed person would have to hear about it and sue, thus advertising the slander and embracing the miseries of litigation. A lawyer would have to take the suit (despite discouraging economics). A court would have to find the comment defamatory, false, and injurious. West estimates that only 80 defamation cases a year are decided;[73] are *any* of these brought by third parties defamed by interviewees?

But nightmares haunt IRBs. An IRB warned a historian not to ask civil rights workers about laws broken during civil disobedience.[74] Did the IRB know that the *point* of civil disobedience is to break the law openly, be arrested, and even jailed? Did it know the "Letter from Birmingham Jail"? Did it know that the statute of limitations on these "crimes" ran out long since? Did it know that civil rights workers are heroes because they defied the law? Did it know that suppressing evidence of that defiance dishonors them?

In sum, social harms—usually the worst nonphysical risks—are rare and modest. People daily handle similar risks. The law has other ways to deter, punish, and exact compensation for them. We are back to "not likely but possible."

But what of psychological harm? What of "depression, altered self-concept, increased anxiety, decreased confidence in others, guilt, shame, fear, embarrassment, boredom, frustration, receiving information about oneself that is unpleasant, and inconvenience?"[75] OHRP thinks "[s]tress and feelings of guilt or embarrassment may arise simply from thinking or talking about one's own behavior or attitudes on sensitive topics such as drug use, sexual preferences, selfishness, and violence."[76] IRBs have objected to research because "subjects might find it distressing even to be asked the questions."[77] Mazur tells IRBs that a questionnaire study of posttraumatic stress disorder "may elicit negative responses" including "suicidal ideation or even suicide attempt [*sic*]."[78] The evidence confutes this stereotype of frail subjects bludgeoned by questions. Furthermore, Mueller observes, psychological research before IRBs "was not rife with misbehavior. Some of us know this from having lived through that era, others can document it by examining the research literature. Furthermore, it was clear in the early days of the IRB literature that the minuscule incidence of negative outcomes was well known."[79]

CASE STUDY: LAST WORDS[80]

Regulationists recoil at research with terminally ill patients. The literature seems to agree "that palliative patients are vulnerable." They have "reached a state of immense vulnerability through the violence of terminal illness, being weakened by losses, and confronted with overwhelming burdens." An NIH consensus conference doubted the decency or propriety "of intruding on patients at a particularly important time in their lives." Annas would bar interviews with the terminally ill: "Desperate, and, therefore, too vulnerable, they are unable to distinguish research from treatment."

These patronizing admonitions rest on shallow ideas about human life, and "there is no empirical research to support" them. Terry's subjects, for example, had days to live. Far from thinking this impaired "the autonomy of their consent," they found "a 'freedom'" in having nothing to lose. And while regulationists fear the dying may grasp at participation hoping to live longer, Terry's patients said they would participate only were there "no possibility of it delaying their deaths." They protested "the usurpation of their autonomy [to choose to speak] by others" and "being treated as already dead." Some yearned to use their remaining days "to do something of enduring value" and thought research let them "give something back to their families and careers and to the community."

IRBs are easily alarmed because they substitute speculations for research on risks,[81] speculations distorted by errors like overweighting single cases, scanting base rate information, and consulting salience, not probability.[82] Bell and Salmon warn that ignorance about illicit drug use leads to using "stereotypes that depict drug users as selfish, irresponsible and unable to make sound judgments." And they find "some evidence to suggest that 'special protections' for drug users have become synonymous with 'over-protection.'"[83] Worse, risk-adverse IRBs tend "to ask for maximum protection" of subjects; e.g., excluding subjects who might become depressed, requiring that subjects be offered therapy, and rewording questions.[84]

So what is the evidence? Take a standard case: IRBs widely fear emotional harm from recalling traumatic events,[85] and "many IRBs" require interviewers to assure interviewees counseling.[86] But as a literature review found, people can and do say no if they fear distress.[87] Even parents who recently lost a child "clearly and unambiguously" decided whether to participate. A third of them declined, and 8% agreed but withdrew later.[88] Furthermore, few interviewers like upsetting people, and it is callous and stupid to hector the distraught, who won't answer well, or at all. No answers, no research.

Researchers considered this problem and years ago responded productively—with research. Their reassuring evidence comes in three stages.

Stage one. Questions upset people much less than regulationists imagine. For example, in a study of trauma, "no participants reported adverse reactions."[89] None of the 9,500 HMO members asked about abuse and other traumas called researchers' 24-hour crisis line.[90] Only 0.3% of New Yorkers questioned about 9/11 asked about mental health services offered them, and not always because of the study.[91] Regulationists mistake the spark that reignites memories and misery. It is not direct questions about abuse, but being in situations like the original event. "[D]aily exposure to media" is likelier than research questions to stimulate memories of trauma.[92]

Stage two. Suppose—against the stage one evidence—that questions often upset people. What would that mean? The *rate* of distress says nothing about its *degree*. People are less upset by questions about unhappy subjects than intuition suggests. Over 80% of parents of stillborn children were not distressed by interviews, and only 1% thought the interviews both distressing and unhelpful; the rest found them distressing but helpful.[93] Furthermore, people are discomfited by different things than IRBs think. In one study, young women more willingly discussed their abortions than their income.[94] In sum, "research is not more stressful, and may be less stressful, than other experiences in everyday life."[95]

Stage three. Assume—against the stage one and stage two evidence—that discussing painful topics often distresses people. How do they feel about their distress? Only "a small proportion" of those "markedly or unexpectedly upset" regretted participating or rated the experience negatively. While a fifth of the people asked about trauma were more upset than they had anticipated, "only one regretted participating." And talking about trauma is "regularly followed by emotional relief that many participants identify as a benefit."[96] For example, 95% of acutely injured adults reported a net benefit from participating in research (and 98% did not regret participating).[97]

Since talking about distress is a standard therapy for it, participants in two studies unsurprisingly "found it useful to reflect on" even painful experiences, and all 29 child and adult refugees "reported relief lasting several days" after interviews. Similarly, after psychiatric inpatients were interviewed, 36% said it "led to new insights," 16% said it was generally helpful, and 12% said it clarified memories. Finally, while OHRP's *Guidebook* warns of stress, guilt, and embarrassment "simply from thinking or talking about one's own behavior or attitudes on sensitive topics," half the seriously injured children and their parents interviewed said participating enhanced self-esteem, and half the children and 90% of the parents "felt good about their altruism."[98]

In short, asking people important questions expresses respect for them, their lives, and their ideas. People discussing troubling things may be sad, perplexed, rueful, dismayed. They talk with families, friends, counselors, and interviewers knowing that is possible but thinking the game worth the candle. Few serious people think life's goal is avoiding these feelings; rather they think them part of living wisely.

I have reviewed the three-stage evidence that asking people about trauma is *much* safer than IRBs apparently think. Regulationists similarly exaggerate other risks. For example, NBAC feared that HIV research that included a blood draw might involve "all the nonphysical risks" of, "for example, learning one's HIV status."[99] Those risks are often put laceratingly. Gostin said in 1989 that patients should be told about false positives; that "[s]ome patients bear an intolerable psychological burden" when told they are positive; that "suicide can result"; that confidentiality can be lost; and that disclosure "can cause ostracism" and losing "a job, a home, a place in school, insurance," and more.[100] Again the evidence is consoling. Even before anti-retrovirals, Moulton's "most striking finding" was that seropositives' distress did not increase significantly when they were told.[101] Asymptomatic people learning their "disease status" do not generally suffer "distress, depression, or suicide." People getting either a negative or a positive result "showed *less* psychopathology" than people declining notification.[102] Some subjects in an HIV vaccine trial had bad experiences, but 94% would participate again, and of the rest, none mentioned social harms.[103]

IRBs see clouds of risk when children buy cigarettes to assess minors' ability to do so, but participating "may be associated with low intentions to smoke" and with efforts to deter others.[104] Regulationists perseverate on how paying subjects might impair their decisions. But Halpern "found no evidence that commonly used payment levels represent undue or unjust inducements," and "the payment level was, if anything, *less* influential among poor patients."[105] Regulationists abhor deception in research far more than subjects: studies find that 90% of participants "perceive social psychological experiments as valuable and valid." In a review of experiments involving deception, participants "reported virtually no annoyance" and "did not mind being misled." One study found that deceived subjects actually enjoyed the experience more and felt they had learned more than undeceived subjects.[106]

Psychological harm is not just rarer than regulationists believe, it is slighter. The IOM grimly warns of "unnecessary risks, however minimal."[107] Mazur ominously tells IRBs that any change in "awareness, concentration, or affect to a degree that the person has not previously experienced may be viewed as a change that makes him or her vulnerable in decision making."[108] Regulationists live blissful lives if they do not daily suffer the harms they fear, like "depression, altered self-concept, increased anxiety, decreased confidence in others, guilt, shame, fear, embarrassment, boredom, frustration, receiving information about oneself that is unpleasant, and inconvenience."[109] One bad class pretty much takes care of all of these for me.

Trivial risks are clad in suits of solemn black: Ending studies poses "considerable risk" because "by definition" successful participant observation "generates feelings of loss in the community" when an ethnographer leaves. So "plans for ending the research should be discussed with participants" *throughout* the study.[110] Levine frets that "researchers may transmit nonverbal expressions of surprise or disapproval upon hearing a patient's response to a question about some aspect of the doctor-patient interaction."[111] And recall the nightmare—that the "researcher's status as a duly constituted 'expert' interpreter of social and psychological phenomena can seriously undermine one's 'inherent authority to interpret' one's experience."[112] Stray outside New Haven, Ann Arbor, or Palo Alto and see what awe that status inspires.

Finally, what are the "dignitary harms" regulationists fear? NBAC says they occur when people "are not treated as persons" but "as mere means, not deserving of respect."[113] Defined so capaciously, what harms are not dignitary? Defined so vaguely, how can one identify and assess them? Affronts to dignity depend on three questions. First, what is the social understanding of dignity? Affronts rest on social norms, not all desirable— like the norms that once led to duels or today provoke honor killings. Second, what harm is intended? If none is intended, is offense appropriate? Third, how is the affront interpreted? If you share the regulationist distrust of researchers, you may think yourself badly used. If not, you may be glad to have helped promote learning.

Is deceiving research subjects a dignitary harm? Two of the social-science studies most commonly used to indict researchers involved deception. Milgram told his subjects he was studying education, not obedience to authority, in the study in which people were told to give larger and larger shocks to someone they thought was suffering them (although he was Milgram's confederate and the machine delivered no shocks). And

Laud Humphreys studied male-male sexual encounters in public toilets by being a lookout for police during the encounters and by interviewing the men later while concealing his having met them and misrepresenting the interviews' purpose.[114] Yet "in a follow-up survey, 84 percent of the subjects told Milgram they were glad to have participated, though some remained angry enough to complain to Milgram or the president of his university."[115] And were Humphreys' subjects harmed if they never knew what Humphreys had done? If Humphreys' work changed the circumstances that led the men he studied to fear discovery?

How should an IRB treat dignitary harms, given their obscurity? Part of the answer depends on my upcoming discussion of what standards IRBs should use to evaluate nonphysical harms. But there is another problem. The IRB remedy for dignitary harms is principally longer consent forms. Yet they can "erode the important personal relationships between subjects" and researchers.[116] Bureaucratic impositions are what people rightly resent.[117] Few people think signing their way through a thicket of paper a compliment to their dignity.

E. THE RISKS OF RESEARCHER MISBEHAVIOR

Men in slaughterhouses, truck drivers, hostlers, cattle and horse owners, farmers and stable keepers, may be taken care of by general legislation; but educated men, devoted to scientific research, and physicians, devoted to the relief of suffering humanity, need some special supervision and regulation!
—John Dewey, *Animals: The Ethics of Animal Experimentation*

Many regulationists think research risks are heightened by researchers' callousness. Justification-by-scandal intimates that only IRBs keep researchers in Austin from acting like doctors in Auschwitz. This intimation is intensified by a trend Anechiarico and Jacobs call the "panoptic vision." It assumes officials (here researchers) tend to be weak or evil,[118] "will succumb to corrupt opportunities," and require "comprehensive surveillance."[119]

OHRP's first director, Greg Koski, preaches the panoptic gospel: "Empirical surveys have shown that too many [scientists] are all too willing to ignore regulatory requirements when they get in the way of 'scientific progress'—by which they mean what they want to do, done when they want to do it."[120] After IRBs arose, Koski laments, "it was as though [all?] scientists had been absolved of their responsibilities ... by delegation to an impersonal third party."[121] Moral obligation should be "more than enough motivation" not to abuse subjects, but, Koski says snidely, "this may be 'too much to expect.'"[122] Koski invokes empirical surveys, but he cites none.

OHRP's present director, Jerry Menikoff, wrote a book titled *What the Doctor Didn't Say: The Hidden Truth about Medical Research.* As McCullough writes, it "suggests that clinical investigators are reckless and not trustworthy," that becoming a "research participant is a 'bad' choice; [that] investigators routinely misrepresent the benefits of clinical research," that "information potential participants need is 'hidden' from them," and that conflicts of interest that cause "'protocol violations are not uncommon.'" McCullough finds Menikoff as frugal with evidence as Koski: "The first sort of claim requires careful ethical analysis and argument, which are not provided. The second, third, and fourth claims are empirical and require justification by adherence to evidence-based standards, which are not met."[123]

IRB manuals also recite the panoptic gospel. Mazur says researchers often will face a study's problems only after IRBs force them to.[124] The bad apples come not as single spies but in bushels: The attempt "is always the same"—to divert IRBs from protecting subjects toward goals like facilitating research. Worse, researchers do so "not to acquire new general scientific knowledge to benefit future generations but to acquire the financial rewards" of research.[125]

Were researchers as debased as panopticism implies, it would intensify research risks. But researchers are much less likely to harm subjects than, for example, doctors are to harm patients. As Fost writes, deaths related to research "since 1973 are extremely uncommon compared to standard care." Fost cites the IOM's estimate of "60,000 to 90,000 deaths a year in doctors' offices. These are preventable deaths." The estimate "is surely exaggerated," but "the unit of measurement is the tens of thousands," while in research, it is "in single digits or possibly two digits."[126] Vaporous as panopticism is in biomedical research, it is embarrassing in social science. As Patullo wrote 40 years ago, "The handful of horror stories notwithstanding, the record of social scientists in protecting human subjects is remarkably good—as, in fact, is that of biomedical scientists." Many millions of subjects have been "'used' in this century. The available evidence strongly suggests that the actual harm done by this vast enterprise is negligible."[127]

Furthermore, the regulationist psychology of the researcher is crude, for it sees only a conflict of interest that would lead researchers to betray subjects' interests. But researchers also have many contrary interests. For example, dragooned subjects rarely cooperate enough to be useful. Furthermore, as van den Hoonaard learned, researchers develop bonds with interviewees. He found that his relationships with some 200 interviewees involved ties that "either evolved out of, or became, natural friendships or relationships involving trust."[128] Similarly, Heimer asked a doctor how he could keep track of so many subjects' data. "'It's not as impersonal as you think,' he replied." Heimer concluded that relationships are not "primarily between scientist and research subject but instead are experienced as relationships between doctor and patient."[129]

F. WHAT IS THE STANDARD FOR EVALUATING RISKS?

Some degree of abuse is inseparable from the proper use of every thing; and in no instance is this more true, than in that of the press. ... [But] better to leave a few of its noxious branches to their luxuriant growth, than, by pruning them away, to injure the vigor of those yielding the proper fruits.
—James Madison, Report on the Kentucky-Virginia Resolutions

While research can hurt subjects, we have seen that serious nonphysical harms are rare and that many nonphysical harms are "trumpery little things." But gravity may be in the mind of the beholder. When is a harm serious and likely enough to justify regulation? I investigate three measures: the standard IRBs seem to apply, the law's standard for intervening to prevent similar risks, and OHRP's minimal-risk standard.

1. THE REGULATIONIST "ENSURE" STANDARD: ZERO DEFECTS

He does have a fairly dynamic zero-defects program.
—General Thomas Kelly, on Saddam Hussein's executing two commanders

Regulationists tend to see even slight risks of small harms as probable and grave enough to require government action—even when they are "not likely but possible." As White says, IRBs try "to prevent *any* imaginable risk, regardless of the magnitude, likelihood, or duration."[130] But many regulationists have a fairly dynamic zero-defects program in another way:

They want IRBs (1) to "guarantee," or "assure," or "ensure" (2) that nobody is (3) ever harmed. So in a 2,400-word pronouncement, the HHS Secretary used "ensure" nine times and "guarantee" and "make sure" twice each. The "system of protections" must "ensure" not optimal but "maximal protection for all human subjects" and "guarantee" not optimal but "the greatest possible protection for every human subject, in every clinical trial and at every research institution in the country." Really and truly: "even one lapse is too many."[131]

The OHRP *Guidebook* is awash in "ensures." Researchers must "ensure that all aspects of the project and follow-up" are proper. Monitoring must "ensure" that research stops when "reliable results have been obtained." IRBs must "ensure" that prospective subjects get information in understandable language. And that subjects know who has "access to the data and who might contact them." And that information "is not improperly divulged." And that participation is "truly voluntary."

The IOM too wants "to *ensure* the protection of *every* research participant."[132] Diligently applying federal "policies and practices will *ensure*" that subjects avoid undue risk, are informed, "and that *all* efforts are made to *ensure* that participants' rights, privileges, and privacy are protected throughout the *entire* research process." Safety "*must* be *guaranteed* from the inception of a protocol, through its execution, to final completion and reporting of results." Not just guaranteed. "[U]ntil evidence is available, ... it is *necessary* to pursue *every* promising mechanism to *maximize*" subjects' protection. An NRC/IOM report[133] thinks its advice will "*ensure* that consent is *truly* informed" by "*ensur[ing]* that parents" understand acres of arcana. That will "*ensure* that the rights of child subjects are protected." It will "*ensure*" that research is "carefully justified." IRBs "should *ensure*" that they have the expertise for "a *complete* and adequate review."

The ensure principle also animates IRBs. It helps inspire them to preserve subjects from faint and fanciful harms. As one of Klitzman's respondents said, "A couple of members tend to come down quite hard on clinical research operations, and shut down more studies if issues don't look really fixed: 'If we can't guarantee that studies are absolutely perfect, we should stop them.'"[134]

This is not responsible policy making. The only way to ensure that no subject is harmed is to prohibit research. As Hyman writes, bad outcomes are "fully consistent with an optimal level of research risk and of research oversight." The alternative is no research and "'children on ventilators after polio.'"[135]

2.   THE LEGAL STANDARD

To try to regulate the internal affairs of a family, the relations of love or friendship, or many other things of the same sort, by law ... is like trying to pull an eyelash out of a man's eye with a pair of tongs. They may put out the eye, but they will never get hold of the eyelash.

—James Fitzjames Stephen, *Liberty, Equality, Fraternity*

Activities as little risky as most (most, not all) human-subject research are generally unregulated, and *much* more dangerous activities are often regulated mildly. Take two close analogies. Clinical medicine is incomparably riskier than research, yet patients are protected primarily by malpractice suits and medical-board discipline, not Treatment Review Boards. Journalism injures more people more awfully each week than social-science research has in its history. Many admired reporters use "hidden cameras, deception of informants, [and] purloining of confidential documents." Their investigations cause "blasted careers, emotional trauma, ruined reputations, lost income, and shattered egos—even the occasional suicide has been attributed to them."[136] Yet journalists are primarily regulated by the laws of defamation and privacy, *much* diluted by constitutional concerns.

The law already provides remedies for some social harms (like breaches of confidentiality) IRBs fear. But by legal standards, few nonphysical harms justify IRB regulation, for "offense, embarrassment, or other mental discomfort" are too "trivial, immeasurable, or subjective" to be taken on by law.[137] So negligently or intentionally inflicting emotional distress is tortious but rarely actionable. Even *intentionally* inflicting emotional distress is actionable only when distress is "severe"[138] and the conduct so "outrageous" and "extreme" that it is "beyond all possible bounds of decency," "atrocious," and "utterly intolerable."[139]

Furthermore, the Supreme Court shields even brutal and base speech if it might be "of political, social, or other concern to the community." *Snyder v. Phelps*[140] shows how far this goes. A group picketed the funeral of Snyder's soldier son carrying signs (like "Thank God for Dead Soldiers") saying that God had killed the son to punish America's tolerance of sin.

The picketers intentionally or recklessly behaved in extreme or outrageous ways that caused acute emotional distress—"severe depression" and exacerbation of Snyder's "preexisting health conditions." The picketing piled anguish on Snyder's "already incalculable grief." But the picketing concerned "matters of public concern" and so was constitutionally protected, however questionable "its contribution to public discourse." We "protect even hurtful speech on public issues to ensure that we do not stifle public debate."

The law also hobbles privacy suits. Disclosure is wrongful only if it is given publicity and would highly offend reasonable people. While IRBs often restrict ways researchers may contact people, the Supreme Court has long "invalidated restrictions on door-to-door canvassing and pamphleteering," even where they were imposed to protect people's privacy in their homes.[141] What clearer dignitary harm is there than losing a constitutional right? A federal statute (42 USC § 1983) makes people who infringe constitutional rights under color of state law liable for the damage they do. But when a court told jurors to "place a money value on the 'rights' themselves," the Supreme Court prohibited compensation for the dignitary affront except when accompanied by "actual injury."[142]

Why does the law permit deliberate and dreadful insults, intrusions, and injuries? Partly, even courts cannot reliably make reasoned, consistent, and fair decisions about them. For example, the law hesitates to protect people against emotional distress "[b]ecause of the fear of fictitious or trivial claims, distrust of the proof offered, and the difficulty of setting up any satisfactory boundaries to liability."[143] People deprived of constitutional rights do not get "damages based on the abstract 'value' or 'importance'" of those rights because "[h]istory and tradition" give too little guidance on valuing them, and "juries would be free to award arbitrary amounts" or "use their unbounded discretion to punish unpopular defendants."[144] And because society's "rough edges" need "a good deal of filing down," people are "expected and required to be hardened to a certain amount of rough language" and "inconsiderate and unkind" acts.[145]

IRBs too lack "sound guidance concerning the precise values" of such interests. When IRBs protect dignitary interests they can (and do) reach arbitrary decisions and "use their unbounded discretion to punish unpopular" researchers and causes. As chapter 3 will show, "caprice" does infect IRB decisions about these harms. And intolerance of "rough language" and "inconsiderate and unkind" acts leads IRBs to impair essential social activities and the liberties of both researchers and subjects.

3.   THE MINIMAL-RISK STANDARD

A third standard for evaluating harm is that research is "minimal risk" when "the probability and magnitude of harm" are no greater than in daily life or in "routine physical or psychological examinations."[146] On that standard, IRBs should rarely act. Families, friends, colleagues, journalists, vendors, pollsters, and strangers on trains ask distressing questions so often that parents teach children about sticks, stones, and words. Researchers' impositions rarely compare with those of many employers. One article says that trolling ("provoking strangers online") has become "vicious" but doubts we want "an Internet where law enforcement keeps watch over every vituperative blog and backbiting comments section," as "it is next to impossible to excise the trolling without snuffing out the debate."[147]

Similarly, humiliation is a TV staple. Candid Camera has yielded to a show that asks people on a lie detector questions like "if you knew you wouldn't be caught, would you commit adultery?" People go on TV to be bullied by Dr. Phil, to hear paternity test results, and to be jeered at by coached audiences. Such shows are far riskier to people (and decency) than social-science research, as they "slither past suicide and accountability."[148] Why is research, which does great good and labors to avoid harm, regulated minutely while entertainment *intended* to injure is barely touched?

Finally, regulationists perseverate on risks arising from the right to make decisions. Levine worries that asking "a patient to choose between therapeutic innovation and an established therapeutic regimen may provoke severe anxiety. And "there may be severe guilt reactions if the risk actually becomes manifest as harm."[149] Leave aside the evidence contradicting these ingenious speculations. If IRBs must protect people from such risks, why do patients have a right to make medical decisions?

In short, most nonphysical harms IRBs try to prevent are harms we risk daily. "As subjects we could be entrapped, exposed, and embarrassed with only the laws of slander, libel, privacy, and contract to protect us. But we are thus exposed already to friends, enemies, journalists, acquaintances, and strangers. Rather than accept regulation that begins to erode freedom of speech, would it not be wiser to return scholars to the ranks occupied by our friends and enemies?"[150]

IRBs once regulated only risks of physical injuries—and in the rhetoric, *serious* physical injuries—to subjects of biomedical research. The IRB standard is now to "ensure" against even small risks to subjects of even social-science research. But both the law's standard and OHRP's risks-of-daily-life standard, sensibly interpreted, would treat most nonphysical risks as beneath regulatory notice.

G. CONCLUSION: "THAT'S NOT LIKELY, BUT IT'S POSSIBLE"

The whole aim of practical politics is to keep the populace alarmed (and hence clamorous to be led to safety) by menacing it with an endless series of hobgoblins, most of them imaginary.
—H. L. Mencken, *In Defense of Women*

Like most human activity, research has risks and can be abused. But overall the costs of regulation outweigh its benefits. This chapter has asked how much scope IRBs have to do good. The regulationist stereotype of hapless subjects and heartless researchers is false. Harms are generally slight and rare. Patients in trials fare at least as well as other patients. Logically so, for only a fraction of research can cause physical harm, only a fraction of that fraction can cause serious physical harm, and virtually none can cause serious nonphysical harm. The system's assertion of authority over social-science research despite its safety suggests the fragility of the argument that IRBs are needed to protect subjects.

Nor can the regulationist stereotype be defended by claiming that it is IRB regulation that moderates risks. First, the rate of research misbehavior was low before the IRB system gathered momentum. And the "fact there are no reports of increasing harm by social science research procedures over time suggests that real dangers to human subjects cannot explain the regulatory surges."[151] Second, research risk is modest because the category "human-subject research" offers so much less opportunity for harm than regulationist rhetoric and behavior imply. Third, some of the safety of research is due to other kinds of research regulation—self-restraint, professional government, institutional and legal sanctions, and the scrutiny of funders.[152]

Could the case for IRBs be persuasively made, surely regulationists would have tried. That they instead recruit rhetoric, stereotype, and aspersion suggests that argument and evidence are scarce. Were research as dangerous as the rhetoric and stereotype imply, IRBs could hardly waste so much time on such trivial risks. And when OHRP's head justifies impeding lifesaving research by invoking possible but not likely risks, the bankruptcy of regulationist risk-assessment has been announced.

In sum, the IRB system's potential benefits must be modest. To justify it, then, regulationists must show that its costs are slight indeed. The next chapter asks if they are.

2

Cost Is No Object

Investigators, sponsors, institutions and IRBs appropriately feel daunted by the array of procedural, ethical, regulatory and logistical requirements ..., and many have expressed concern that critical research may not be done, thereby depriving individuals and society from [sic] the potential benefits for which they look to science with hope. We cannot, however, allow the interests of science, sponsors or society take [sic] precedence over those of individuals who are taking the risks for the rest of us.

—Greg Koski, *Imagination and Attention*

Regulation is never free. Regulators must be funded, complying with regulations can be expensive, and regulation can degrade regulated activities. Yet regulation's cost depends on its form and culture. However inadvertently, the choices that shape the IRB system characteristically increase its cost. Most basic is the choice of a "command and control" model, one that assumes that people follow rules because they will be punished if they do not (or, sometimes, rewarded if they do). Deterrence is the modal command-and-control mechanism, but the IRB system uses a yet more costly one—event licensing, which condemns IRBs to review *every* inquiry to prevent bad outcomes that are generally unlikely and rarely severe. IRB members' time is often valuable, and IRBs use their time (and their staffs') ever more profligately. Finally, IRB regulation can distort, slow, and stop research whose "potential benefits" can be precious lives protected, health restored, and welfare promoted.

Worse, the IRB system's structure and culture encourage indifference to cost. First, IRBs are assigned to think only of subjects and not of cost. Shamoo recites the creed: "The regulatory mandate is clear: human subject protection, first, foremost, and last."[1] NBAC invokes Hans Jonas: "[P]rogress is an optional goal," and its tempo, "compulsive as it may become, has nothing sacred about it."[2] A regulationist can even say that one way "to assure serious attention to the ethical, regulatory and scientific aspects of research involving cognitively impaired subjects is to have fewer researchers conducting such research."[3]

Second, regulators can ignore costs because they do not pay them. OHRP does not fund IRBs, nor IRBs researchers, and the benefits foregone when research is impaired are obscured. Third, IRBs have reasons to ignore costs. Saying yes can lead to scandal, suits, and sanctions; saying no may incense researchers, but they can do little. Fourth, IRB regulations and OHRP's supervision fetishize paperwork, afflicting both IRBs and researchers. Fifth, lacking procedural and substantive rules, IRBs make inefficiently ad hoc decisions, and researchers must guess what is wanted. Sixth, IRBs are unaccountable and need not justify even pointless costs.

A. INTRODUCTION

Because research on human subjects is how we produce the innovations that improve health, reduce morbidity or mortality, and alleviate human suffering, preventing or delaying research results in vastly more suffering and death than occurs from researchers' ethical lapses.
—Carol A. Heimer, *The Unstable Alliance of Law and Morality*

This chapter first reviews the evidence that IRB regulation reduces research's benefits and provides an example of that effect. It next explores three costs IRBs impose: First, the subtraction from funding of resources diverted by regulation. Second, the reduced efficacy restrictions on research cause. Third, the damage that regulation does the infrastructure of research and the work of hospitals and universities. Finally, the chapter asks whether IRBs' benefits justify their costs.

1. THE LOGIC OF COST

There is yet ... the incredible loss and detriment that this plot of licensing puts us to; ... it hinders and retards the importation of our richest merchandise, truth.
—John Milton, *Areopagitica*

Regulating research is so costly because it inhibits activities that can do so much good. Curing disease and preventing death, Dewey said, make possible "all social activities" and preserve "human affections from the frightful waste and drain occasioned by the needless suffering and death of others with whom one is bound up."[4] American parents once feared polio, diphtheria, typhus, typhoid, tuberculosis, tetanus, mumps, measles, chickenpox, and more. In the last century, war killed 150 million people; smallpox 500 million.[5] A century ago, American life expectancy was 47 years; now it is 77. Deaths from cardiovascular disease dropped two-thirds between 1950 and 2000. The twentieth century's medical revolution "produced economic value about as large as the increase in all other goods and services."[6]

Much remains to do. "[R]ecent improvements in social welfare appear to be more strongly related to growth in public and professional biomedical knowledge" than (as once) to economic development.[7] Many diseases, like malaria (250,000,000 cases and 1,000,000 deaths annually), are unconquered. New infections arise, old pathogens invade new areas and grow more virulent and harder to treat.[8] The need is desperate in the third world, and the world's poorest continent is scourged by AIDS and tuberculosis.

Regulation impedes research first by "taxing" it, by exacting resources from researchers to pay for compliance. Second, regulation's "supervision" is supposed to improve research but too commonly impairs it. Both taxation and regulation divert resources from research: Researchers assemble applications, wait for IRB reactions, and respond to IRBs' demands, many of which slow or distort research. Taxation and supervision can harm research by, for example, making samples unrepresentative or inhibiting use of epidemiological data. Taxation and supervision can stop research.

Research being valuable, regulation must be thrifty. Yet IRB regulation is extravagant, since it is an extreme form of the expensive command and control method. That method typically relies much on deterrence—which research has widely found both costly and minimally effective. It is costly partly because it requires so much monitoring and surveillance. IRBs' event licensing multiplies that monitoring and surveillance. First, IRBs license every research project, not just ones that abuse subjects. Second, surveillance so intensive tends to alienate the regulated from the regulators, thus increasing the need for and cost of surveillance.

In the chapter's epigraph, Koski implicitly acknowledges that IRBs impede research. Researchers bleakly agree. They—like regulationists—have their own axes to grind, but no one knows better how IRBs hobble research. Stewart and Kurzrock include IRB regulation in the "regulatory burden" in clinical trials that "is to the war on cancer what World War I mud was to trench warfare." That "burden is onerous, misguided, and expensive, with little value added."[9] At a meeting of senior orthopedic surgeons, 90% said the threat to research of "regulatory obstacles" was "moderate or severe." Asked if their IRB was "(1) cumbersome, bureaucratic, and difficult to deal with; (2) more interested in protecting the institution than the patient; and (3) causing delays and unnecessary costs," two-thirds said "all three."[10] As Wootton writes, "thousands of unnecessary deaths may be caused by undue regulatory barriers or consent requirements that reduce enrollment in trials of effective therapies or that obscure their treatment effects due to selection biases or delays in treatment."[11]

2.   THE EXAMPLE OF EMERGENCY-MEDICINE RESEARCH

A certain man ... fell among thieves, which ... [left] him half dead. ... But a certain Samaritan ... went to him, and bound up his wounds ... and set him on his own beast, and brought him to an inn, and took care of him.
—Luke 10:30–34

The regulation of emergency-medicine research whose subjects cannot give consent exemplifies ways regulation can constrict inquiry with dubious benefit to subjects but undoubted harm to life, health, and welfare. An expert panel said in 2005 that "resuscitation rates are currently unsatisfactory," "treatments are unsatisfactory," and much standard care is poorly tested. IRBs could once authorize deferred or implied consent, but in 1993 OHRP's predecessor (OPRR) and the FDA forbade research without prospective consent. The blow to resuscitation research was "far reaching and devastating."[12] During three years, *one* protocol was permitted.[13] So "innovative therapies either have not been developed" or lack "well-designed trials," which often long delays discovering that innovations are "toxic, inefficacious or both."[14]

In 1996, "growing concerns" that "high quality acute care research" had become "difficult or impossible"[15] evoked new regulations[16] that prohibit some research, permit some in principle but not practice, and allow some at crippling cost. IRBs may waive consent only if researchers leap three sets of hurdles. First, (1) subjects' lives must be threatened and treatments "unproven or unsatisfactory." (2) Informed consent must be unfeasible. (3) Preclinical studies must show potential for "direct benefit" to subjects, and risks must be "reasonable." (4) The research must be impractical without the waiver.

Second, the subject's (or surrogate's) consent must be sought if possible, and IRBs must be kept informed about such attempts. Failing prior consent, researchers must expeditiously seek permission to continue.

Third, researchers must (1) "consult" with "representatives of the communities" where research will be done and (2) "disclose" the plans, risks, and benefits. Minimally, this means a

summary of the research protocol, study design, and a description of the procedures ...; [a] summary of other available treatment options and ... their risks and benefits; [a]n estimate of how long the study will last ...; [a description of how] subjects will be identified; [i]nformation about the test article's use, including a balanced description of the risks and expected benefits ...; [a] statement that informed consent will not be obtained for most research subjects; [t]he rationale [for waiving informed consent] ...; [a] copy of the informed consent document; ... information that would be part of the informed consent process ..., e.g., available treatments for the condition under study; risks/potential benefits of participating in the research; [the] possibility that FDA might inspect the subject's records; [a] description of the therapeutic window ... and the portion of that window that will be used to contact the subject's LAR [legally authorized representative]; [a] description of the attempts that will be made to contact the subject's LAR to obtain consent, or, if no LAR is available, a family member to provide an opportunity to object ..., both before and after the test article is administered ...; [a] description of how someone might decline to participate ...; [r]easons why community input is important; [k]nown community perceptions/concerns ...; and ... individuals to contact for more information. ...

Furthermore, where "appropriate," the IRB should consult the community. The FDA advises IRBs to, for example, consider "a public meeting," a "separate panel" of community members, IRB consultants from the community, community representatives to the IRB, or "other mechanisms." There must be an "independent data monitoring committee." And the community must get the study results and demographic data about the subjects.

Yet many regulationists find these rules lax: One writes sarcastically that you should know that if rushed to an ER, "[you] may be entered into an experimental research project" without consent, "compliments of the [FDA] and [DHHS]."[17]

These baroque rules introduce regulatory "cost." Cost is calculated first in resources, like space, money, and time. IRBs must assess, approve, and monitor the requirements; researchers must "consult" the "community." When Dix sought to manage brain trauma better, the IRB decided the "community" was Mississippi. An IRB member was the "community liaison," attended all seven community meetings, and distributed, collected, analyzed, and refined questionnaires.[18] The regulators' costs were pennies compared to the researchers'. Dix's whole team, including two neurosurgeons, attended all meetings whenever possible. They met groups four times in Jackson and traveled 150 miles to the Delta for a fifth meeting. And the IRB wanted still more meetings and quarterly reports on community consultation to "verify continued community support."

The regulations not only devour resources, they damage research. By slowing it they postpone its benefits; Dix's community consultation, for example, delayed her a full year. The regulations can cause "selection bias" by excluding people too ill to consent, i.e., those most needing help. Even researchers who have poured resources into their work have just given up. Kremers wanted to compare a pneumatic vest with standard CPR. He advertised a community forum in newspapers. Of the 1.4 million people invited, 25 attended (15 of them health care workers).[19] The IRB accepted Kremers' protocol "pending approval of the informational brochures and posters." But the posters called the vest "innovative," which the IRBs said could cause "recruitment bias." The IRB wanted the admitting nurse to "point out the brochure to each new patient and encourage the patient to read it and ask questions." The posters had to be videotaped to prove that patients really could see the information. *None* of the 1,750 relevant patients admitted wanted exemption or raised concerns. Four underwent cardiac arrest and were enrolled. The direct cost of the community consultation was $5,600, $1,400 per subject. Kremers quit.

Yet emergency-medicine research is needed urgently. For example, children's brains may be protected from cardiac arrest's consequences by methods like hypothermia. But "1) What is the optimal temperature … ? Does it vary by age group or etiology … ? 2) What is the … therapeutic window? Are there factors that affect this? 3) What is the optimal duration of hypothermia?" Yet "[n]o large-scale RCT has been conducted."[20] The regulations make such research heroic.

The emergency-medicine establishment urges researchers to serve on IRBs "to educate" them, to "perform research to ask the community how it defines the success of community consultation," and to study the rules' effect on research.[21] So regulation drives doctors away from what they do well—conducting research and saving lives—toward what they do poorly—analyzing policy.

In short, these liberalized regulations hardly change the prohibition they supplant. In their first decade, the FDA received 60 requests to conduct research and approved 21, "a pittance, considering the scope of the acute illnesses and injuries for which we currently have unsatisfactory or no treatment."[22] Damschroder says that many IRBs interpret the ambiguous criteria conservatively, causing "less health services research in many settings."[23] Sponsors, investigators, and IRBs just give up, since interpreting and implementing the rules are "too confusing, time-consuming, and cost-prohibitive for many sites."[24] Nichol observed in 2004 that "the number and proportion of randomized trials" of treatments for sudden cardiac arrest fell significantly during the last decade because of the regulations.[25]

Even in this corner of research, the stakes are disturbing. Roughly 300,000 people annually have cardiac arrests out of hospitals. Five percent of unselected patients survive, so "a one-year delay of a new therapy that improves survival by 1% may cost approximately 3,000 lives."[26] Halperin says that in many emergency situations like "cardiac arrest, mortality may exceed 90%." Because sufferers are numerous, "even small increases in survival could save many lives." Even if research reduced "mortality only from 90% to 80%," more than 20,000 lives would be saved yearly.[27]

Worse, cardiac arrest is changing, and the survival rate is *dropping*. Research has focused on ventricular fibrillation, but equally lethal cardiac rhythms (pulseless electrical activity and asystole) are increasingly common. Survival remains dismal without "large, well-designed studies."[28] And in Seattle (with nationally admired emergency services), survival of cardiac arrest from the research moratorium into the emergency-waiver era has fallen: Between 1977 and 1981, 17.5% survived to hospital discharge; between 1998 and 2001, 15.7%.

So what good do these regulations do? Consulting communities is otiose, since communities decline to be consulted. Salzman, for example, wanted to test two devices to improve survival "with good neurologic outcome" after CPR. He sent a press release to four TV stations, four talk-radio stations, two metropolitan newspapers, and many community newspapers. He was interviewed by some of these, bought notices in 10 newspapers, and addressed the city council and the county commissioners. A video was aired on five cable stations. He invited 136 organizations to a meeting and called and e-mailed nonresponding groups. Only 84 people attended, 43 with "EMS/public health" affiliations; 15 more with IRB affiliations. Ignoring researchers' time, Salzman paid $4,150 to reach 26 unaffiliated people.[29]

Insofar as communities respond, it is generally "fine with us." Eighty percent of Contant's respondents approved of emergency research without consent.[30] When Dix surveyed the few people who came to hear about head injuries, all approved.[31] All the 25 people at Kremers' forum supported his study,[32] none had questions. A study of public-access defibrillation included consultation involving 24 IRBs, 20 demanding revisions, 10 more than once. There were "1030 meetings, attended by at least 8169 individuals (median 88 participants per meeting); 475 press releases; distribution of 9270 letters, brochures, newsletters, or e-mails; 231 radio, television, or print advertisements; posting of 459 notices; 286 feature news stories; and 75 radio or television appearances." The negative response was 1%.[33]

These "liberalized" rules painfully illustrate regulation's cost. Researchers sacrifice time and money. Some are denied waivers, others give up, many never try, almost no research is finished. Thousands of patients die and suffer who might have been helped. Considering how few lives the IRB system can save, regulating emergency-medicine research alone surely costs more than the system's benefits.

B. TAXING RESEARCH

[T]he power to tax involves the power to destroy. ...
—U.S. Supreme Court, *M'Culloch v. Maryland*

Consent waivers show IRBs both taxing and supervising research. This reduces researchers' funds and time and hobbles research, obscuring ways to save lives, cure illness, and enhance welfare. The system taxes research in many costly ways. In other contexts, claims that funds spent on regulation would be better spent elsewhere are often empty because the money rarely reaches the elsewhere. But resources IRBs divert already are dedicated to research to save lives, cure illness, and soothe distress. These are the true costs of the dollars this section counts.

1. RUNNING IRBS

It is not merely the IRB members whose time and energy are wasted. Consider the consequences of imposing on investigators the obligation to comply with some of the regulations I have called defective and ... the pointless documentation requirements. ...
—Robert J. Levine, *Ethics and Regulation of Clinical Research*

What does administering the IRB system cost? First and least, the agencies that regulate IRBs must be paid for. OHRP is by federal standards small and cheap. (In 2011 it wanted $7 million for a staff of 29.) Second, however, the thousands of IRB members include expensive people like doctors or scientists (e.g., $600 an hour for consulting in a malpractice suit). IRB members at the hundred institutions receiving the most NIH funding meet for many hours and spend 275 hours yearly outside meetings.[34] IRB members are so numerous that "[m]any social sciences and humanities departments are smaller" than IRBs.[35]

Third, IRB staffs are populous, proliferating, and prosperous. There has been "tremendous growth in what can be termed the 'IRB industry.'" The Northwestern "Office for the Protection of Research Subjects grew from two full-time professionals in the late 1990s to 25 professionals and an administrative staff of 20."[36] Columbia has five IRBs of some dozen members each with 28 staffers.[37] A 2007 estimate concluded that medical schools' IRBs cost averaged about a million dollars annually.[38] The National Cancer Institute's central review board costs $1.9 million yearly.[39]

The cost of IRB labor is hinted at by a 1998 study of 491 IRBs doing 284,000 reviews, "including 105,000 initial reviews," "116,000 continuing/annual reviews, and 63,000 reviews of amendments."[40] IRBs also responded to reports of harmed and complaining subjects and to legal actions, trained researchers, recruited members, made policy, and managed records, personnel, and technology.[41] Reviewing protocols took 1.7 million hours: 122,000 by chairs, 516,000 by members, 472,000 by administrators, 498,000 by administrative staff, and 62,000 by institutional officials.[42] These costs soar if OHRP audits an IRB to see if it is operating properly or in response to a complaint. Klitzman writes that audits can be triggered easily "and cost millions, yet in the end find little, if anything." One of Klitzman's interviewees described an audit sparked "by a disgruntled former faculty member" who might have had "some mental health issues." OHRP found no evidence to support the complaint, "but it took *four years*!"[43]

Fourth, IRBs require support. Members and staff are increasingly trained and certified; IRBs use space, supplies, and services (like the general counsel and HR). Fifth, a small industry provides IRB-related specialists, including consultants, bioethicists, academics, and trainers. Sixth, IRB accreditation is spreading, and obtaining it is costly in fees and work, like a self-study requiring "documentation of goals and procedures for all dimensions of IRB operations" that takes "some institutions several years to complete."[44] In sum, after a sturdy childhood, Big Ethics is enjoying its teenage growth spurt.

2. RUNNING RESEARCH

We have long endured online tutorials, reams of paperwork, and advice from our [IRBs]. … Through the questioning of small segments of proposals, IRBs have caused delays, missed deadlines, and reduced productivity for our graduate students, postdoctoral fellows, and ourselves.
—Stephen J. Ceci & Maggie Bruck, *Do IRBs Pass the Minimal Harm Test?*

Thousands of researchers and their staffs prepare materials for IRBs both before and during research. Review can be long and arduous. One report estimates that more than 80% of proposals are sent back for changes; one experienced observer estimates 90–95%.[45] Multiple rounds of modifications are possible. After approval, researchers must report even trivial changes and get annual reapproval. IRBs tax research in other ways. They can make recruiting subjects costlier. A study of respiratory care for very premature infants had to pay about $200,000 for research nurses to get consent to routinely performed procedures.[46]

Even regulationists have long deplored paperwork minutely documenting minor topics. NBAC bemoaned its "overwhelming burden" on both IRBs and scholars. "Free Parking" shows how much paperwork even a small, riskless study may need. As IRB authority expands, paperwork proliferates. In a national study, the mean pages per application doubled from 2002 to 2008.[47] In an eight-IRB study using essentially the same protocol in 2002 and 2007, pages per application went from 86 to 104.[48] Thus clinical research coordinators are coming to specialize in handling IRBs. Thus to "ask a few children whether they recognised Tinky Winky or Jake," an English doctor needed statistical advice and a pilot study to see how many subjects to have. He "filled out the rather lengthy ethical approval application form" and then was told it had been supplanted. "If you never read this study written up in any journal don't be surprised."[49]

IRBs and researchers must increasingly submit to education. NBAC: Education is the IRB system's foundation and essential to protecting subjects.[50] IOM: "Research investigators and key personnel should be versed in the ethical foundations underlying research participant protection, the regulatory requirements …, research administration and management skills … [, and] GCP and medical ethics." Otherwise "serious errors" could compromise subjects' safety and data's integrity and interpretation, all creating "unnecessary risks, however minimal the risks may have been."[51]

Many people must learn much. NBAC: Researchers, IRBs, and institutions frequently do not understand "research ethics."[52] It is "important to educate prospective participants and the general public." Researchers must recurrently be retrained, or at least retested, and institutions must pay for the "development and oversight of this training." The proportion of hospitals requiring training doubled from 2002 to 2008, with 12% newly requiring "HIPAA training specific to their institution." And NBAC wants "education, certification, and accreditation systems that apply to all researchers, all IRB members and staff, and all institutions."[53]

A final set of administrative costs is unnoticed but noteworthy—research subjects' time and trouble. Even when consent forms were shorter, an average of 30 minutes was spent discussing them.[54] Aggregate the time, and the sum is enormous.

3.   COST AND THE EVIDENCE OF MULTISITE STUDIES

[Chairs (87%) and members (83%)] agreed that "This IRB runs with reasonable efficiency."
—NIH Report

Increasingly, major biomedical studies require multiple sites.[55] Sometimes to investigate differences among sites. Or to replicate results in one center in others. Or to accumulate enough subjects. Even 15 years ago a third of initial IRB submissions were from multisite studies.[56] These studies have evaluated many treatments for many diseases, preventing "several tens of millions of premature deaths and much suffering."[57] These studies not only do much good, they provide some of the best evidence about how IRBs work, since they reveal how different IRBs handle identical protocols.

Multiple review has no apparent benefits,[58] and the regulations sensibly permit single IRB review.[59] Yet IRBs tenaciously reject it. Scores of American and British reports show that (1) multiple review is hideously wasteful, (2) many IRBs are dilatory and cumbersome, (3) IRBs' obsession with forms devours everyone's time, and (4) different IRBs' decisions about the same protocol are often irreconcilable and unfounded in discernible principles. In Humphreys' "eight-site observational substance abuse treatment study," review "*after* the home IRB had approved the project" consumed 17% of the research budget. First, IRBs often disagreed about the particulars of forms. Second, review was required by more than one IRB from the same institution. Finally, the study's coordinators were often prohibited from contacting IRB staffs at the sites, nor would IRBs talk to each other. Yet the study's basic procedures were never substantially altered, even after 15,000 pages were exchanged.[60] Similarly, in Vick's mailed survey and medical-records review of ventral hernia repairs, IRB issues cost roughly 13% of the 30-month budget, 25% of the first year's budget, and 30% of the project's calendar.[61]

C. SUPERVISING RESEARCH

If parents of children dying of some of the diseases we encounter in neurology understood how much more cumbersome and expensive research is as the result of this system, the system would be in big trouble.
—Survey respondent

The IRB system discourages, delays, degrades, and destroys research, often for ghostly gains and wraithly reasons. The ways are many.

1. RESEARCH DELAYED

[Society] is under definite obligations to see to it that physicians and scientific men are not needlessly hampered in ... the inquiries necessary for ... their important social office of sustaining human life and vigor.

—John Dewey, *The Ethics of Animal Experimentation*

IRBs protract research. It cannot start until an IRB reviews and licenses it, and permission is needed to modify research. IRBs slow research by restricting its conduct.

CASE STUDY: MY PORTION OF PARADISE[62]

Anybody who wants to save me from kidney stones is a fine, fine fellow. Such is Dr. Fredric Coe. In 1969, he began using his patients' urine samples to analyze their risk of stones and to seek treatments. In 1987, he began saving samples (now for 4,500 patients) and getting IRB permission to use them. The IRB's confidentiality obsession baffled Coe, since each patient was a dot on a graph, unidentified by name, address, or age. The results were averages, never case studies. Nobody "out there" cared about cases; they wanted numbers. But Coe memorized HIPAA's "eighteen personal health identifiers." He told "people in charge" that no identifiers appeared and that they were only seen by the people who already took care of the patients. Coe could freely use the samples to treat patients, but when he used them for research, he suddenly had to rebut a presumption that he would breach a patient's confidentiality.

Soon, Coe got "'Pending Conditional' status, meaning more information was needed." Eventually the IRB told him to get oral consent from "all future patients to have their data used in your publications" by reading a script to them. Since the study used no identifiers and had "no risk the script should be very simple. This oral script will need to be voted upon at another fully convened IRB meeting." Since "discussion for your protocol was quite lengthy at the last meeting," the IRB "strongly suggest[ed]" sending the script to the same panel of the IRB. Otherwise, "new stipulations may arise." By the time approval came, months had elapsed, "months during which I was not permitted to analyze my own data."

Yearly Coe completed tables of the number of patients in the program, the number of measurements of blood and urine in his records, and papers published. In 1998, Coe's two-page request for re-approval was summarily granted. Next year requirements were more involved, including "an amendment to add an additional investigator who would isolate proteins." In 2002, the IRB wanted a bibliography and literature summary on urine proteins, which took much time. Next year, another bibliography. In 2004, one that included the search criteria.

In 2005, Coe had apparently "used far more than our original 100 urine samples specified in 1997 and could not account for all of them. How many in 2002? 2003?" Since this was "scrap urine, it is hard to be sure; a sample may show up in several notebooks because it is merely a substrate for extraction of molecules." Coe consulted his notebooks. "This took real time—hours and hours. ... In addition, there were questions about how the grant from the NIH that funded the research might relate to this protocol." Coe "could not understand why our grant would matter to an IRB," and the IRB eventually agreed it did not. But 2005 was "expensive."

Next year, the IRB reviewed

all of our past submissions and found worrisome irregularities. Questions soon followed. Why does our research pose no more than minimal risk to subjects? Why will a waiver of consent not adversely affect the rights and welfare of subjects? Why is it impractical to do the research without a waiver? Will pertinent information be provided to subjects, if appropriate, at a later date? Then there was the vexatious matter of how many urines. We needed to submit an amendment to increase the numbers—we really have used too many. Finally, the grants became relevant. On reading our program project grant—over 1,000 pages in all—it appeared that some grant work might have used these scrap urines. If so, the IRB needs a copy of the grant for its files.

Coe "submitted the usual continuation application, with its bibliography, search criteria and summary of changes to the risk–benefit ratio." And "an amendment to use more urine." And "a supplemental form W waiver of consent-authorization," since getting each patient's consent would be "Herculean." (Coe did not know beforehand when he would need urine.) When last heard from, he was waiting to see if he could "use the scraps of urine? Or, to save our patients from harm, need we pour it down the drain?"

Coe wonders why the tiniest protocol change requires so many forms, why so much bureaucracy is needed to change the time of a meal or blood draw. "Does a decision to put up signs to recruit normal subjects somehow impose a heightened risk of an allergic reaction? The latter change required not only submitting the request, but clearing the text on the signs, and even having each sign stamped with an official stamp."

So Coe recites his little speech to his patients. They think he is daft. He says that "it is HIPAA, it is the IRB." Most of his patients say "what is HIPAA? What, indeed, is the IRB? My world, I tell them. My portion of paradise."

IRB approval can take months. An extreme example is Gittner's trivially risky health-service research—8 *years* of negotiation with several IRBs.[63] More normally, McWilliams' genetic epidemiologic research study "took 9 to 252 days for approval by 31 IRB committees." Dziak's health-services research "took 5 to 172 days by 15 IRB committees." Stair's "clinical trial took 26 to 62 days for approval by 44 IRB committees." Sherwood's median time between enlisting an investigator at a site and IRB approval there was 14.7 months. Preparing materials took a median of 9.5 months; the average wait after submission was over 3 months.[64] Some research is "exempt," but IRBs insist on approving exemptions. IRBs may (but need not) "expedite" some research (allow one IRB member to say yes but not no),[65] but only if it fits one of nine categories and is minimally risky. And research occasionally "suggests that 'expedited' review can actually be slower than standard review."[66]

Delay can degrade research. For example, delay in epidemiological research diverts funds and scientists.[67] New infections are often ill understood, and outbreaks are often seasonal and geographically unpredictable. Despite the urgency this creates, in a multisite study of West Nile virus IRBs variously asked from zero to 269 questions. Topics "ranged from grammatical and editorial requests to mandated inclusion of site specific language."[68] Because it took so long to develop and approve protocols, (1) they reached sites after the viral season had started, (2) most sites could not enroll subjects at peak season "for lack of IRB approval," and (3) "a number of sites lacked IRB approval even after the season ended." Such delays "make clinical trials impracticable" and "severely restrict" clinical trials' capacity to respond quickly to new infections.[69]

Social scientists suffer too. Stern studies terrorists, and the Harvard IRB's review has sometimes been so protracted that research had to be abandoned. For example, radical black Muslims agreed to speak to her, but after six months waiting for IRB approval, they declined.[70]

2. RESEARCH RESTRICTED

[W]e should not have a system in which thousands of lives might be lost because we have an outmoded conception of human-subjects research that leaves little room for riskless studies aimed at improving medical practice.

—Thomas L. Beauchamp, *Viewpoint*[71]

IRBs alter protocols in ways that reduce research's reliability, scope, and utility. The problem is extensive and expensive.

IRBs damage research by impeding recruitment. IRBs forbid the use of whole categories of research subjects, restrict the ways subjects are approached, and impose requirements that discourage participation. This diverts resources to recruiting, keeps numbers too small, and creates selection bias, as in this

CASE STUDY: LAST BREATH[72]

A fatal asthma attack begins like any other. The child has been wheezing more and using her inhaler more, with less benefit. Her airways are inflamed, in spasm, plugged with mucus; her body labors to get air into them. She becomes anxious and tells her mother she can't breathe. Going to the emergency room, she struggles more violently but less successfully. She panics, her breathing worsens, her lips turn blue. At the emergency room, her chest muscles are so exhausted that little oxygen reaches her brain. Her terror recedes as she loses consciousness. Oxygen can be forced through a tube down her trachea, but not deep enough into the lungs. She dies.

Asthma afflicts 7.5% of us. "In 2000, asthma exacerbations accounted for approximately 1.8 million emergency department visits, 465,000 hospital admissions, and 4,500 deaths." Since 1980, deaths have increased more than 50%; among children under 19, 80%. The disease is slightly more common among African Americans than among whites, but they are three times likelier to die from it. "Ethnic differences in asthma prevalence, morbidity and mortality are highly correlated with poverty, urban air quality, indoor allergens, and lack of patient education and inadequate medical care."[73]

But what precipitates an asthma death? Since little is known, Clark proposed a fatal-asthma registry. She worked "closely with HIPAA experts and one of the four IRBs" to develop a protocol. She thought it qualified for a waiver of authorization from next of kin for access to data, but the four IRBs disagreed with her. They disagreed with each other about contacting next of kin. Two allowed contact by phone following a contact letter; the other two let researchers call only if their letter was answered. It took three months for Clark to get IRB clearance, and IRB review changed the protocol in ways that made the registry less representative and thus less valuable.

IRBs constrict access to subjects. One regulationist thinks subjects should only be approached by letter or a third party.[74] Some IRB members insist that people first return a signed card agreeing to participate, which devastates recruitment (in one study, success fell from 92% to 31%). Such low participation promotes selection bias and stops epidemiological research.[75]

IRBs often make consent so burdensome to researchers or alarming to subjects that recruitment is slowed and skewed. Some IRBs impose inflammatory language,[76] like lists even grislier than Viagra ad side effects. Legal trappings alone can alarm recruits. Morahan describes evaluating a program to help senior female medical and dental school faculty with their careers. Mid-study requirements reduced participation from 100% to 84%. Every dropout who gave a reason blamed the consent form. Because of (fatuous) phrases like "[t]his is a long and important document," "[y]ou should take your time and carefully read [it]," and you can discuss this form "with your family member, physician, [or] attorney." Because of (insulting) warnings of "anxiety or stress when answering questions about success or failures in leadership" serious enough that the researchers would "be happy to refer you to counseling."[77]

Somewhat differently, Harvard's IRB made Stern (the terrorism researcher) warn subjects that she would tell the authorities of specific plans for violence. She didn't wish to know about such plans but didn't "want to be so explicit," since it "just reminds them that they have done bad things" or that "maybe I'm not on their side."[78] IRBs often tell those studying "hospitalized psychiatric patients, marihuana smokers, homeless black men, or pool hustlers" to get signed consent. But "[m]ost ethnographers establish trust only through gaining rapport," so requiring consent first usually severs "ties before trust can begin to be cultivated." Thus government "shields us from knowing the truth about ghettos, tearooms, marihuana users, and abuses of patients in psychiatric hospitals."[79]

Likewise, a Canadian stroke registry had to spend C$500,000 on consent issues during its first two years and hire neurologic research nurse coordinators and reached a participation rate of only 40% to 50%. Many patients died or were discharged before being approached. Selection biases were severe: 7% of the enrolled patients but 22% of the stroke victims died in the hospital.[80] In Gong's study of the genetic risk of acute strokes, less damaged patients were overrepresented because 40% of the IRBs prohibited surrogate consent. Gong concludes that such requirements "may severely restrict and bias needed research in critical illnesses" and in "conditions that can affect a patient's decision-making."[81] In Greene's mailed survey of psychosocial consequences of prophylactic mastectomy, IRBs set varying "physician consent requirements, invitation letter content and signatories, incentive type, and mailing protocol,"[82] which obscured the nature and degree of bias.

Selection bias not only makes research less useful generally, it makes it less useful to the neediest specifically. Inhibitions on recruitment tend to exclude the sickest patients. The more IRBs protect people from risk, the less researchers can study people at risk.

IRB regulation has impaired kinds of research that are fruitful yet cheap. For example, medical care generates information, and blood and tissue samples may be taken. These data can be stored in biobanks—collections of biological material (even, say, genetic material from intestinal microorganisms or colonies of disease-causing bacteria) and information. Biobanks let researchers do in months what might otherwise take years. Even more can be learned when archives are linked to other medical data sources, both traditional (like death certificates) and novel (like DNA databases), or to nonmedical data, like air samples or lists of toxic dumps.

Such research has lovely advantages. It is efficient because databases already exist. Smaller groups (say, ethnic minorities or patients with rare comorbidities) are likelier to be adequately represented. And such research "studies (messy) real experience."[83] For example, cancer registries' "output is impressive" by "any standards, and often in the face of limited resources." They have contributed "most of the evidence" justifying multidisciplinary care and specialization.[84] Epidemiology especially mines them. Until Doll and others identified cigarette smoking as a cause, the spike in lung cancer deaths was baffling. Since tobacco-related mortality this century may average 10 million people annually, a 1% reduction saves 1,000,000 lives per decade. And research on clozapine for schizophrenia linked the Clozaril National Registry's mortality data on almost 70,000 patients with data in the Social Security Death Files and the National Death Index.[85]

IRB interpretations of HIPAA corrode archival research. This "significantly reduced" consent for a follow-up questionnaire in a registry study of patients with acute coronary syndrome, perhaps producing a damaging selection bias.[86] Chart reviews are "critical to evaluating medical treatments, detecting harmful drug interactions, uncovering dangerous side effects," and "developing new therapies." But they are impossible with "anonymous information, because the detailed data that researchers require will always include information that could be used to identify a specific person."[87]

Not only can IRBs make archival research costlier, longer, and harder; they can stop it. Fost reports that HIPAA reduced medical-records research at the University of Wisconsin 77%. Multiplied nationally, "tens of thousands of important epidemiologic studies" are stopped.[88] Yet there is scant evidence that archival research is unsafe. As one investigator wrote passionately, constraints on it "are a major set back in science and I hope all those at OHRP and the ethicists die of diseases that we could have made significant progress on … USE OF THESE SAMPLES IN NO CONCEIVABLE way harms the study subjects. It is a bureaucratic legalistic impediment to research that only HURTS people and protects no one."[89]

IRBs particularly impede research the vulnerable need. IRBs restrict access to group members, make consent forms scarier, require special confidentiality measures, and otherwise make research so much more expensive and arduous that less research can be done, that research is less reliable, and that researchers give it up. Bell and Salmon say, "Ironically, concerns expressed in the name of protecting drug users may actually harm individuals by inhibiting research that is beneficial to them and their communities or disallowing study procedures that participants themselves endorse as ethical and respectful."[90] Programs to reduce lead-paint risks for poor children demand sound research, but the NRC and IOM advocate restrictions so burdensome that IRB approval would be virtually impossible and that sensible researchers would avoid the field.[91] "Intimidated for several years" by rules restricting research with the vulnerable, "almost no one" at Northwestern outside education, psychology, and linguistics studied children, and researchers in those fields usually stayed in easily controlled situations.[92]

The problem is harsh because the federal regulations instruct IRBs to specially restrict research with the vulnerable and because IRBs are fertile in anticipating risks to them. We need to understand adolescent "sexual activity and contraceptive practices, smoking, and alcohol and drug use," but some commentators think research condones or encourages "such behaviors in young people" or yields knowledge that might "weaken the social fabric of society" and perpetuate harmful practices. "Evidence-based guidelines on the care of pregnant women and the mentally ill are rare." But IRBs impede research that might help them. Park and Grayson say that "stringent restrictions on pediatric research make major advances" in well-founded knowledge "rare at best." This is one reason "that as many as 80% of drugs" pediatricians prescribe have not "been systematically studied in children." Thus "specific data regarding dosing, efficacy, or risk" are unavailable. And most pediatric therapies rely on studies "that are inherently subject to bias, inferences from studies of adults, or, worse, anecdotal evidence." For example, addressing some of the important questions about pediatric asthma "head-on is almost impossible within the current framework of 'ethical research.'"[93]

African-American infants are likelier to be born with extremely low birth weights and twice as likely to die. The SUPPORT study asked how different respiratory care affected lung disease, retinopathy, and survival in ELBW infants. All 18 IRBs required that consent be obtained, even though the tested regimens are routinely provided without specific consent. Getting consent cost $200,000, and if 75% of the eligible but not enrolled infants had been included, recruitment could have taken 18 instead of 48 months. Mothers of unenrolled infants were less likely to be white, insured, high-school educated, and recipients of prenatal care. And their infants were likelier to die. In short, IRB restrictions inhibited doctors trying to save their disproportionately black patients from suffocation, blindness, and death.[94]

The children of incarcerated adolescent girls "are among the most vulnerable and least well served" American children, but little is known about their "numbers, health, developmental, and placement status." HIPAA's stringency and IRB ignorance "make obtaining permission to conduct institution-based case file reviews a long and expensive process."

Acoca reports the "increasing difficulty—if not impossibility—of obtaining permission to conduct face-to-face interviews."[95]

Even scholars not working with vulnerable groups are steered by IRB pressures away from some populations and toward rigid methods.[96] So because Feld could not meet IRB "demands for a more detailed recruitment strategy and interview protocol," he decided not to interview police and only to listen to audiotapes of interrogations, thus losing "part of a potentially groundbreaking project."[97]

Most notorious is the IRBs' tendency to treat all research like biomedical research. Biomedical protocols commonly test hypotheses and resist variation. But in many fields, researchers need "[t]o be open to novelty and anomaly." Questions "suddenly take on pressing importance." Questions evolve fitfully,[98] work progresses by trial and error, hypotheses metamorphose, and relations with subjects deepen. Yet many IRBs require unalterable questions, so that researchers cannot shift direction, respond to subjects' comments, or have normal conversations.[99] So you are asking college students to solve math problems and three weeks before the academic year ends, you realize that your work "on simple addition needs to be buttressed by another experiment, say one testing subtraction problems."[100] Not without new IRB authorization. Similarly, a student doing "an exempt observational study of children who actually joins their game of tag" must "fill out the same protocol violation form, heavily laced with medical and legal terms, and phrased in the language of rebuke, as a researcher who accidentally doubles a patient's radiation dosage in a medical trial."[101]

IRBs also tend to apply regulationist ethics, like the rule against deceiving or harming subjects, rigidly. That can "preclude valuable forms of critical inquiry," like interviewing and observing police officers "to learn about police racism (or corruption, sexism, excessive use of force, etc.)" or investigating other "high-profile, contentious issues involving powerful people or agencies."[102] Or finding out what mental hospitals are really like or how apartheid really worked.[103]

IRBs review research's substance and methods but (chapter 4 shows) generally not well. Sometimes researchers dissuade IRBs from mutilating research (at a cost in resources and delay), but sometimes research must be done badly if at all. For example, Gittner wanted to improve substance-abuse screening. Because IRBs caused "large additional study costs, delays and inaction," because IRBs "seemed more concerned with minimisation of institutional legal risk" than ethics, and because of IRB-mandated methodological changes, the final "protocol was not translatable into clinical practice and the generalisability of the results was seriously compromised."[104] Similarly, Thompson notes that "researchers risk sanctions and public stigma from being accused of running afoul of the research regulations" and thus may design "less robust and, thereby, ineffective QI studies."[105] Van den Hoonaard observes that making researchers destroy data has become a "fetish" and notes the American Anthropological Association's "great concern" about IRBs' tendency to require destroying data or identifications. He argues that this makes longitudinal and comparative research impossible and keeps researchers "from conducting an ongoing analysis" of data.[106]

3.   RESEARCH DENIED

IRBs started out in part as a way to stop the next Joseph Mengele from physically torturing humans ..., but have ended up chilling valuable social science that might ... explain how someone gets to be a Joseph Mengele.
—Dale Carpenter, *IRBs, Regulatory Incentives, and Some Modest Proposals For Reform*

Regulationist doctrine holds that IRBs rarely prohibit research, but they often kill it by a thousand cuts, by requesting revisions so persistently that researchers give up. As Robert Levine said, "The way disapproval is accomplished de facto is that requirements for revision are made that the investigator chooses, for any of a large variety of reasons, not to accept."[107] For example, a graduate student wanted to study how prison affects women. She completed her IRB application "honestly and accurately and finally heard back that I had to make substantial revisions." She frequently consulted the compliance coordinator and the secretary. Her second form "was rejected on a whole other set of criteria that [the] IRB never mentioned" before. She finally changed her topic enough to escape IRB jurisdiction "because they had pushed back the start date of my research so far."[108]

IRBs can make research prohibitively costly. For example, budgets for observational health-services research "are typically very modest" and cannot absorb delays and unexpected expenses caused by "multiple re-submissions and conflicting reviews."[109] IRBs can impede relationships with funding agencies: "I decided to forego a grant because the deadline was short and I would need IRB approval to ask for the money."[110] One can only guess how often researchers abandon ideas because they think they cannot get IRB permission in time, on tolerable terms, or at all. Proposing and initiating research can cost so much that researchers hesitate to invest in projects IRBs might thwart.

Because of IRBs, some research will not be done at all, some will be done but be damaged, and some might be done by someone outside IRB jurisdiction. Some biomedical research can be done by profit-making enterprises. Some social-science research will be done by journalists. This can have two unhappy consequences. First, the work may be done poorly. Researchers working for profit-making enterprises may lack the time and freedom to follow the data; they must accommodate business constraints. Journalists are untrained in the substance and method of the social sciences. Second, research driven out of the academy (and even out of the country) may be done by people unhampered by the ethical codes and norms of academic disciplines. (Would you rather be investigated by a reporter or a sociologist?)

So Hamburger asks whether a researcher today could expose a Tuskegee or whether the IRB would protect the subjects (the researchers) by requiring informed consent and suppressing of their identities. Would the researcher "end up exposing an unspeakable study by unnamed persons concerning an unmentionable disease in an undisclosed location"?[111]

4. HARMING RESEARCH SUBJECTS

Perversely, IRBs can raise subjects' risks and lower their benefits. Sometimes, as Beauchamp writes, this happens because of the "prevailing assumption that research using subjects is *dangerous*, exists for the benefit of *future patients* and is aimed at scientific knowledge, *not benefit for immediate subjects*." Yet subjects may not "see research as burdensome, but as potentially beneficial." For example, AIDS groups have long argued strenuously that protectionist law and policy denied "benefits to a segment of the population deeply in need of" them, which "certainly looks like a moral failure."[112] Beauchamp calls the Pronovost case "stunning in this regard, because the activities produced *no risk whatever* for patients" and followed "the safest *practices* known to exist," practices "already proven safe and efficacious." Yet "OHRP made the wooden judgment" that "the whole apparatus of federal requirements" was required, delaying "effective preventive measures" and possibly causing avoidable deaths.[113]

Sometimes IRBs cause subjects direct and physical harm. In a study of ELBW babies, one IRB wanted researchers to inject a placebo into control-group infants, even though the study was double-blinded in other ways and the placebo's effect on 1-pound people was unknown.[114] Sometimes subjects' purses and preferences suffer. Flowers' IRB made her specify an interview site, preferably on campus, even though her impecunious subjects had trouble getting there.[115]

IRBs can endanger subjects' confidentiality. In Green's 43-site study, 12 IRBs asked for names, increasing subjects' risks and violating promises made them.[116] One IRB wanted a list kept of African child-soldiers that local authorities might find. Flowers avoided learning phone-sex workers' names, but her IRB demanded signed consent forms. (A few subjects used their pseudonyms, creating "consent forms signed 'cum-monger' and 'snow-white.'")[117] In a random audit, Perrone's IRB sought keys linking pseudonyms with biographies and an audiotape of the interview,[118] making it likelier that subjects' "illegal drug use would become known" and forcing Perrone to violate promises to the subjects.[119]

IRBs can also decrease subjects' benefits from research. Some subjects seek help from a treatment or from the superior care research may provide. Sometimes a trial is a last hope, however wispy. The IRB in "Free Parking" harassed a program offering mothers of ELBW babies $500 (a 50% chance of $1,000) to visit their children. While some people find talking about painful events therapeutic, IRBs often prohibit or inhibit such conversations. The benefit might simply be a pleasant day for children (see "Down on the Farm" in chapter 4). Sometimes the benefit is payment that an IRB sometimes lowers or eliminates. Some subjects could use researchers as a megaphone but encounter IRB resistance, as when Bradley proposed to give young people video cameras to record their experiences.[120] Subjects' reward can be helping other people, like the families in "Last Breath" (this chapter) or the dying patients in "Last Words" (chapter 1).

D. UNDERMINING THE INFRASTRUCTURE OF RESEARCH

[S]o far to distrust the judgment and the honesty of one who hath but a common repute in learning, and never yet offended, as not to count him fit to print his mind without a tutor and examiner ... is the greatest displeasure and indignity to a free and knowing spirit. ...
—John Milton, *Areopagitica*

IRBs not only delay, damage, and destroy research projects. They harm the research enterprise. As Schrag writes, because "of IRB oversight, society as whole has fewer books and articles, and has fewer scholars willing to interact with other human beings." And "ever more students" are "discouraged from academic careers that depend on talking to other people."[121]

The IRB system makes training students—graduate, undergraduate, and even high school—harder and worse. This even though IRBs should lack jurisdiction over most student research, since it is rarely "a systematic investigation ... designed to develop or contribute to generalizable knowledge." Assignments rather teach students about a subject and about what research is, how to conduct, interpret, and report it.

IRBs have hobbled and halted teachers' attempts to teach research. Slow and unpredictable IRBs discourage semester-length projects. Even a student who began planning her senior honors thesis in her junior year spent a semester and a half struggling with "bureaucratic review committees," including two IRBs. She "was repeatedly misguided about forms I should submit, when, and to whom." So she had too little time "even to begin the actual testing of my subjects, let alone conduct the project."[122] A professor "spent hours reviewing IRB forms" and half the semester getting them past the IRB chair, even for harmless interviews and questionnaires. Students "found the IRB debacle to be nitpicking nonsense. Many of them ultimately received an 'incomplete' for the course." Yet the IRB chair was not only "highly competent and cooperative" and "an established social scientist, but also an extraordinarily cooperative friend of mine. In short, the IRB fiasco is not about persons, but a system."[123]

IRBs especially deter students from studying crucial kinds of problems. "Any mention of sex set off alarms. Patricia Adler and Peter Adler watched in dismay as IRBs put so many conditions on studies of gay teenagers, public sex, and sexually transmitted diseases that graduate students abandoned the topics; one student left the university in disgust."[124] One faculty member "now restricts his students to 'bland topics and archived records'" because of the IRB's "delays and limitations."[125]

Graduate students picking thesis topics have more than a semester, but more to lose. Dismal reports abound. Feeley helped two generations of graduate students navigate "the minefields of IRB review." IRBs' "costly delays and changes" drove many to less troublesome research.[126] One student's IRB conditioned even constricted interviews with treated and released sex offenders on approval from "correctional and mental health facilities," which would grant it only after he got IRB approval. He gave up.[127] One graduate student's review took so long the university waived two semesters' tuition.[128]

Professors have discouraged students from doing research because they feared IRB delays or lacked time to help students get IRB licenses.[129] A dissertation supervisor had to undergo CITI training before a student could conduct research. Some professors tell students just to go along with inappropriate or nonsensical procedures.[130] (Berkeley graduate students call the "Committee for the Protection of Human Subjects" the "Committee for the Prevention of Research on Human Subjects."[131])

Many physicians think scholarship is "essential to intellectually vital medical practice." Students once learned research through chart reviews, which could be "scholarly and insightful" and lead "to clinical insights and additional research." But now students cannot, even with substantial help, "prepare the multiple complex forms required by an IRB, submit them, and have them reviewed, revised, resubmitted, and approved" during one rotation. So "too many students" do research that spares them IRB bureaucracy.[132] Similarly, the Infectious Disease Society of America fears "HIPAA's effects on medical-record reviews" because they often introduce trainees to research and need not take long. But "[e]ven expedited [IRB] review often requires 1–3 months," killing projects.[133]

Van den Hoonaard describes a "crisis brought on by research-ethics review"—"the decline of methods that have traditionally been at the heart of social research," including "fieldwork/participant observation, covert research, [and] action research." He studied Canadian master's theses before and after ethics review had proliferated and found a decrease in theses involving research subjects from 31% in 1995 to 8% in 2004. Of those theses, 40% included fieldwork in 1995, but only 5% in 2004.

One of his informants observed "an immense decline at the Qualitative Analysis Conferences (that has a high attendance of graduate students) of subcultural research."[134] And at the main Canadian conference for qualitative researchers, a third of the papers were based on fieldwork in 1999, below 19% in 2002, and 15% in 2007.[135]

New academics may also forsake fields in which IRBs delay, damage, and prevent research. As Fost says of IRB "micro-regulation" of language in consent forms, "it's endless, and is really a great deterrent to research, and it is discouraging some people from going into the field."[136] One report found many researchers believing HIPAA led scholars to rethink "certain studies" and discouraged clinicians and students "from research careers in view of the complex regulatory burden."[137]

Thomas Vogt, a member of two IRBs, admonishes "students to think twice" about human research. The regulatory "focus on minor details has diverted discussions from substantive to trivial. It is also diverting scarce funding from research into indirect costs and discouraging talented young scientists from doing human research." Coe teaches young faculty to battle IRB difficulties "that are legion, demanding of time, and that often impose insuperable barriers to research."[138] With the tenure bomb ticking, assistant professors must publish rapidly and richly; IRB supervention is costly, disapproval disastrous.

Even tenured professors lose. Bledsoe found that IRB delays and intrusion into each step of research keep many social scientists away from "topics, methods, and populations that IRB frames in the mode of risk." One scholar said, "It is very discouraging, and I find myself thinking of EVERY new research project as it relates to the possibility of IRB approval."[139] One physician says the "incredibly burdensome IRB system" drives scientists to give up human for animal research even though "treatments developed in animals rarely succeed in humans," because IRBs are "far less efficient, more costly, and impose a more intricate, arbitrary and difficult regulatory burden" than the committees regulating animal research.[140]

People in institutions that receive federal money but have not created an IRB cannot do human-subject research. For example, some of the hospitals in the Keystone (ICU checklist) project could not have met OHRP's demand for IRB approval because they had no IRB. Even people whose institutions receive no federal money may find that journals will not publish research without an IRB's imprimatur. One enterprise studied why people leave chronic-care programs, how intensive diabetes management affects health care costs, the honeymoon effect when people enter intensive diabetes programs, and how employee incentives affect diabetes patients. But it did not publish results for want of an IRB. And a several-hundred-person medical practice abandoned their review board "because it was 'too much trouble.'"

We saw earlier that IRBs can distort research in ways that injure vulnerable groups. Bledsoe sees professors steering students away from "topics or populations that the IRB considers 'touchy'" and hesitating to let students tackle major social issues like "abortion and crime, or have them collect data from populations that IRB defines as vulnerable," like immigrants and children. Regulatory sensitivity is so delicate that one scholar worries about "'any population that is not adult, well-adjusted, crime-free, middle class, heterosexual, white.'"[141] An IRB official said that "'[s]ome faculty have learned to become strategic about projects, to avoid IRB review, and don't study vulnerable populations.'" [142]

Collaboration helps researchers amass large samples; do interdisciplinary work; and compare phenomena in different geographical, social, or cultural settings. But requiring approval from each scholar's IRB disrupts and even destroys collaboration. And in "an increasingly globalized, comparative political-social science, possibilities for cross-national collaborations become increasingly constricted as researchers need to satisfy [IRB] policies that conflict with each other (e.g., one requiring data storage, another prohibiting it)."[143]

I argued earlier that the IRB system delays, damages, and denies research. I am now arguing that it corrodes the institutions and practices that sustain research. It drives people away from scholarship. It impels students and scholars from people toward molecules and mice. It diminishes the research students can learn and scholars practice. It pushes scholarship toward the blandness that leave IRBs unperturbed.

E. HARMS OUTSIDE RESEARCH

As the system reaches beyond "research," costs increase, not least because IRBs must exceed their competence. One example illustrates classic IRB imperialism, the second the unexpected niches into which IRBs intrude.

IRB jurisdiction is intruding into administrative work, like quality improvement. Instead of investigating treatments, "QI asks how best to put knowledge into practice." QI is part of a hospital's administrative duties (like instituting Pronovost's checklist). But "the growing consensus" calls QI research that IRBs must approve.[144] This imposes all the costs of dealing with IRBs that we have canvassed on health care institutions desperately trying to control costs. It slows, discourages, and prevents efforts to improve care. And it makes it harder to hold hospitals accountable for the quality of their services.

Curriculum is classically the faculty's responsibility, but faculties often solicit students' opinions. However, medical educators increasingly wonder whether IRBs must approve "faculty scholarship derived from student assessment and curriculum evaluations activities."[145] For example, did the Association of American Medical Colleges' 2004 graduation questionnaire constitute unapproved research? "[M]any allegations were not upheld," but the AAMC agreed to submit future questionnaires for IRB review.[146]

Tomkowiak and Gunderson[147] describe a medical school that reformed its geriatrics curriculum under IRB standards, even though the dean of research said IRB approval was unneeded and the IRB never answered requests for exemption. The faculty used surveys to assess the reform, which "quickly became a nightmare." The "innovative and nontraditional geriatrics curriculum" was attacked by some students and faculty. "Formal allegations of research misconduct were brought against the geriatrics curriculum" two years after it began. The IRB announced that students had been made to answer unapproved surveys "for research purposes." Without telling the faculty, the IRB "suspended all activities involved with the geriatric mentor program" and discussed it at a meeting which excluded faculty. The IRB allowed "mentor visits and related planned activities" but not surveys. The geriatrics faculty had to provide many documents describing how the curriculum was evaluated and surveys were used. "Detailed and individual responses were also developed for each allegation made against the curriculum, accompanied by examples of evidence to support the curriculum evaluation components." Ultimately the faculty decided that to save "the reform" and end "the personal and institutional allegations, all data associated with this curriculum would be destroyed."

F. CARELESS PEOPLE

They were careless people, Tom and Daisy—they smashed up things and creatures and then retreated back into their money or their vast carelessness. ...
—F. Scott Fitzgerald, *The Great Gatsby*

This chapter has reviewed the IRB system's costs. All agencies have costs, and they can be justified by their benefits. But regulationists and IRBs often seem careless of wasteful burdens they inflict. First, regulationists have not seriously evaluated the IRB system. They do not know how IRBs operate, whether IRBs prevent desirable while permitting undesirable research, what ethics and regulations IRBs apply, how IRBs treat researchers, whether IRB decisions improve consent, or what consequences IRB censorship has. Such questions responsible agencies must ask.

Second, event licensing is extravagant. IRBs must review all research to prevent bad outcomes that are rarely severe and generally rare. Event licensing profligately taxes both regulators and regulated. Third, IRBs drown researchers and themselves in paperwork requiring attention to trivial details about trivially risky research, as in "Free Parking" or "My Portion of Paradise." ("Surely it is nearly insane to require any procedure at all to perform research using what is destined for the nearest toilet. ...[148]) Soldiers call this *chickenshit*, "petty harassment of the weak by the strong." It "is small-minded and ignoble and takes the trivial seriously."[149] IRB members themselves say "nobody likes going through bureaucracy," "administrivia detract from sound ethical analysis," I spend "every waking moment reading applications," and I'm "spending too much time on irrelevant details."[150]

Fourth, researchers repeatedly find IRBs as indifferent to exactions from them and their subjects. They describe questions that applications already answered. One researcher thinks IRBs have a quota for questions. The application answers 90% of them, so when IRBs ask them, you just copy and paste. "When the quota of questions has been reached—you have approval! (usually 3 volleys)."

IRBs seem unfazed by the costs of undisciplined decisions. "Blatant inconsistency did not seem to trouble members of ethics committees." Approved projects became dangerous, approved questionnaires became risky, and venerable standardized instruments were declared harmful.[151]

Lincoln's IRB approved her advanced fieldwork methods course but during the semester re-reviewed it and ordered it to "stop March 7!"[152] Another scholar found each exchange raising new issues, more questions about old issues, and "issues beyond the pale of the original submission."[153]

Heedlessness also grows out of following rules rigidly. How else explain Flowers' weird experience? Forbidden to use her field notes, she interviewed herself about them, which "seemed to calm the IRB considerably."[154] Or a sociologist's needing "consent to 'study my own life'": "I hereby grant myself consent to utilize all of my own past, present, and future writings, drawings, and other of my own personal records and creative products for the purpose of research and publishing purposes. I understand that since this is an overtly autobiographical study and my identity as the author will be publicly knowable, I will be identifiable in all published accounts."[155]

Heedlessness polluted "Free Parking" (chapter 1). That IRB protected mothers who could not afford to visit their babies against a 50% chance of about $1,000 in parking. The IRB rained down petty demands. Yet the hospital could have given parking away unimpeded if only it had avoided learning its program's results.

Fifth, indifference to needless costs is dramatized by the prolonged failure to resolve the shameful multisite-study problem. IRB review at each site confronts researchers with disagreements about forms, procedures, levels of review, substance, method, and consent, with endlessly duplicative work, all to no apparent benefit. While OHRP has at last suggested addressing the multisite problem, it has long just told IRBs that they are free to be reasonable. Little reveals OHRP's indifference to the lives and health that research can save more than its tolerance for this madness.

For example, all fourteen IRBs in Sherwood's project called the research minimum-risk and had few questions about subjects' safety. But each IRB had its own application form "in addition to the protocol document." All required supplemental forms (e.g., on biosafety and child research). Sherwood sought to keep forms few by incorporating each institution's HIPAA language in the consent form, but three IRBs refused. Four IRBs required no assent form, some demanded separate forms for three age ranges. Almost two-thirds edited grammar. One IRB insisted on two consent forms, one for "you" and one for "your child." Others wanted forms changed from second to first person, which meant reworking the document.

Sixth, mission creep exacerbates waste by giving IRBs work already done better elsewhere. They review scholarship's methods and substance, which they do poorly and funders' and journals' peer reviewers do better. IRBs increasingly regulate institutions that are already regulated in other, better ways. For instance, hospitals are accountable for the care they provide to a battery of governmental and nongovernmental regulators. Under that regulation, hospitals try to improve the care they provide. When IRBs call such efforts research, they not only add another layer of regulation but take on work they are ill-placed to perform, as OHRP's attack on Keystone suggests.

Obviously, not all IRBs are so careless, but much in the system's structure, culture, and incentives encourages indifference. Not least, as we will see, IRBs are lawless and cannot be held accountable for their acts.

G. CONCLUSION

Our catalog of costs has included the IRB tax (resources diverted from research) and IRB supervision (damage to research). This means lives that could have been saved, illness that could have been treated, and welfare that could have been enhanced. How much? Nobody knows. Partly because regulationists have not troubled to make a case for their system. And partly because the system's cost would be brutally hard to calculate. Even if you knew what research IRBs had impeded, you might not know what it would have done. However, IRB taxes and supervision are ubiquitous, and research can help billions of people.

We have already seen regulation's cost in lives and health in emergency-medicine research. Collins' ISIS-2, a multinational trial of thrombolytics (blood thinners) for hospitalized heart-attack patients is another example.[156] American (unlike other) researchers had to get patients to sign a 1,750-word form detailing participation's risks and benefits, the side effects of aspirin and streptokinase, and subjects' rights. ISIS-2 recruited 17,200 subjects in 16 countries. Collins estimates that American consent requirements slowed the study about 6 months. Thrombolytics lowered vascular mortality at 5 weeks by 42%. Because heart attacks are common, that enormous reduction in mortality meant thousands of lives.

Collins calculates that regulatory delay caused "at least a few thousand unnecessary deaths."[157]

More precisely, in 1987, 760,000 Americans were hospitalized with heart attacks. From 1994 to 1996, 31% of them were eligible for thrombolysis—roughly 235,600 patients in 1987. Within a few years, it was used for about 75% of eligible patients, so the delay easily cost thousands of lives. Discounting the loss of lives to account for the gradual adoption of thrombolytics suggests about 6,500 deaths could have been prevented, with a probable range from 3,600 to 20,000. This excludes deaths outside the United States. But just aspirin (available even in poor countries) reduced vascular death by 23%. The researchers commented, "If one month of low-dose aspirin were to be given to just one million new patients a year—which is only a fraction of the worldwide total with acute MI [heart attack]—then a few tens of thousands of deaths, reinfarctions, and strokes could be avoided or substantially delayed (and these benefits could be doubled if low-dose aspirin were continued for at least a few more years)."[158]

Regulation also inhibits research showing that a standard treatment is harmful. For example, head injuries were once treated with steroids; research found they *increased* death rates.[159] As Chalmers notes, consent requirements "slowed recruitment," delaying the "discovery that this widely used treatment is lethal."[160] The Cardiac Arrhythmia Suppression Trial (discussed earlier) is another example.

Most research neither discovers new therapies nor discredits old ones. But much research edges medical care and social welfare forward. IRB regulation annually costs thousands of lives that could have been saved, unmeasurable suffering that could have been softened, and uncountable social ills that could have been ameliorated.

In this chapter's epigraph, Koski speaks of the fear that IRBs' "procedural, ethical, regulatory and logistical requirements" stop "critical research" and deprive "individuals and society from [*sic*] the potential benefits" of science. This chapter confirms those fears. Koski says the benefits cannot "take precedence over the interests of those who are taking the risks for the rest of us." But chapter 1 found those risks far slighter than regulationist rhetoric implies and generally no greater than risks people daily assume without government supervision. And this chapter finds that losing those benefits is critical. First, the system's regulatory choices—especially event licensing—are almost ingeniously expensive. Second, the system taxes and regulates research in ways that damage, deter, and even prevent it. Third, restricting research costs lives, keeps illness untreatable, leaves suffering unsoothed, and inhibits social understanding, thereby diminishing the decency and dignity of human lives.

The IRB system's purpose is to save lives and prevent injury, but if it produces more deaths and distress than it could save, it is tolerable only if it is worse to die from a researcher's mistake than from a disease research could subdue. If so, regulationists have not said why. At this point, therefore, the case has been made: The IRB system was instituted to protect human life, health, welfare, and dignity. Since its costs in human life, health, welfare, and dignity outstrip its benefits, the system cannot be justified and thus ought not be retained.

Part II
The Quality of IRB Decisions

For I am a man ... having soldiers under me: and I say to this man, Go, and he goeth; and to another, Come, and he cometh . ...
—Matthew 8:9

Part I concluded that IRBs had modest scope to do good and much scope to do harm. But good and harm depend on how well IRBs make decisions. Part II suggests they err too often and thus that their costs outweigh their benefits even more seriously than part I concluded. Chapter 3 summarizes evidence that IRBs make decisions badly and starts to explain why. Chapter 4 argues that bad decisions are driven by the IRBs' indeterminate and perverse ethics. Chapter 5 shows how lawlessness—the lack of substantive and procedural rules—and unaccountability degrade decisions. Chapter 6 finds that IRBs' task of censorship leads them astray.

IRBs irredeemably make decisions inadequately because regulationists (like most people) believe Matthew's centurion. They overestimate regulation's effectiveness and underestimate the challenge of structuring regulation well. But regulation in a complex society is stubbornly hard to organize and administer. Learning to build organizations that make good decisions has been one of modernity's great projects, and good regulation requires studying its lessons. The IRB system, however, was initiated with little attention to those lessons and has grown more by inadvertence than deliberation.[1] In short, because regulationists (like most people) do not appreciate regulation's complexity, they have constructed and tolerated regulation that cannot work satisfactorily.

Because many of my readers need not study regulation, this introduction to part II briefly sketches its fundamentals and frustrations. For simplicity's sake, I particularly consult the long, illuminating effort to help judges toward sound decisions. Courts have many advantages over IRBs: Judges are specifically chosen for their profession and guided by many well-tried rules, substantive and procedural. Judges are subject to review, criticism, and discipline. Yet there is much disturbing evidence about the quality even of judicial decisions, evidence that applies *a fortiori* to IRB decisions.

For example, nobody thinks judges just "apply the law." The issue is how much they follow it. One reason, Judge Easterbrook notes, is that courts have so much work and so little expertise that their understanding "both of the rules they apply and the social situations the law regulates" is limited.[2] For example, Eric Posner finds courts "*radically incompetent*" to understand "relational contracts"[3] and little more competent to grasp "the simplest of business relationships."[4] Vidmar reviews, for instance, studies suggesting that only 5% of 400 trial judges comprehend the basics of the test for evaluating expert testimony.[5]

Furthermore, interpreting legal rules requires considerable aptitude, training, and practice. Yet even the finest analysts are distracted by factors like their experiences, preferences, and interests. These include not just political beliefs but "costs such as effort, criticism, and workplace tension" and "benefits such as leisure, esteem, influence, self-expression, celebrity," and chances for promotion. Decisions are also shaped by "collegial and other group effects" (like "panel composition, dissent aversion, and opinion assignment") and relations within the judiciary and with other branches of government.[6]

In addition, the decisions of all professionals—"doctors, real estate appraisers, engineers, accountants, options traders, military leaders, and psychologists"—are distorted by cognitive illusions.[7] Research "suggests that even highly qualified judges inevitably rely on cognitive decision-making processes that can produce systematic errors in judgment."[8] Thus federal magistrate judges (who are selected especially well) are plagued by problems with anchoring, framing, hindsight bias, the representativeness heuristic, and exaggerating their abilities.[9] Judges "rely heavily on their intuitive faculties" in many circumstances, like "awarding damages, assessing liability based on statistical evidence, and predicting outcomes on appeal." They are misled by "absurd settlement demands, unrelated numeric caps, and vivid fact patterns."[10]

More specifically, Englich asked "experts in criminal law" with "considerable experience in similar legal cases" to sentence hypothetical criminals. Some of the experts were given a prosecutor's proposed sentence, others rolled dice before choosing a sentence. The latter were as much influenced by the "anchoring" number as the former.[11] And Danziger found that the likelihood that Israeli judges would grant prisoners parole "steadily declines from ≈0.65 to nearly zero and jumps back up to ≈0.65 after a break for a meal."[12]

Such deficiencies afflict even good judges, but there are a dismaying number of bad ones.[13] They "lack even slight command of the law." They procrastinate. They are inefficient. They overstep their authority. They abuse litigants and employees. They "display bias, prejudice, and stereotypical thinking." They "are untruthful."[14]

In short, regulation is an essential but troubled enterprise, for it endows with power people who—however bright and beneficent—make decisions in ways they do not understand, would not want, and cannot justify. Responsible lawmakers understand these dangers and seek structures and rules to mitigate them. For example, skepticism about judicial capacity animates "many legal doctrines, including the business judgment rule in corporate law, which restrains courts from second-guessing managers and directors, and the many contract doctrines that restrain courts from second-guessing parties to contracts." Judges are constrained by role demands like "impartiality, suppression of personal predilections, [and] attention to legal doctrine."[15] Judges are guided by precedent. One study was "captivated by the excitement, the devotion to legal analysis, the depth and rigor of constitutional analysis, and, yes, the true pleasure revealed by the judges" engaged "with a meaningful legal problem."[16] Thus helped, for example, judges are less prone than other people to some kinds defects in reasoning.[17]

Part II shows, however, IRBs rely on amateurs to make expert decisions and use few if any of the standard ways of mitigating regulation's problems. Worse, the IRB system is so structured that adopting most of them ranges from impractical to impossible.

3

Arbitrary and Capricious Decisions

The reviewing court shall ... hold unlawful and set aside agency action, findings, and conclusions found to be ... arbitrary, capricious, [or] an abuse of discretion. ...
—Administrative Procedure Act

The IRB system is built to fail. Founded on an exaggeration of research's risks (chapter 1) and a denigration of regulation's costs (chapter 2), it can hardly do more good than harm. But how much good and how little harm depends on how well IRBs work. The evidence is that they often work badly. Not because members are indolent, wicked, or foolish, but because their task is unmanageable. Event licensing and mission creep saddle IRBs with impossible loads. Evaluating research's substance and methods demands more expertise than IRBs can muster. Their poverty of rules leaves IRBs with less guidance than agencies need.

Because IRBs need not report what they do or why, evidence must be indirect. But indirect evidence can persuade, and this does: regulationists themselves distrust IRB decisions, when OHRP acts as an IRB it has been imprudent, and (most tellingly) multisite studies show IRBs handling identical cases inconsistently. IRBs lack time, knowledge, and skill to understand their choices; IRBs assess risk ignorantly; and IRB incentives are warped. In short, the IRB system is so poorly constructed that—in the classic legal phrase—IRBs are chronically arbitrary and capricious.

A. THE EVIDENCE OF ERROR

[M]any of the "horror stories" told by social science and humanities researchers are true: these situations are taking place because of "IRBs that a) don't understand social and behavioral research, b) don't know how to use or are afraid to

use the flexibility in the regulations, and c) don't pay sufficient attention to the efficiency of their procedures."
—Jerry Menikoff (Director, OHRP), *Where's the Law?*

IRBs are studied little, their decisions less. But we have already reviewed many poor decisions, and more systematic evidence shows pervasive problems. Sometimes IRBs get things right, sometimes IRBs stop or improve bad research, sometimes IRBs find appreciative researchers. But the proportion and gravity of their poor choices are unacceptably great. I review first the distrust of IRB decisions that OHRP, IRBs, and regulationists themselves evince; second, the improvident decisions OHRP makes when acting as an IRB; and third, the multisite studies showing IRBs recurrently making irreconcilable decisions. Then I begin to show why poor decisions are inevitable.

The IRB system's own opinion of its work is skeptical, even harsh. OHRP, IRBs, and regulationists have good reasons to prove their usefulness but have hardly tried, and they often castigate IRBs' work. Regulationists can frankly admit they have little evidence that IRBs work well. Questioned, IRBs typically call themselves "quite successful," but asked why, they "almost invariably pointed to the lack of serious problems or complaints."[1] OHRP's first director could cite no "direct evidence" that IRBs prevented harm.[2] Canadian officials "simply put forward a passionate belief that they *must* be doing their job effectively, expressing a gut-level sense or 'intuition' that all is as it should be, unable to point to any evidence for that claim."[3] One said ingenuously, "'I would have to think it's effective since I've been there thirteen years, wouldn't I!'"[4]

The regulationist literature is drenched in dismay. Elliott (a prominent bioethicist) thinks that "[b]y any reasonable estimate, that oversight system has been a failure."[5] More than a decade ago, IOM saw "significant doubt" about the system's capacity "to meet its core objectives" and found IRBs "'under strain' and 'in need of reform.'"[6] Elite organizations describe understaffed, undisciplined, and undertrained IRBs. The system "is not functioning as intended, a message that this [IOM] committee as well as a long line of analysts and observers have delivered."[7] OHRP has audited many IRBs and found them failing so badly that OHRP has closed all federal research in excellent universities, including Duke and the University of Pennsylvania.[8]

IRBs routinely decline to trust other IRBs—they refuse to accept other IRBs' work in multisite studies despite pressing reasons to do so. When Canadian IRBs (REBs) were asked about this problem, their major concern was that "one REB cannot trust another. One participant stated bluntly, 'We don't trust the ethics process at other institutions.'"[9] Some IRB members also distrust OHRP. Some of Klitzman's interviewees thought the "federal focus has increasingly shifted to assessing forms, rather than protecting subjects." Klitzman quotes an IRB chair: "New regulations may also not really help the patient. With OHRP and accreditation bodies like AAHRPP, the focus is much more on: do you have the right forms and policies?"[10]

A second insight into IRB decisions comes when OHRP acts like an IRB. In prominent cases it has made poor decisions and persisted against ample evidence. In Keystone (the checklist), for example, OHRP's risk assessment was "not likely but possible" and its rulings were a triumph of literalism over sense. Similar is the following

CASE STUDY: LIFE AND BREATH[11]

In adult respiratory distress syndrome (ARDS), lungs fail. Patients not ventilated die, as do a third to a half of those who are. Those who survive do well, so ventilating properly means life or death.

Respirators have multiple settings (for frequency of breathing, depth of breathing, oxygen percentage, and more). The optimal combination depends on factors like the patient's age, sex, size, and sickness. More breathing might seem better but isn't, since excessive ventilation can tax bodies without additional benefit. Respirator settings also affect fluid balance. Too much fluid floods the lungs and the patient drowns; too little means inadequate fluid for circulatory functions, so blood pressure drops, then disappears.

In 1999, a National Heart, Lung, and Blood Institute study was stopped early when lower ventilator settings led to about 25% fewer deaths. But that study did not show how low settings should be or how patients' fluid status should be handled. So the NHLBI got eminent ARDS specialists to conduct a multisite randomized trial of ventilator settings and fluid management.

In November 2001, two pulmonologists and two statisticians at the NIH Clinical Center sent OHRP a letter criticizing the study design.

Pressed by OHRP, the NHLBI suspended enrollment in July 2002: the federal institute with expertise in lung disease bowed to an agency with no such expertise. NHLBI convened a panel approved by OHRP. It found the study well-designed and vital. OHRP announced its "serious unresolved concerns" and demanded that the trials remain suspended. Meanwhile, clinicians had to struggle.

Eight months later, OHRP loosed its hold, without comment on the costs, misery, and death it had caused. Rather, it berated IRBs for approving the study without adequately evaluating its methodology, risks and benefits, and consent practices. It did not explain how an IRB could do better when OHRP and NHLBI had bitterly disagreed.

Much effort is now devoted to "prospective, randomized comparative effectiveness research." Attractively, "there is no additional risk to being randomly assigned to one or another equally well-supported treatment option that falls within the standard range of care in clinical practice."[12] A rewarding recent example addressed a painful problem: Very premature infants are kept alive partly with oxygen, but it can cause vision loss from retinopathy of prematurity (ROP). From 2004 to 2009, the "SUPPORT" study sought in 23 sites (including many major research universities) to ascertain the best level of oxygen saturation. At the time, a "range of 85 to 95% was becoming standard clinical practice, and the American Academy of Pediatrics (AAP) later recommended this range in its 2007 guidelines." SUPPORT therefore divided its subjects into two groups, one at the higher end of the standard range (91–95%) and the other at the lower end (85–89%). In other words, all the SUPPORT infants received standard therapy; as the SUPPORT sample consent form said, each of the "possible combinations of treatments is considered by some units to represent their desired approach. ..."[13]

The study found less ROP in the lower range, but "contrary to what was known at the time, the study also showed a slightly but significantly increased incidence of death—19.9% versus 16.2%—among infants assigned to the lower" range. The "AAP amended its guidelines, citing SUPPORT, and physicians treating very premature infants are starting to use higher saturation rates to reduce the risk of death," despite "the potentially higher risk of ROP."[14]

Each study site's IRB had approved the study and the consent forms. However, in 2011, OHRP began to investigate SUPPORT's consent process. Eventually, OHRP "determined" that the IRB-approved consent forms "failed to include or adequately address" the study's "reasonably foreseeable risks and discomforts" because they did not warn parents that their children might die because of the study. But as Magnus and Caplan write, "Given that there was variation in clinical practice at the time the study was mounted, it is not clear how randomization among treatment options could have created novel risk over random physician preference." There was "absolutely no evidence to support the claim that the infants enrolled in the study were exposed to greater risk than infants outside the study."[15]

The *New York Times*, Public Citizen, and some bioethicists endorsed OHRP's "determination." But NIH aggressively defended SUPPORT;[16] prominent bioethicists (including many with fine regulationist credentials) said OHRP had improvidently attacked crucial research;[17] and a *New England Journal of Medicine* editorial was "dismayed" by OHRP's response to "a model of how to make medical progress."[18] John Lantos acidly wondered why OHRP was promoting a world in which "doctors would misrepresent the risks of the studies, frighten parents away, prevent responsible research and continue to treat babies based on their non-validated beliefs about what is best."[19] SUPPORT was a major study conducted by eminent scientists supported by NIH and approved by IRBs at some of the country's best research institutions. Had they *all* misunderstood OHRP's rules for research? "[I]n a remarkable move," OHRP suspended "its compliance actions" and promised new guidance.[20]

The best evidence that IRBs make unreliable decisions is multisite studies where different IRBs receive the same protocol and treat it in wildly erratic ways. As one IRB manual blandly admits, "there is much variation regarding functional and operational processes among IRBs."[21] As Green says dryly, a "high degree of inconsistency" among IRBs "has long been observed."[22]

These studies are typified by the report of prominent researchers whose IRBs generally objected to their research but could not agree on why:

CASE STUDY: VITAMIN A[23]

Extremely low birth weight babies weigh less than 1,000 grams (35 ounces). They are too tiny to keep warm, too weak to suck from breast or bottle, and too unformed to get enough oxygen from air. Even in neonatal intensive care units they often die, and survivors often have chronic lung disease.

Of the thousands of neonatologists in the United States, a few work at the medical schools where most neonatology research is conducted. The ablest neonatologists at these schools serve on the Neonatal Research Network, which NIH sponsors. To maximize their resources, Network members debate: Which unsolved questions matter most? Which are likeliest to be solved?

In the 1990s, the Network considered a trial of supplemental vitamin A. Premature babies risk complications if they get too little vitamin A, but too much can be toxic. Small studies had shown supplements might reduce stroke, lung disease, and infection, but the Network thought the evidence only suggestive. It planned meticulously. Jon Tyson, professor of pediatrics at the University of Texas, was the principal investigator. A Network subcommittee assisted him in trial design and the biology and pharmacology of vitamin A; colleagues offered comments, as did external reviewers. The Network Steering Committee and an external advisory board reviewed the protocol. The protocol then went to investigators at 14 centers for submission to 18 IRBs.

Infants eligible for the trial lived on the thinnest of margins. All needed supplemental oxygen, and 90% were on ventilators. Of the 807 infants in the trial, 133 died before hospital discharge, and brain damage, sepsis, and chronic lung disease plagued the rest. The average hospital stay, for those alive at hospital discharge, was 3 months. The infants were randomized into a treatment group receiving vitamin A three times a week and a control group receiving standard care without supplemental vitamin A. All were monitored for vitamin A toxicity. To help the IRBs, the protocol thoroughly discussed the trial's background and design.

Despite this extravagant exertion and expertise, IRBs had manifold objections. Sixteen of the eighteen required changes in the consent form. One objected to saying (truthfully) that NIH provided funding. Several IRBs opposed saying (truthfully) that infants would benefit from additional examinations and monitoring in the NICU and over the next two years. One IRB wanted the form to say that collecting blood samples has risks like fainting. And there was chaotic disagreement about the study's science.

One IRB thought the risks of supplemental vitamin A so outweighed the benefits that giving it would be unethical; another thought the benefits so outweighed the risks that withholding it would be unethical. The Network's IRB submissions discussed this issue and said that the evidence of benefit was only suggestive and that few physicians routinely used supplements.

Several IRBs withheld approval because they wanted the study to control for the amount of vitamin A in feedings. The Network's IRB submissions had discussed this issue and argued that doing so was impractical and undesirable. For example, vitamin A in breast milk varies from one mother to the next, varies between one feeding and the next, is affected by storage, and is absorbed differently from vitamin A administered intravenously. Furthermore, the study's goal was not to ascertain the effect of different levels of vitamin A; it was to ascertain whether supplements helped ELBW infants in the NICU.

Two IRBs withheld approval because the infants' blood was not monitored for toxic levels of vitamin A. The Network had considered this issue. There are no accepted blood levels for vitamin A in people less than two pounds, and glucocorticoids—which most ELBW infants receive—alter the vitamin A distribution in ways that might lead to confusing blood-level results. The most sensitive sign of vitamin A toxicity in infants is increased pressure in the skull's soft spot—which the study monitored daily.

One IRB withheld approval because it wanted the control group to receive real, not sham, placebo injections. The Network's IRB submissions had discussed this issue and said that giving a shot to tiny infants causes stress and that the placebo might harm them. The researchers kept families and NICU staff blinded by using a tiny needle and pacifier to minimize crying, placing a screen around the bed, making the injection site hard to detect, and bandaging both real and sham injection sites.

One IRB withheld approval because it wanted interim outcome data, presumably so it could stop the study if it seemed to be producing dispositive results. But interim data from one of multiple sites rarely justify aborting a study. This fact, well known to statisticians, was demonstrated in this study: The results at each center varied, with a relative risk of bad outcomes ranging from 0.66 (vitamin A reduced bad outcomes by one-third) to 1.11 (vitamin A increased them by 11%), a range no more than would be expected by chance.

One IRB withheld approval because it imagined that making infants less than 500 grams (18 ounces) eligible would lead to trying to keep infants alive to have more research subjects. The Network had not considered this possibility. Experienced neonatologists, they thought that pediatricians—no likelier than IRB members to torture patients—would not say, "We really shouldn't treat him at all, but he would be great for the vitamin A study. Let's resuscitate him."

After many struggles, all the IRBs conceded all these points (and others I have spared you). The study showed that supplemental vitamin A reduces chronic lung disease in ELBW infants.

Some variation in agencies' decisions is inevitable. But this case study describes flatly contradictory decisions, finds IRBs stating different objections to the protocol, and shows IRBs making objections they had to withdraw.

Inexplicable variation is a persistent pattern. Singer and Levine report it in the late 1970s.[24] In 1982, Goldman and Katz sent three protocols to IRBs at major universities. All were disapproved, but with "substantial inconsistency" in IRBs' reasons and "substantial inconsistency" in applying "ethical, methodological, and informed-consent standards."[25] Boards disagreed diametrically: some disapproved and others approved placebos in breast cancer research.[26] Variation was due not to local differences but to "inconsistent application of standards within each IRB." A "substantial number" of IRBs "approved designs that we had deliberately made unacceptable." In sum, "IRBs approve inappropriate investigations and inhibit appropriate investigations. Deficient protocols may be modified, but only the most glaring problems are identified." This "cast doubt on the adequacy" of IRB decisions.[27]

Multisite studies continue to report flagrant inconsistencies. Sometimes IRBs flatly contradict each other. Recall that one thought vitamin A supplements necessary and another thought them unethical. Similarly, faced with Stair's study of inhaled fluticasone supplementing standard emergency asthma treatment, one IRB said all patients should receive it while another thought it "hazardous and therefore unethical."[28]

IRBs differ about whether a protocol must be reviewed and at what level. About whether an inquiry is human-subject research.[29] About whether research is exempt.[30] About expediting review.[31] About protocols' risks.[32] About cost-benefit analysis.[33] About risks of blood draws.[34] About minimal risk.[35] About risks of chart reviews.[36] About whether paying subjects is a benefit.[37] About whether psychological testing is a benefit.[38] About whether the special attention subjects receive counts as a benefit.[39] About making PI and staff always available.[40]

IRBs disagree about who may be a subject. About enrolling a child who cannot assent.[41] About approaching people by phone.[42] About using opt outs or opt ins.[43] About enrolling prisoners.[44] About paying subjects and how much.[45] About paying children and how.[46] About monitoring HIV-infected adolescents' health without parental consent.[47] About what literacy forms.[48] About who signs invitation letters (the local PI, the PI and the primary physician, or the director of the health plan's breast cancer screening program?).[49] About getting a treating physician's consent before contacting subjects.[50] About whether the IRB should be named in a reminder letter.[51] About surrogate consent for the disabled.[52] About including the disabled in minimal-risk studies.[53] About requiring competence assessments of people likely to have "impaired decisionmaking."[54]

IRBs disagree about requiring consent.[55] About what a form must say.[56] About children's assents and documenting them.[57] About the age at which assent is required.[58] About describing conflicts of interest.[59]

IRBs disagree about whether research staffers must update their ethics training by calendar or fiscal year.[60] About responding to young survey respondents who say they do risky things.[61] About consulting communities about waiving informed consent.[62] About whether each site needs a PI.[63] About naming the IRB in an invitation letter.[64] About letting a study's coordinating center contact local IRB staff.[65] About whether a central PI must have an institution's own HIPAA training.[66]

IRBs within a single institution disagree. I described Green's experience of an IRB disagreeing with itself.[67] Decades before, there was "little consistency in detecting consent problems within each board. Often, what appeared appropriate to a particular review board for one consent form was not considered appropriate by the same board for other forms." Even on objective issues "little affected by the nature of the research" (like including a compensation statement), "individual IRBs demonstrated no consistent pattern" in interpreting guidelines or applying "standards for approval."[68] Coe was warned to resubmit a form to the same IRB panel lest "new stipulations" arise.[69]

Even single IRBs can fluctuate. Goldman and Katz thought it hard "to find consistent responses to ethical issues within a particular board."[70]

Recently, a respondent said, "Different IRBs at our institution feel totally different."[71] Another said that people moving internally among IRBs were "astounded that we're at the same institution."[72] Klitzman found inconsistencies not just over different protocols, but over "the *same* protocol." Even "a single member may also make seemingly inconsistent decisions on similar protocols over time."[73]

I have canvassed situations in which IRBs reach contradictory decisions about the same protocol. For instance, in Green's 43-site study of practice guidelines, "IRBs varied widely in the standards" for deciding what level of review to require. One exempted the study, 10 expedited review, 31 demanded full review, and 1 disapproved the study.[74] One board granted an exemption the study was ineligible for. When Green's protocol was reviewed by the *same* IRB "acting on behalf of two different sites," it was "approved as minimal risk with waiver of consent in one case and rejected pending revision and with formal written consent required in the other."[75]

IRBs assess risk erratically. Green's study was designed to meet the "minimal risk" criteria, but only a minority of IRBs agreed, despite "guidelines and expert advice" urging IRBs to adjust review and monitoring to a project's risk and complexity. A majority of IRBs did full-scale reviews. Many "imposed all the usual regulatory requirements for clinical research," like medical care for study injuries and HIPAA consent for physicians, "even though the IRBs themselves acknowledged to us the irrelevancy to our study" of doing so.[76]

IRBs balance risk and benefit disparately. "[A]pplication of the federal risk and benefit categories is variable and sometimes inconsistent with the federal regulations and actual risks to children." A single blood draw was the only procedure a majority of IRB chairs thought minimally risky. About half thought electromyography minimally risky or a minor increase over minimal risk, while roughly 40% thought it more than a minor increase. About a quarter thought allergy skin testing minimally risky, 43% thought it a minor increase over minimal risk, and about a quarter thought it more than that.[77]

IRBs disagree about paying subjects. "IRB policies and practices on payments to parents and children varies [*sic*] considerably." Many permit reimbursement for time and expenses, a few permit "incentives." Some prohibit payments to children, others encourage them, and others want alternatives like toys.[78]

Another measure of IRBs' unpredictability is that, despite research-ers' incentives to comply with an IRB's wishes, applications rarely satisfy IRBs. Goldman and Katz found outright approval "rare." *None* of the 166 initial full-board protocols received by the IRB that Jaeger studied was approved outright.[79] *Every* IRB in Sherwood's study had objections requiring a response.[80] Especially after researchers have applied to and satisfied many IRBs, subsequent IRBs should have "no or few recom-mendations," but Sherwood and many others had learned otherwise.[81] One survey found that protocols are primarily rejected for "clarification and process concerns."[82] Even first-rank researchers going to extremes can fail. When the American Society of Clinical Oncology undertook a National Initiative on Cancer Care Quality, it got approval for a protocol and consent forms from IRBs at Harvard, Rand, and the National Cancer Institute. Yet 35 of the 65 IRBs in the study modified the consent forms and 20 modified the protocol.[83]

Schlaff's IRBs not only responded inconsistently, but when Schlaff re-peated the *same* study seven years later, "the major barriers to IRB ap-proval were quite different at each site." Worse, IRB variability "appeared to be much greater" the second time around.[84] Similarly, in Helfand's two-stage study, IRBs responded no more quickly in the second round and required almost twice as many changes, even though IRBs knew it was a standard protocol from a steering committee for an NIH-sponsored clinical trial that "had been approved by an independent data and safety monitoring board."[85]

Erratic decisions seem to be international. At least before the British at-tempt to reform multisite reviews, variation was "the rule." For one trial, "between 1 and 21 copies of a protocol were required by each of 125 lo-cal research ethics committees [RECs], with two thirds" requiring amend-ments.[86] In another trial, agreement was "probably better than chance" but "slight."[87] Finally, an experienced observer described RECs' "incon-sistent working practices": one opposes telling patients that an REC had approved the research (that would be "coercive"), another requires giv-ing the information. One opposes paying subjects, the next supports it. One accepts family members as translators, another wants "accredited professionals."[88]

Nor is variation driven by local circumstances. None of the editori-al revisions imposed on Green "addressed any special local cultural or language issues."[89] Klitzman rejects IRBs' and staffs' attribution of variability to local circumstances: "no data have ever been published supporting the claim."[90] Even some regulationists concede that "no data substantiate the value of such local knowledge."[91] And a former OHRP head convincingly argues that "a psychologically oriented explanation of factors contributing to that variability should also be considered."[92]

In sum, the multisite studies reveal IRBs regularly making incompatible decisions, so that if some are right, others must be wrong. Variation among IRBs is so dramatic and ubiquitous that decisions cannot be based on consistent principles. When a single protocol is submitted to 44 IRBs and 40 of them require widely differing changes,[93] the plausible range of interpretive variation is far outstripped. Cowan's conclusion is much more convincing—that decisions turn on "the personal backgrounds, experiences, and biases of IRB members."[94]

We have already encountered many poor IRB choices; the cases from chapter 2 in which a decision's costs plainly outweighed its benefits is just one category. The multisite studies also abound in plainly poor decisions. One survey (in an IRB administrator's thesis) asked questions with answers in OHRP guidance. Not only did variability "permeate" the responses, but the IRBs were right "only 55% of the time."[95] Multisite studies also show boards refusing approval because of objections IRBs eventually had to withdraw (as in the vitamin A study).

The multisite studies also report IRBs fixed on trivialities. As Bosk says, "bureaucratic organization leads workers to ignore goals and focus on, even sanctify the means or operating rules and procedures." Goal displacement flourishes because "ultimate goals are difficult to keep in view; their achievement is near impossible to measure," and it is hard to tell whether means serve ends efficiently.[96] Thus IRBs (and OHRP) notoriously dwell on paperwork and forms. Almost two-thirds of Sherwood's IRBs revised grammar (e.g., changed a form from the first to the second person).[97] In another study, thousands of dollars went to things like changing "description of study" to "study description" and replacing Helvetica with Times New Roman.[98]

Not only do IRBs say no when they should say yes; they may say yes when they should say no. This would produce the worst of worlds—a costly system that permits bad but blocks good research. Given flawed protocols, "only two IRBs raised objections in all three cases. Seven committees consistently failed to find such flaws. The remaining 13 boards rejected only one or two projects."[99]

IRBs may not even understand the problem with inconsistent decisions. Klitzman's "interviewees generally defend[ed], ignore[d], or downplay[ed] these variations, the subjectivity involved, and the problems that might ensue."[100] One chair said, "Each of our IRBs has its own feel or flavor. That's good."[101] It's not. When the Supreme Court encountered a test ("reliability") that lower courts applied inconsistently, it was indignant: "Reliability is an amorphous, if not entirely subjective, concept." Much might affect reliability, so a statement's reliability depended "heavily on which factors the judge considers and how much weight he accords each of them. Some courts wind up attaching the same significance to opposite facts."[102] Saying that the standard was manipulable, the Court forbad it.

In sum, there is much evidence that IRBs make decisions badly. First, regulationists not only cannot show that IRBs work well, they excoriate them. IRBs distrust each other's decisions. OHRP has judged IRBs so grimly that it has halted federal research in major universities and frequently execrates IRB performance. Second, when OHRP acts as an IRB, it has made poor decisions poorly defended. Third, multisite studies show IRBs reaching contradictory decisions about identical protocols. When IRBs are so consistently inconsistent, when they act more like random-number generators than agencies applying reason to rules, their decisions are not good enough for government work.

B. INFORMED CONSENT

[T]he legitimacy of much of our system of human subject research in large part turns on how good a job we are doing in obtaining informed consent.
—Jerry Menikoff (Director, OHRP), *What the Doctor Didn't Say*

The IRB system's success *does* turn on informed consent, for superintending it preoccupies IRBs. Lidz found that while IRBs frequently ignore many regulatory criteria, they attended carefully "to consent forms and processes. They almost always discussed the consent forms, and nearly 9 in 10 protocol reviews" had questions about them, confirming research finding "that IRBs regularly and often exclusively recommend changes to consent forms."[103]

The IRB system is *not* doing a good job with informed consent. The evidence shows IRBs making inconsistent decisions, despite the effort devoted to consent. Nor have regulationists confronted the evidence that informed consent is a regulatory technique that cannot achieve its goals.

1.   THE TROUBLES OF INFORMED CONSENT

[C]onsent in the research setting bears ... a great weight on its shoulders. Perhaps we should refer to it, in comparison to clinical consent, as ... consent on steroids.
—Jerry Menikoff, *Void for Vagueness*

Informed consent is a species of perhaps the most common but least successful regulatory genus today—"mandated disclosure." It fails because disclosees do not notice disclosures, do not read them, cannot read them, do not understand them, do not use them, and do not make better decisions with them. The empirical evidence on information policies, including "disclosure policies, suggests that they have not made consumers significantly better informed and safer."[104] Ben-Shahar and Schneider so recently analyzed mandated disclosure so lengthily that this section can briefly summarize its ills.[105]

Mandated disclosure fails because too much is asked of it. And unrealistic as hopes for it are, hopes for informed consent in research are higher, as Menikoff's "consent on steroids" suggests. OHRP thinks "[i]nformed consent assures [again] that prospective human subjects will understand the nature of the research and can knowledgeably and voluntarily decide whether or not to participate."[106] The "standard account" requires that subjects "fully understand the nature of scientific rationale and procedure," have "insight" into risks ethicists or regulators identify, and "have motives for participation that are not 'false.'"[107] From the "prevailing ethical and legal viewpoint," patients can understand "the often complex and voluminous medical information" they get and put it in "accurate, clinically usable perspective."[108]

The history of informed consent is a history of failure. In 1980 Cassileth wrote that studies showed "that patients remain inadequately informed, even when extraordinary efforts are made" and no matter how much information is provided, how it is provided, or the treatment involved.[109] In 2003, the NRC acknowledged that there "appears to have been little progress" in improving forms and procedures.[110] Lidz asks if informed consent has "produced the rational autonomous decisions" expected and finds the answer "pretty simple. There is very substantial empirical evidence that the large majority of both research subjects and patients do not carefully weigh the risks and benefits."[111]

Informed consent disappoints even in optimal circumstances. Joffe lavished labor on subjects in cancer trials who consulted "additional sources of information and had support from family or friends. Nonetheless, knowledge varied widely and there were important misunderstandings. Major deficiencies included not being aware of non-standard treatment, the potential for incremental risk or discomfort, the unproven nature of treatment, and the uncertainty of benefits to self."[112] Many "did not realise that the treatment being researched was not proven to be the best for their cancer, that the study used non-standard treatments or procedures, that participation might carry incremental risk, or that they might not receive direct medical benefit from participation."[113]

In another study, over half thought consent was used "to protect the investigator and/or affiliated institution from liability."[114] Many regulationists agree. Two IRB authorities think consent more concerned with protecting institutions than subjects.[115] And a two-stage multisite study concluded that many parts of the consent forms numerous IRBs require seem aimed more at "avoiding liability" than explaining research.[116]

Informed consent's theory is that people read, understand, rely on, and use forms to make better decisions. But as Appelbaum says, given how much information must be disclosed, its complexity, "the exponential growth in length" accompanying "attempts at simplification, and the inherent limitation of those involved in the consent process (many of whom have lost whatever ability they once had to communicate intelligibly to lay people)," that theory is dubious.[117] And when Lidz asks about informed consent's success, he rightly answers that if its goal is subjects fully participating in decisions, it "has largely failed." Only unusually are "subjects likely to understand enough … to be equal partners with the professional."[118]

As Ben-Shahar and Schneider write, mandates like informed consent depend on a long chain of weak links: Lawmakers must correctly see and say what disclosees need to know, disclosers must interpret instructions accurately and follow them faithfully, and disclosees must notice the disclosure, read it, interpret it, and apply it. But OHRP regulations give IRBs poor guidance, and IRBs are expert neither in the research described nor in explaining arcana to novices. There is rarely a *via media* between easy but incomplete and complete but confusing forms. The disclosees (research subjects) rarely study forms carefully enough to meet regulationists' standards of learning. Illiteracy, innumeracy, and inexperience make forms incomprehensible. Reasoning from disclosure to decision is littered with confusion and error. I do not say that informed consent *never* makes *any* difference of *any* kind or that *no* improvement is possible. But it cannot do what regulationists want.

Nevertheless, the conventional wisdom "overwhelmingly, staunchly" supports informed consent.[119] OHRP Director Menikoff writes, "Admittedly, there is evidence that these forms currently play a relatively small role in the decision making process of many people who decide to enter research studies. But that in itself is likely [*sic*] a reflection not of the futility" of informed consent "but rather of how poorly currently used consent forms are written."[120] So OHRP determination letters criticize complex forms and say complex language violates the regulations.[121] OHRP's *Guidebook* insists that IRBs "ensure [again] that information" is understandable.[122] OHRP's rule-making notice wants forms that are "shorter, more readily understood, less confusing, that contain all of the key information, and that can serve as an excellent aid to help someone make a good decision."[123] Regulationists, like the NRC, routinely see poor progress after "decades of research" but tell "[s]ocial, behavioral, and economic science researchers" to study "procedures for obtaining and documenting informed consent that will facilitate comprehension of benefits, harms, and risks of harm."[124] Similarly, IOM wants "a new approach"—"clear, simple, unclouded, unhurried, and sensitive disclosure" of "all the information a reasonable person would need to make a well-informed decision."[125] Who doesn't? Who gets it?

2.   IRBS AS CAUSE, NOT CURE

There are [*sic*] a wide array of problems [in consent forms], ranging from failing to disclose that randomization is taking place in the study to failing to describe what standard care is and how being treated in the study differs from standard care, to probably the most common (but far from least significant) failing, writing a consent form that is mind-bogglingly dense and incomprehensible. ...

—Jerry Menikoff, *What the Doctor Didn't Say*

As we just saw, regulationists criticize forms' length and density but want them longer and denser. Menikoff says forms elide complex issues *and* are "dense and incomprehensible." But OHRP regulations demand *at least* (1) a statement that research is being done, an explanation of its purposes and the length of subjects' participation, a description of the research procedures and experimental aspects; (2) a description of "risks or discomforts"; (3) a description of "benefits" to subjects and others; (4) disclosure of alternative treatments; (5) a confidentiality statement; (6) if risk is more than minimal, an explanation of the compensation or medical treatments for injured subjects; (7) a name to contact to learn more, a statement about subjects' rights and "research-related injury"; and (8) assurance that participation is voluntary and may be abandoned. So researchers must address fifteen topics (and many subtopics), and the regulations list *more* disclosures for IRBs to consider. OHRP's *Guidebook* says grandly, "Information *could* be deemed 'material' if it *might influence* the decision of any reasonable person."[126] Not to mention conflict-of-interest and HIPAA statements. And IRBs can require more disclosures *ad libitum*.

As IRBs have regulated every word in every consent form in all human-subject research, forms have grown longer and denser. Unsurprisingly, the changes IRBs require often make the forms less understandable.[127] In 1984, Appelbaum criticized the "tendency to cram ever more information into consent forms."[128] In 1983, the mean length of one VA hospital's consent forms had nearly doubled over seven years and the forms required "college-level reading ability."[129] In 1989 another VA's forms were 58% longer than the former's had been in 1982. Their mean readability was at the 13.4 years grade level, and 17% reached the hardest level (at least a college sophomore's or junior's).[130]

In 2010, Albala concluded that one IRB's forms increased "an average of 1.5 pages per decade." In the '70s, the average form was less than a page, by the mid-'90s, over 4.5 pages.[131] In 2011, an eight-IRB study found forms over two times longer than 7 years before, for a virtually identical protocol.[132] That this irrepressible growth is instinct in regulationist ideology is suggested by its ubiquity. A Norwegian study found that oncology consent forms grew significantly over ten years.[133] And Australian consent forms' median went "from seven to 11 pages between 2000 and 2005."[134]

IRBs preach brevity and promote breadth. IRB exemplars flout IRB standards: only 8% of the IRB templates and samples in medical schools with specific standards met them, and the mean readability score was 2.8 grade levels over the norm.[135] Breese examined HIPAA templates from one hundred major medical centers and fifteen independent IRBs. Almost all "had inappropriately complex language." So "[d]espite the regulatory requirement for 'plain language,'" nearly all forms were as complex as "corporate annual reports, legal contracts, and the professional medical literature."[136] Not only do IRBs preach virtue and practice vice, they "do not, as a general practice, enforce even those standards they themselves set."[137] Forms describing "oncology protocols at a large, university-based, comprehensive cancer center [were] too complex to be read by most patients and their families." The center's "Research Committee, the hospital's IRB, and the national cooperative groups" all failed to make the forms "readable with an eighth-grade education."[138]

IRBs do not just issue bad exemplars and endorse unreadable forms. They make forms worse. Burman[139] evaluated the way IRBs evaluated two protocols in a 25-site trial in "institutions oriented toward clinical research." IRBs demanded a median of 46.5 (3–160) changes per form, 85% of which did not alter meaning but tended to degrade the form. Forms stretched, sentences swelled, the active voice faded, and difficulty worsened.

Yet regulationists incite IRBs to meddle more. One manual tells IRBs that they "understand the issues the best" and so "should accept the role of editor" and "not blindly accept criticism that they are just nitpicking at the grammar or punctuation."[140] They should warn researchers that there will "be a thorough edit of the consent document for readability" and "that there will likely [sic] be more than one set of revisions."[141] Another manual finds "no substitute" for IRBs' subjective decisions about language.[142]

Ultimately, OHRP is responsible for decades of IRB subjective decisions and objective failure. Burris and Welch's review of OHRP enforcement letters "indicates no substantial change since NBAC described OHRP's counterproductive focus on paper compliance." OHRP "continues to nitpick consent forms" and thinks "the remedy for most problems" is "more." OHRP demands consent forms "both readable and larded with boilerplate." Yet, Burris and Welch say, OHRP's director blames IRBs for instituting burdensome new rules that are not required: "Consent forms used to be 2–3 pages that people may have read, and now they are 20–30. I've seen them over a hundred pages long. ... That's a burden that we don't create, but the institutions trying to escape liability [*sic*]."[143] As Robert Levine once said mordantly, "There is no more expensive or less competent redaction service available in the United States than that provided by an alarmingly large number of IRBs."[144]

The multisite studies are again illuminating. Green's 43-site project showed IRBs minutely editing forms to no common, or even evident, purpose. More than half required completing parts of forms that the IRB acknowledged "did not apply to our particular survey."[145] IRBs demanded revisions "at an undiminished rate even late in the recruitment phase of the study, when the study protocols and consent forms had been refined through revisions at multiple previous centers." Three-quarters of the sites required at least one resubmission; 15% required three to six. The revisions had no pattern but "comprised a wide range of requests for deleting or adding sentences or paragraphs, phrasing, tense, and word choice."[146]

IRBs not only make forms more littered and less lovely, they make them wrong. In Burman's study, IRBs inflicted "an error of protocol presentation or a required consent form element" in two-thirds of the forms. Many errors were minor, but over a quarter were "more substantive," like deleting significant side effects, making "major errors" describing study procedures, or removing a mandatory part of the form.[147] At the extreme, IRBs make researchers mislead subjects. The study of senior women in medical and dental schools had to admonish them that they might be driven into "counseling" and exposed to "legal problems." Those are absurd things to tell senior faculty, but they seem to have led 18% to leave the study.[148]

IRBs make forms less readable and less accurate (partly) because IRB ideology and practice misguide them. The "ensure" principle inclines IRBs to fear the wispiest possibilities. The tendency to invent risks, to treat unlikely risks as likely and slight risks as serious exacerbates this. Regulationist suspicion of researchers teaches IRBs to distrust researchers' forms and make them warn subjects against themselves. In addition, copious warnings and paperwork look like ways to avoid lawsuits, scandal, and OHRP displeasure. So 94% of the IRBs that McWilliams encountered insisted on their own consent forms,[149] and some made her use templates unsuited to her study. One IRB wanted information about data safety and monitoring in the consent form even though the study had no intervention to monitor. Yet the templates omitted relevant facts, like "assurances of confidentiality for family members."[150]

Finally, good writing does not flourish in the IRB world. I have read thousands of pages from IRB chairs, members, and staff; from OHRP; and from regulationists, pages rich in sentences like this: "However, how IRBs discharge their duties is not clearly spelled out in the regulations, neither is there specific algorithmic guidance at the present time. As such, there is much variation regarding functional and operational processes among IRBs."[151] Or: "OHRP finds that, given that the project involved non-exempt human subjects research, JHU failed to ensure that the requirements for obtaining and documenting the legally effective informed consent of the subjects or the subjects' legally authorized representative under HHS regulations at 45 CFR 46.116 and 46.117 were satisfied."[152] Physician, heal thyself.

In short, even if subjects wanted to and could achieve the understanding regulationists want, IRBs would cripple informed consent: IRBs have steadily lengthened and complicated forms. But consent on steroids does not accomplish and even thwarts its own ends. OHRP's director says that "the legitimacy of much of our system of human subject research in large part turns on how good a job we are doing in obtaining informed consent." The IRB system is not doing a good job. It seeks to do the impossible and, inevitably, fails.

C. THE ENGINES OF ERROR

IRBs should not accept responsibility for performing functions that they are by design incompetent to perform.
—Robert J. Levine, *Inconsistency and IRBs*

This chapter's first part surveyed the evidence that IRBs make poor decisions unacceptably often; the second part surveyed the evidence that IRBs' crucial method—informed consent—fails unacceptably often. This third part begins to ask *why* IRBs err (and thus how far error can be reduced). One answer has already emerged: IRBs review too much research too intensively and review expert work without expert knowledge.

Regulatory choices increasingly overburden IRBs. As the introductory chapter said, the regulations define IRB authority broadly and loosely. As we have repeatedly seen, event licensing is an extravagant way to regulate. As the Conclusion will show, IRB imperialism amplifies both the scope and intensity of scrutiny. In one study, submissions increased 42% in five years. Burman assumes a university with 500 new and 1,000 continuing studies annually reviewed by two IRBs, each meeting for three hours twenty-two times annually. If new protocols take twice as long as continuing studies, IRBs have eight minutes for the former and four minutes for the latter. Another study found meetings averaging 2 1/2 hours for "18 initial review, 9 expedited reviews, 43 amendments, and 21 safety reports."[153] And in one two-stage, 25-site study, IRBs made 2,347 changes in the consent form alone,[154] a median of 46 per form (range, 3–160).[155]

IRBs' must create, collect, and store an Everest of paper, including intricate records of IRB proceedings and reams of forms from researchers, like "[c]opies of all research proposals reviewed, scientific evaluations, if any, that accompany the proposals, approved sample consent documents, progress reports submitted by investigators, and reports of injuries to subjects."[156] Fost and Levine say that OHRP "has insisted that a quorum be documented" for each "of 100 or more actions [*sic*] items on the agenda of a single meeting of a typical IRB." An accreditation agency wants a nonscientific member's presence "documented for every action item." Another agency "threatened a warning letter because the institution was defining a quorum as 'more than one-half' rather than 'one-half plus one.'"[157]

These regulatory choices burden IRBs not just with too much work, but with work requiring expertise IRBs lack. Simon Whitney's travails illustrate a common problem:

CASE STUDY: FIRED PATIENTS

Doctors sometimes fire patients. The decision can be mechanical (a fixed number of missed appointments or payments). Sometimes it can be discretionary. Perhaps the patient makes sexually suggestive comments about a staff member, is too recalcitrant to work with, or seems likely to sue (or has sued but continues to expect care). How do patients react to being fired? Does it change their feelings about themselves, their new physicians, or medical care? Do physicians have criteria for firing patients? Do they give formal warnings?

I hypothesized that certain patients (like those with stigmatized illnesses or coexistent physical illness and drug abuse) are particularly likely to be fired. I knew that talking with patients and physicians about this would provide insights that would never occur to me. A literature search produced nothing, but I found a note from a CBS news producer on a message board about fibromyalgia and chronic fatigue syndrome inviting fired patients to contact her. I suggested we might cooperate in our separate inquiries.

The IRB was hostile, peremptory, and contemptuous. I say "IRB," but was it the chair (a plastic surgeon) or someone else? What process produced its response? The IRB wrote, "Please justify how this is considered research and not investigative journalism." This was puzzling: if this was not research, the IRB lacked jurisdiction, since IRBs license only research, not journalism. Did the IRB share the methodological parochialism common among biomedical IRBs—not understanding (even despising) qualitative research? Such parochialism cannot be cured with a few supplicating paragraphs. The IRB also demanded more risk-benefit information. Any risk seemed speculative and trivial, and I had already described the project's importance. But I tried to assuage the IRB's concerns.

The IRB responded with belligerent comments, questions, and commands. I gleaned a bit more about what the IRB was thinking. For example: "This research does not qualify for risk category 1. The information obtained could potentially place the subjects at risk for criminal or civil liability, or be potentially stigmatizing." Which crime? Which tort? How would a prosecutor or plaintiff locate and recognize anything of interest in highly anonymous descriptions of widely scattered subjects published in an almost anonymous medical journal?

I answered the question about investigative journalism as best I could. "I am afraid you have formed a false impression that this is a sensational project, not legitimate research. This is not at all the case. I have a four-year AHRQ K08 award and spend all my research time on topics like this."

The IRB became angrier. They seemed offended by my association with journalists and doubtful about qualitative research: "As currently written, the risks of this protocol outweigh the benefit of the knowledge that may be gained. Please include further information on the benefit to society of the knowledge that will be gained since there is no plan to quantify the data."

I asked to present my case in person but was sent to the public affairs office. It suggested explaining again that this was research, not sensational journalism, and that subjects' confidences were safe. I had already done that more than once and had invested so much so fruitlessly that persevering seemed pointless. My tenure clock was ticking, the research was unfunded, and dealing with the IRB was ghastly. I said I thought "the comments indicated lack of understanding of social science research methods, unwillingness to consider qualitative research as being capable of producing useful results, and just plain hostility. ... I just don't have the heart to pursue it."

IRBs' decisions are supposed to rest on the educated opinions of all members.[158] For the IOM, education means "skills and knowledge, ranging from technical scientific design expertise to a strong working knowledge of the ethical literature."[159] So members "should understand the ethics and history of research with humans," the "structure and funding" of research, and research regulation, "including local laws." And "be able to read scientific literature and protocols at some level, understand scientific methods for various disciplines, assess" research's effect on "the community and vulnerable populations," do risk-benefit analysis, and appreciate and enforce informed consent.[160]

IRB manuals concur. Amdur tells IRBs to assess proposals' science, researchers' qualifications and resources, and studies' methods.[161] Mazur warns that reviewing protocols can be "extremely complex."[162] IRBs must analyze protocols *scientifically* and *ethically*[163] and need "in-depth knowledge of the history and ethics of human subject protections and the regulations."[164] They must judge research's importance.[165] And evaluate "scientific issues" like the "significance of preliminary data, feasibility of specific aims, and data analysis plans."[166] And review "the drug dose and route of administration."[167] And "fully consider" a study's procedures, its timing and setting, and the researchers' qualifications. And demand "well-conceived, well-formulated, and appropriate plans for interpretation of data and statistical analyses," including "adequate stratification factors and treatment allocation plans for the study design after study completion."[168] And gauge risks' "probability, magnitude, and duration."[169]

IRBs are also supposed to be expert in research ethics. Even assuming such expertise is possible, do IRBs have it? Regulationists widely doubt it. Many members seem to know little of the regulations, to say nothing of ethics. Van den Hoonaard's observation of four REBs confirmed his data "from interviews, other notes, and what scholars have said in general about ethics-committee members' knowledge of federal policies: they are unfamiliar with them or have too little familiarity."[170] Staffers are, "next to the chair, vital" to IRBs and usually "serve as ex-officio members at meetings." But they "have no research experience, and many still do not have expertise in ethics."[171] Ethics training can be embarrassingly crude. Spike calls it "minimal," with a short (often under ten hours) training course (often online) and a multiple-choice quiz (so simple many people can pass without training).[172] Nor is there "clear evidence of *any* relationship between ethics education for health care professionals and either moral competency, moral development," or better behavior in clinical ethics contexts.[173]

IRBs evaluate not just ethics but science. Mazur says many ethical questions "cannot be adequately formulated or even addressed" without grasping "the science behind the study's hypothesis."[174] Levine says that judging benefits' likelihood and scope requires "technical expertise."[175] OHRP's *Guidebook* wants "*thorough* assessment of information with respect to *all* aspects of the research and *systematic* consideration of alternatives." OHRP instructs IRBs to "distinguish the 'nature, probability and magnitude of risk.'" And to evaluate researchers' estimates of harm or benefits in terms of "known facts" or "available studies."[176] Thus in the vitamin A study, IRBs told eminent neonatologists that their issue was settled, that vitamin A toxicity could not be properly handled, and to give ELBW infants placebos. And in the ARDS study, OHRP persistently preferred its science to the National Heart, Lung, and Blood Institute's.

Why is an ethics board reviewing science? OHRP's *Guidebook* says "invalid" research "exposes subjects and the institution to unnecessary risk."[177] More, it requires *good* research: An institution's policies and officials should insist upon "well-conceived and -conducted research."[178] IOM wants review "by neutral scientific experts to ensure that the question(s) asked are important," "that the protocol is feasible, well designed, and likely" to answer the research question,[179] and that "data analysis" is "of high quality and free from bias."[180] Stark found IRB members asking whether proposals were "good science"[181] and thinking IRBs helped "strengthen research."[182] Again, the test is "good," not "invalid," or even "poor," or even "adequate" science.

IRBs' scientific competence must be so great that they can usefully review research even after "neutral scientific experts" have done so. Schlaff's study was conducted by a committee established by the National Institute of Child Health and Human Development "to design and conduct multi-center trials." Its steering committee comprised experienced investigators from seven sites, the PI of their data coordinating center, and an NIH-appointed "project office and committee chair." An advisory board and a data safety monitoring board critiqued the protocols. But eight IRBs plunged in with the usual "huge amount of variability between the various sites."[183]

Regulationists, then, believe IRBs need broad and deep expertise. Do they have it? Consider Simon Whitney's IRB service:

CASE STUDY: TONSILS

I woke up vomiting blood. This is what normally happens to eight-year-olds after a tonsillectomy. But I didn't know that. My parents had promised ice cream, but by then I didn't care. I was violently ill and scared to see blood. The nurse told me that it was fine and I would be fine. And of course she was right.

Decades later, when I was on the Stanford IRB, a researcher proposed to give pediatric tonsillectomy patients an unlabeled pain medication. Half the bottles with pink syrup would contain Tylenol with codeine, half plain Tylenol. By that time I was a family doctor committed to relieving suffering. When I saw this protocol, I thought "Plain Tylenol?" Right after an operation? How could the pediatric ENT people justify this barbarism, denying a kid decent pain relief? I knew it was just wrong and said so at the meeting.

That was the high point of my IRB service. The low point was the next meeting. The chair had called the pediatric ENT (Melinda Moir), who told him that all kids normally got was plain Tylenol and that she wanted to see if adding codeine helped. So my brilliant ethical idea, far from improving things, was slowing down the protocol that might improve pain care. I was chagrined.

It gets worse. When I recently searched for articles on postoperative care of patients I found thousands. Had I searched for these articles before challenging Moir's study? No. Did I know they existed? No. Did I know about the 70 articles specifically on managing tonsillectomy patients? No.

It gets worse. During that literature search, I found Melinda Moir's article reporting the research I had impeded. One graph shows that the kids who got plain Tylenol had less pain than the kids who got codeine. The next graph showed that kids without codeine maintained oral intake better than kids with it. Of course. The codeine was nauseating some of these kids. My postoperative memory is not of horrible pain. It's of throwing up. So I, on the IRB, had been convinced that the IRB was ethically obliged to require more kids to take a medication that did not help their pain but did make them vomit.

IRBs are novices evaluating experts. Disciplines comprise minutely specialized scholars with abstruse knowledge, so "judgments about scholarly significance can be made only by those who have great expertise regarding the current state of knowledge"[184] in, say, gastric pH, axonal degeneration, and cell mosaicism. As Shapin writes, experts are inexpert about "claims of *different* expert groups."[185] Furthermore, there is "little cross-disciplinary consensus" about excellence and its achievement. As Lamont puts it, "disciplines shine under different lights" and "are best located on different matrixes of evaluation," since "their objects and concerns differ so dramatically."[186] C. P. Snow's "'gulf of mutual incomprehension'" separating scientists from literary intellectuals also divides "many interpretative from more positivist researchers."[187] So physicians often cannot imagine fields whose "aspirational model" is not the hard sciences.[188]

Worse, even specialists disagree, since standards of "quality or excellence can be differently weighted and are the object of intense conflicts."[189] Thus empirically grounded fields like political science and sociology battle over "formal theory and quantitative research techniques in disciplinary standards of excellence."[190]

Scientists can differ fundamentally and furiously. As Shapin says, "You name it, it's been identified as the Scientific Method." Some scientists think there is no "special, formalized, and universally applicable Scientific Method; others insist with equal vigor that there is." The latter disagree about what it is. "Some scientists like Francis Bacon, some prefer René Descartes; some go for inductivism, some go for deductivism; some for hypothetico-deductivism, some for hypothetico-inductivism."[191] Shapin thinks "no small part" of the natural sciences' "enormous success" may arise from "the relative *weakness* of formal methodological discipline."[192] And Geertz thought it one of anthropology's advantages that practitioners don't quite know "'exactly what it is.'"

Some core IRB questions—like whether benefits exceed costs—even experienced supervisors of research dare not answer. An industrial lab manager, Shapin says, thought it impossible "to foresee the results of true research work." Another "defined research as 'systematic inquiry into the unknown,'" so that "'a certain amount of freedom on the part of the investigator' is implied by the very idea of research."[193]

So how can "at least five members" with "varying backgrounds," including at least one with no background in science, "complete[ly] and adequate[ly] review" research? "[M]ost institutions have a 'one-size-fits-all-but-nobody-knows-much' panel."[194] But how can they not? IRBs reviewing Helfand's study of minimally invasive urologic surgery contained "physicians, researchers, nurses, lawyers and pharmacists." Ten of the sixteen IRBs had at least one surgeon, but only one had a urologist, and one had no physicians at all.[195] They evaluated risks, "including the surgery itself, anesthesia, infection and other surgical complications." Helfand drily says that IRBs "unfamiliar with surgical procedures may have difficulty assessing the risk-benefit criteria." Likewise, in a study of "a well-defined genetic disorder" (cystic fibrosis), IRBs seemed "confused" about what subjects should know. "Genetics introduces probabilistic risk information that incorporates the concepts of penetrance and variable expressivity and often, unconfirmed estimates of risk perception, which further complicates determining risk-benefit ratios." This was "illustrated by considerable variability in how IRBs dealt with DNA banking within their consent forms."[196] And how is an IRB chair who specializes in "the effects of hydrophobic and hydrophilic glass coatings" on driving to assess proposals to study terrorists?[197]

The problem of inexpert review of experts is exacerbated when IRBs do not realize how their ignorance limits them. Like the IRB chair who was "a professor of foods and nutrition" and could think "that conducting oral history interviews was 'not different from creating a database of DNA'" and that because scholars in the humanities "'are evaluated on their research'" they are "'engaged in the same activity as a biologist.'"[198]

Nor can IRBs well evaluate researchers' competence (as the OHRP *Guidebook* wants). Universities labor learnedly to select faculty. Nothing in IRBs' composition, experience, knowledge, or judgment fits them to decide that specialist departments hiring specialists have erred.

Even regulationists deplore IRBs' ignorance (and researchers' laments are thick as leaves in Vallombrosa). HHS's inspector general, for example, finds many IRB members and staffers too inexpert to assess protocols adequately.[199] Amdur concedes that many IRB members are poorly equipped "to effectively evaluate scientific issues."[200]

Nor can IRBs be rescued by outside help. Consultants are uncommon.[201] IRBs cannot practically add members to fill gaps in expertise because there are too many gaps. For example, Hunt wants IRBs to have an expert in billing, since it "is virtually unintelligible."[202] But how many other gaps would thus need filling?

Some problems might be avoided if IRBs did not itch to interfere in matters which they do not understand. But this overtaxes self-denial. Sears chaired the UCLA IRB that reviewed research of a thousand professors and several thousand graduate students from many departments. The IRB's "'data'" included protocols without expert evaluation from sources like outside letters, committee reports, or departmental votes. The IRB's "analysis, usually (but not always) well-meaning, was generally amateurish," since members rarely had "up-to-date knowledge."[203] And Stark found that criticism of scientific quality often came from specialists in a different field.[204] Even less informed must be nonscientist members, 47% of whom recognized in one study that "they lacked sufficient training or education in science and ethics to do their job."[205] Many IRB members acknowledge their limits: in one study "a substantial minority felt less than fully competent" to evaluate research's originality, feasibility, method, and analysis.[206]

Furthermore, evaluating challenges to conventional wisdom requires resources amateurs lack. For example, mammogram screening reduces breast cancer deaths of women in their fifties.[207] Could IRBs countenance research questioning the screening imperative and using a control group receiving no mammograms? Kalager did such research in Norway. The death rate from breast cancer fell, and Kalager concluded that mammography caused about a third of the improvement.[208] But if mammography reduces deaths 10%, 2,500 fifty-year-old women must be screened for ten years to save one life. Good, but 1,000 of them will have an abnormal mammogram, and 500 will have a breast biopsy. Between five and fifteen of them will have breast cancer and be treated, but some would die from other causes first and others would have cancer incurable whenever it was caught. Welch thinks mammography probably reduces the 10-year risk of death from breast cancer for a 50-year-old American from about 4.4 to 4.0 per thousand. So without screening mammography, after ten years, 995.6 women do not die of breast cancer; with screening mammography, 996.[209]

The paucity of lives saved, false positives, and unneeded treatment might not matter. Zelen, a statistician, said that were he a woman he would be screened. Kalager, who *is* a woman, disagreed because of "the small chance of benefit in light of the larger chance of finding and treating a cancer that did not need to be treated."[210] If experts duel, can inexpert IRBs subdue their assumptions enough to understand the arguments?

If IRBs are not competent in their work, staffs are less so. Academics have long scholarly training and experience; staff rarely do. Yet as HHS grew exigent, "universities placed ethical review in the hands of a new class of administrators."[211] Staffs are intermediaries between IRBs and researchers, present cases to boards, and claim ethical and regulatory expertise.[212] They are professionalizing—seeking barriers to entry, educational prerequisites, licensing requirements, certification, professional associations, and continuing education. A new credential—Certified IRB Professional—promotes the shift toward more influential staffs (and away from IRBs as peer review).[213]

In sum, Sears is right that research university IRBs cannot evaluate research responsibly.[214] And Zywicki is only a bit unkind to say that the argument for IRB review of science "appears to be a rationalization rather than a justification for this practice."[215]

IRBs have yet more personnel problems. Able and admirable people serve, but as NBAC acknowledged, it is hard to get and keep them.[216] First, academics are not picked for skill in committees. Deans dislike diverting serious scholars from the research that they do uniquely well and that builds universities' reputations. Or fine teachers from classrooms. Or adroit committee members from more fruitful work (like hiring faculty). Second, why serve? Scholars strain for time for the research, teaching, and (for some) practice that are their true and rewarding callings. In large institutions, IRB workloads are like a part-time job stacked on your full-time one.[217] Serving can be onerous and thankless.[218] Turgid accounts of usually harmless research on abstruse topics sicken the academic soul, especially when "primarily bureaucratic and focused on unimportant minutiae."[219] Fear of sanctions and suits deters some people from serving.[220]

Third, why join so unloved a committee? Commissions, commentators, and even courts indict a "system in jeopardy" that recklessly lets researchers abuse subjects. One state supreme court leapt to scourge not only the researchers before it but an IRB which was not. "In the instant case, as is suggested by some commentators as being endemic to the research community as a whole," a Johns Hopkins IRB failed to protect subjects, "instead suggesting to the researchers a way to miscast the characteristics of the study in order to avoid the responsibility inherent in nontherapeutic research involving children."[221] And OHRP treats IRBs like children from whom the rod is too much spared, with "heavy-handed shaming and criticism."[222]

IOM suggests that workloads make it hard "to recruit and retain knowledgeable IRB members."[223] Once, Case Western Medical School's IRB comprised its dean and departmental chairs.[224] Today, Fost and Levine say that "[s]enior faculty commonly avoid serving."[225] Of twenty "experienced senior faculty thought to be especially suitable" to chair one IRB, none acceded. "Even among the entire IRB membership there are virtually no full professors."[226] At Northwestern, many faculty once "willingly participated," but "resentment of the IRB process" and "skepticism of its agenda" changed this. Fost, an IRB chair, describes trouble recruiting "senior research faculty" and "a massive disincentive" to serve.[227] He lost "two very valuable members." One left a meeting never to return, saying "'this is not why I'm here.'" He would gladly protect human subjects but not "spend time documenting compliance to rules" little related to that goal.[228]

IRB amateurism contrasts with academic professionalism. Scholarly journals typically have expert editors. Manuscripts that survive their screening go "to three or four specialists in the exact area of the study's expertise."[229] The editor reviews their reviews. Funders recruit peers to "mobilize" experts' "connoisseurship and judgments."[230] These reviewers do not challenge "disciplinary traditions" but use "the epistemological and methodological standards of the applicant's discipline."[231] Finally, personnel decisions are ordinarily sedulous. At one school, tenure decisions begin with letters from eminences in the specialty and evaluations from knowledgeable colleagues. A committee scrutinizes the candidate's writing, the outside letters, and the inside evaluations and prepares a detailed recommendation to the tenured faculty. It meets twice and usually discusses the scholarship, even down to the footnotes. The provost reviews the faculty's recommendation. Strong, even passionate, but informed disputes about substance and method proliferate.

In all these processes, expertise is recruited *relatively* easily. Scholars feel an obligation to the enterprise of screening and editing books and articles, awarding grants, and granting tenure. Evaluators may benefit from their task. Being on a prestigious competition's panel can be like an executive's annual bonus.[232] Influencing competitions and other scholars' work can be satisfying.[233] And fun. Some of Lamont's panelists like "the highly pleasurable opportunity" to learn about other fields.[234] Some like working "with 'other really smart people.'"[235] Lamont describes "moments of individual or collective effervescence during deliberations,"[236] pleasure in reading good proposals, and rewarding relationships.[237] Unlike IRB work, most academic decisions rest on criteria evaluators respect. While IRB staffs are increasingly powerful, evaluators in most academic situations act personally. IRB members are "trained," but academic evaluators "are presumed to be responsible professionals who set high standards for themselves" and have "full or nearly full sovereignty."[238]

Yet even the best peer review is flawed. Reviewers may be "dramatically influenced" by things like the research's outcome, and agreement among them "may be extremely low."[239] Even in the elite decisions Lamont describes, "[e]valuators often favor their own type of research," since they "are necessarily situated in particular cognitive and social networks."[240]

In short, IRBs lack the time, care, and expertise to make their decisions and are less and less able to recruit well. The contrast with ordinary academic decisions highlights these inadequacies. Predictably, then, IRBs seem to deliberate poorly. Van den Hoonaard found in extensive research that "virtually no time" was spent discussing ethical principles.[241] Members felt "more at home discussing professional" matters, tended "to weigh in with disciplinary and individual viewpoints," and appealed "to what sounds 'reasonable.'"[242] Van den Hoonaard includes among the many factors leading to "idiosyncratic and inconsistent decisions" the uneven attendance at meetings, the interjection by committee members of disciplinary paradigms and individual perspectives (i.e., private reflections about ethics), discretionary judgments, the attitude of what is "reasonable," varying desires about what it means to protect research participants, unfamiliarity with ethics policies, the use of distancing mechanisms, the tendency for committee members to work as manuscript editors, and the influence of jealousies and, sometimes, vendettas.[243]

Fitzgerald, another of the best-informed IRB observers, says that because most members have not studied applications and some would profit little from doing so,[244] they "respond to the précis—not the application."[245] Deliberation can be free-form and get "off on tangents."[246] Fitzgerald thinks this helps explain why IRBs demand information they already have (recall "Vitamin A"): "The committee could not, or would not, resolve" an issue or "the discussion got away from the actual application," and demanding information let them "move on."[247]

Jaeger too learned that the majority of members read only proposals they were asked to review, not every proposal.[248] Generally, the meetings Candilis "observed consisted of long descriptions of the protocol by designated reviewers" with "a few short exchanges with other members and a significant number of contributions from the chair." The other members were "a 'silent majority.'"[249] Jaeger confirms Mazur's intimation that some members "remain unclear about what it is they actually did."[250]

More specifically, for example, we have repeatedly seen IRBs assessing risk badly. But how could they do it well? A huge literature[251] finds people misunderstanding risk. Most lack good information about it.[252] Human psychology distorts perceptions of and reasoning about it. "[U]nderstanding is most moved by things that strike and enter the mind together and suddenly, and so fill and inflate the imagination; and it then imagines and supposes, without knowing how, that everything else behaves in the same way as those few things with which it has become engaged." So "understanding is slow and awkward" unless constrained "by strict rules and a powerful authority."[253] Given "competing accounts of danger, people tend to move toward the more alarming account." Strong emotions can have "nearly the same effect as a 2,000-fold increase in risk." So people will pay more for flight insurance against losses from terrorism than for losses from all causes (including terrorism).[254] Such defects in reasoning and multitudes more infect IRB decisions.

Group dynamics exacerbate the defects of individual psychology. Like-minded people deliberating "typically end up accepting a more extreme version" of their views. "Social cascades" exaggerate risks. Groups can be "more fearful than individuals" and prone to "moral panics." Examples "prove memorable." If people are predisposed to think the risk is serious, group dynamics lead people to consider the example highly revealing. Thus "a tendency toward fear breeds its own amplification."[255]

So (Agrawal and Emanuel say) IRB "members frequently rely on their intuitions" in evaluating the risks and benefits of Phase 1 oncology studies.[256] Van Luijn observes that while "most IRB members set great store by the risk/benefit ratio and scientific issues, they also find them difficult to evaluate."[257] Most IRB discussions do not weigh risks and benefits systematically, but "involve gaining an overall impression (20%), considering what alternative treatments are available (15%), or considering whether one would be willing to undergo the trial-based treatment oneself or would advise a family member to do so (10%)."[258] With decisions made so sloppily, the inflation of risk chapter 1 describes may be inevitable. Hence the gulf between the data on harm from asking questions and the regulationist alarm about it. Hence "not likely but possible." And since IRBs' "[p]redictions of danger to patients could not be based on a strong empirical base," they are "very vulnerable to the professional, cultural bias of IRB members."[259]

If IRBs poorly understand the research they evaluate or the risks it poses, why not educate them? An ethnographer wants to do so.[260] An anthropologist thinks "boilerplate" can do so.[261] Child psychologists think PIs must do so.[262] A literacy researcher wants "tools" to educate IRBs about "non-postpositivistic research."[263] Community-based participatory researchers hope to educate IRB staffers.[264] A palliative-care specialist sees that young field "educating IRBs."[265] People studying pregnant women agree that "educating IRBs is crucial."[266] Researchers surveying scientists recommend "educating IRBs to accord researchers greater respect and fair treatment" by collaborating with specialists in organizational development who have "in depth understanding" of IRBs.[267] Primary-care practice-based researchers describe a "feasible and useful" way to educate IRBs.[268] A working group on genetics and microbial issues in women's health thinks "[e]ducating IRBs" is required.[269] Scholars working with refugees want IRBs educated about cultural differences.[270]

This long list briefly samples the many specialties jostling to "educate" already burdened IRBs. That several could succeed is improbable; that many could is preposterous. Consider what success can take: The rarity of the disease (recurrent respiratory papillomatosis) Sherwood studied "required educating each IRB about the entirety of the disease process," yet still "few IRB members" could assess a biopsy's risk. Sherwood's efforts made IRB approval more efficient, only after 30 months of teaching staff and members about the federal regulations.[271]

A distinguished jurist asks "[w]hat happens when you turn a generalist loose in a complex world? An ignorant or unwise judge will be unaware of his limits and is apt to do something foolish. A sophisticated judge understands that he is not knowledgeable and so tries to limit the potential damage." IRBs are hard-pressed to limit the damage they do because they increasingly face issues beyond their competence and workloads beyond their capacity. And as the next chapter argues, little in IRBs' ethics or ethos encourages them to recognize their limits or the damage they can do.

In sum, IRBs face such a range of recondite issues that managing them well would be miraculous. They require knowledge possessed by few, that cannot be analyzed without long training and experience, that involves more issues than novices can keep in mind, that demands judgments about which people disagree, and that requires speculation about uncertain facts and unknown consequences. And IRBs generally act when other people are better situated to do so. Thus an AAUP report could "see no reason to think IRBs are more capable of assessing the importance of a research project than researchers" or "more capable of assessing whether research projects would impose a more than minimal risk of harm."[272] It did not think that IRBs could judge social harms to subjects nor that IRB members were "especially competent" to judge ways of protecting data, for that "requires experts."[273]

Originally, IRBs were to run a superior peer review (recall Case Western's IRB comprising the medical school dean and department chairs). This goal has become increasingly unrealistic. Rather, anyone who spends years reading regulationist writing finds that the IRB empire has become a third-rate enterprise. It understands regulation crudely. Its literature generally falls short of academic standards. Its ethics are often puerile. It seems to repel first-rate people. And while professionalization may help the empire's officers, it seems to repel people drawn to rigorous disciplines.

This chapter has reviewed several kinds of evidence that IRBs make bad decisions badly often. Regulationists themselves denounce the process and product of IRB deliberations. IRBs distrust other IRBs. When OHRP reviews research, it makes decisions it has struggled to justify. IRBs make dazzlingly inconsistent decisions about identical proposals without apparent reason. Poor decisions are built into the system. Event licensing, the imperial imperative, and bureaucratic diktat overload IRBs. Amateurs make arcane judgments with poor resources, guidance, and expertise. Their decisions are consequently inconsistent, inexplicable, and indefensible at a rate intolerable in a government agency.

4

The Misshapen Ideology of the IRB System

Did you anticipate at that time that the Belmont Report, decades later, people would be saying that this is probably one of the best reports that's ever been written by ... a commission for the government?
—Bernard A. Schwetz, (then) Director of OHRP, to Norman Fost

In part II's introduction, I said that regulationists have underestimated regulation's difficulty and the need to consult the law's experience with it. Chapter 3 summarized the evidence that IRBs make decisions unsatisfactorily and said that one reason is that IRBs make kinds and quantities of decisions beyond any agency's capacity. Chapter 4 now considers another of the law's lessons—that courts and agencies improve decisions through rules (statutes, regulations, precedents). This chapter (4) and the next (5) argue that IRBs generally lack rules or have rules too superficial and obscure to be helpful. This chapter examines IRBs' ethical rules and finds their ethics incoherent and their ethos impoverished. The next chapter examines the rules required by what lawyers call due process and finds IRBs essentially free to ignore them.

A. AN INCOHERENT IRB ETHICS

As unconscionable as it may seem, even today many active investigators ... have not read the Belmont Report and cannot identify or explain the three fundamental ethical principles discussed therein.
—Greg Koski, *Research, Regulations, and Responsibility*

The IRB system is not an engine for abstract ethical thought. It is an agency regulating research. It thus needs, but lacks, a coherent, legible, and defensible ethics.

CASE STUDY: TERROR[1]

Scott Atran is one of "very, very few scholars who directly talk to terrorists." With "a considerable sum" from NSF and the Defense Department, he and a "cross-disciplinary, multi-university, international team (including researchers from Michigan, MIT, Harvard, Northwestern, Germany, France, Israel, Palestine and Indonesia)" sought "to interview jihadis in different settings, and run experiments with them" about questions like "how group dynamics can trump individual personality in motivating suicide bombers."

A University of Michigan IRB forbade Atran to "interview failed suicide bombers or their sponsors who are prisoners, because prisoners cannot, in principle, freely give informed consent." The IRB insisted that parole boards be told everything Atran was doing (although there are "no parole boards in Indonesian military prisons") and that lawyers accompany him "to verify that questions weren't potentially prejudicial to the prisoners." Even if its conditions could be met, the IRB said, the research was "'in principle' incompatible with the rights of human subjects and therefore 'never' likely to be approved." Atran's argument that the prisoners and their organizations "are more than willing to give their consent and eager to get their ideas out" changed nothing.

Nor would the IRB let Atran interview unimprisoned subjects, who might jeopardize themselves by revealing their plans. It did not matter that Atran would warn them "not to talk about operations" and give "well-accepted guarantees of complete anonymity." Atran had once heard "vague plans" and had reported them, but this "did not seriously compromise the health or welfare of the suicide bombers." And Atran had trouble understanding the "UM's moral logic" that he would be "ethically remiss by disrespectfully violating the bombers' wishes in helping to save their lives and the lives of their intended victims."

Atran also failed to show that his research's benefits outweighed its costs. He vainly argued that any lives saved when his "interviews with radical Islamist leaders resulted in fruitful contacts during a crucial Middle East ceasefire negotiation" were a benefit and that learning why people "want to blow up Manhattan, London, Tel Aviv or Jakarta," thus helping to keep them from being blown up, "would be a pretty good benefit."

After "many months," the IRB released emergency funds the NSF had awarded for "high risk research" to do pilot interviews with "freely operating jihadis." But "no group identifications should be registered" (in a project comparing jihadi groups) nor personal details collected (in a project to understand what motivates jihadis). Ultimately, the IRB decided that its permission "to carry out the truncated emergency research could not be pursued further, even on matters that had been previously approved, and against which no new objections had been raised."

Atran thinks "most of this is nuts." It is "getting next to impossible to even talk to people who are dying to kill in order to better understand why they die to kill." And the "IRB expressly forbids even thinking about trying to stop them from actually doing what they want because that could interfere with their rights. 'Don't ask, don't tell' isn't enough—IRB wants guarantees that the opportunity for discovery can never arise."

1. THE PROBLEM OF THE SACRED TEXTS

Investigators well versed in the Belmont Report and more technical IRB procedures rarely need to dispute decisions.
—J. Michael Oakes, *Risks and Wrongs in Social Science Research*

How would a conscientious IRB member ascertain and apply research ethics? In the noble tradition of Mr. Valiant-for-Truth, Squire Allworthy, and Mr. Knightley, and to honor the seriousness of many IRBs, call him Earnest Member. He begins in the system's Sacred Texts. The principal Text—the Belmont Report—says that documents like the Nuremberg Code and the Helsinki Declaration "assure" (again) that research will be ethical. But, the Report rightly says, they "often are inadequate to cover complex situations; at times they come into conflict, and they are frequently difficult to interpret or apply."

Not least, the Texts conflict among themselves and with other authorities. "The World Medical Association, for example, rejected the Nuremberg Code as a jurists' attempt to establish standards for criminal prosecution."[2] Lie writes that many people accept Helsinki's "prohibition of clinical research studies in developing countries that do not provide the worldwide best standard of care" but that "every other commission and body that has considered this difficult issue" has disagreed.[3] Thus the Declaration "lost its moral authority" in perhaps "the most contentious [recent] debate in research ethics."[4] And the FDA stopped incorporating the Declaration in its regulations because it conflicted with American law.[5]

In addition, the Texts "often are inadequate to cover complex situations." Justice Holmes said "[g]eneral propositions do not decide concrete cases."[6] The Texts are heroically general. Their rules are too few and foggy to tell government what it may do or researchers what they may not do. In short, Fost says, the Texts "first of all, say different things," and worse, "say incoherent things; that is, have guidelines that are widely thought to be ethically incoherent."[7]

"Fortunately," Sieber writes, IRBs have the "Belmont principles, which require the use of common sense."[8] The Belmont Report has "quasi-legal force"[9] as "the central source of ethical judgment." It enjoys a "shared reverential admiration,"[10] even veneration.[11] It proffers three "[b]roader ethical principles"—respect for persons, beneficence, and justice—from "which specific rules may be formulated, criticized and interpreted." The principles are "comprehensive" and "stated at a level of generalization that should assist scientists, subjects, reviewers and interested citizens to understand the ethical issues" in research. Their "analytical framework ... will guide the resolution of ethical problems." Belmont "clearly explains the three principles that are the main tools that all IRB members should use to evaluate the ethics of specific research proposals."[12]

Belmont is more invoked than read and more read than analyzed. This "[v]aguely worded and hastily finalized"[13] document *cannot* "guide the resolution of ethical problems." As Beauchamp writes, its principles are "not even principles at all, but 'headings.'"[14] And the Report fundamentally fails to define those principles.

But can we rescue, say, "respect for persons" by defining it as "autonomy"? As regulatory language, autonomy is hopelessly vague and endlessly expansive. Even the Supreme Court has struggled. Autonomy "is notoriously a greedy concept, but the Court cannot define its limits. Autonomy is notoriously one good among many, but the Court cannot articulate a sound method for accommodating it to other goods."[15] Justice Scalia acidly said that the Court must try to explain it by rattling off "adjectives that simply decorate a value judgment and conceal a political choice."[16]

Nor does the Report define "beneficence." The Report explains that promoting well-being falls under the principle, which implies that beneficence is a larger category than seeking well-being but does not describe the category. There follows so confusing a discussion of whether beneficence is an "obligation" that I dare not interpret it. Then we read that "[t]wo general rules have been formulated as complementary expressions of beneficent actions," namely, "(1) do not harm and (2) maximize possible benefits and minimize possible harms." Do these "complementary expressions" encompass all that beneficence requires? Why are they complementary and not contradictory, since one prohibits harm while the other permits it if it is minimized? And why must benefits be maximized? In what relationship must one person *always* maximize another's welfare?

Nor does the Report define "justice." Ordinary definitions tend toward tautology: "a moral value commonly considered to be the end which law ought to try to attain."[17] Holmes said he "hates justice, which means that I know if a man begins to talk about that, for one reason or another he is shirking thinking in legal terms."[18] The Report says that "injustice occurs when some benefit to which a person is entitled is denied without good reason or when some burden is imposed unduly." This begs the question, since "good" and "undue" turn on the meaning of justice. The Report then says that "[a]nother way of conceiving the principle of justice is that equals ought to be treated equally." But how is this different? Is it a definition of justice or a component of it? The Report also says, "Who ought to receive the benefits of research and bear its burdens? This is a question of justice, in the sense of 'fairness in distribution' or 'what is deserved.'" So, is this the definition of justice or merely an example of one aspect of it?

The Belmont principles mean different things among and within fields. "Respect for persons" is a philosophers' term of art that can mean treating people as ends, not means. Does Earnest Member know that? He treats people and is treated as a means daily, and so much the better. Nor can the philosopher's special meaning practically be taught to the IRB members, IRB staff, and researchers. And even philosophers disagree about what respect for persons means. Some "suggest that respect incorporates considerations of well-being. Others suggest that concern for well-being lies within the purview of beneficence and nonmaleficence" and that the ambiguity about "well-being is one reason the principle of respect for persons is unhelpful." This must confuse Earnest Member, especially since there is "a sense in which both are correct."[19]

Thus the Report's method is not reason, it is *ipse dixit*. It does not explain why its principles were chosen, why they are right, what they mean, or how to infer rules from them. It just announces conclusions. For example, one of the "complementary expressions" of beneficence is "do no harm." But instead of explaining why, the Report says, "The Hippocratic maxim 'do no harm' has long been a fundamental principle of medical ethics. Claude Bernard extended it to" research. But Miller and Wertheimer rightly question how far "'do no harm' is operative even for medical care."[20] It can only be "operative" with arduous interpretation, since much care inflicts harm to do good and/or risks doing more harm than good. And who was Bernard, why did he "extend" the rule to research, and why does he matter?

A final measure of the Report's helpfulness is a rare judicial reaction to it. One appellate court thought a trial court reasonably decided that submitting the Report to a jury "would unduly arouse its emotions of prejudice, hostility, or sympathy, and would tend to confuse the issues and mislead the jury."[21]

Defeated by Belmont, Earnest Member reaches for OHRP's *Guidebook*. But it essentially restates the Report and similarly prefers announcement to argument. Thus it asserts that the "principle of justice mandates that the selection of research subjects must be the result of fair selection procedures and must also result in fair selection outcomes."[22] It does not explain why, what "fair" means, or how to achieve fairness if fair procedures do not. It says: "The 'justness' of subject selection relates both to the subject as an individual and to the subject as a member of social, racial, sexual, or ethnic groups." Justness may "relate" to these (often conflicting) things, but *how*?

Continuing in the *Guidebook*, Earnest Member finds OHRP less interested in "the subject as an individual" than as a group member. But is research unethical when it *excludes* minority groups (denying them research's benefits) or when it includes them (exposing them to research's risks)? When OHRP uses a Belmont principle to help Earnest Member "understand the ethical issues," OHRP not only eschews analysis, it clouds it.

In sum, Belmont's "principles" are not principles but labels. They have no clear meaning in daily discourse, philosophy, or even regulationism. At most they express amorphous aspirations. As regulatory guidance, they are empty.

The Report is not only obscure; it is often wrong. First, respect for persons. The Report says little of autonomy's limits. Consider Keystone's doctors (research subjects, OHRP thinks). They ceded autonomy by agreeing to work for the hospital, which was entitled—obliged—to oversee them and protect its patients. They ceded autonomy by virtue of the role (doctor) they chose and the power (to harm patients) they had. They could not ethically claim a right to prevent a hospital from studying the presumptively desirable improvement at issue in Keystone. Nor did they; that they might was Director Pritchard's intimation.

Second, researchers should *not* always be beneficent. Like journalists, social scientists study bad things and bad people. Sometimes they—like journalists—want to prevent evil and thwart evil people. What researcher would not expose, say, the White Aryan Resistance to odium? What sociologist investigates prisons and says nothing to wardens' disadvantage? Even social scientists who "want to spare human feelings whenever possible" are happy to see researchers uncovering "gangsters and Klansmen."[23] Social scientists have duties even to deplorable subjects, but a social science indentured to its subjects is unethical.

Third, as a principle of research ethics "justice" is inapt. Justice is ordinarily the *government's* duty, not the citizen's. Principal constitutional provisions intended to promote justice—like the due-process and equal-protection clauses—apply only to the state because of its unique power and duties. Imposing governmental duties on citizens undesirably limits their freedom. For example, the government must treat everyone equally; individuals may choose their friends and promote their own causes. Nor *can* citizens meet governmental standards of justice, if only for want of resources to (for example) treat similarly situated people similarly. We hold government to standards of justice but people to individual standards believing that the sum of individual decisions is better socially, intellectually, and economically than holding everyone to the state's duties. Government should distribute research resources justly; individual researchers cannot tell what justice requires and may lack the means, knowledge, and ability to do justice. Nor does Belmont tell us why doing research makes you more responsible for justice than anyone else.

Belmont concedes that justice has "not generally been associated with scientific research" but says that ideas about it were "foreshadowed even in the earliest reflections" about research ethics. But neither the fact that some unethical behavior is unjust nor the fact that "ideas about justice" were "foreshadowed" makes justice a foundation of research ethics. Belmont argues that "the exploitation of unwilling prisoners as research subjects in Nazi concentration camps was condemned as a particularly flagrant injustice." But Nazi "research" was not primarily condemned as "injustice." It was condemned as brutal and savage. To call it exploiting the "unwilling" depreciates the evil and muddles analysis.

Suppose Earnest Member applies the Belmont principles to a standard problem? Archives house libraries of data: millions of patient records in thousands of hospitals; biobanks of tissues, organs, and excreta; DNA databases; and more. These data can be used efficiently and have often facilitated "great advances in medical knowledge" with "important benefits for mankind."[24] HIPAA requires researchers using "protected health information" to get consent, but contacting all the relevant donors is rarely practical.[25]

IRBs may waive the consent requirement if three criteria are met. First, there must be "minimal risk" to patients' privacy (researchers must "protect the identifiers from improper use," "destroy the identifiers," and assure "that the PHI will not be reused or disclosed"). Second, the research must be "impractical" without the waiver. Third, it must be impractical without the PHI. IRBs' attempts to define HIPAA's terms—"minimal," "adequate," and "impractical"—and to impose HIPAA's conditions have produced "extreme variability." Can the Report's "analytical framework" help Earnest Member solve the ethical problems of applying HIPAA?

Earnest Member starts with respect for persons. Winickoff and Winickoff conclude that people whose genetic material is used in research are treated respectfully by telling them the purposes, risks, and benefits of each project.[26] Donors might "disagree with a particular commercial or scientific use of their material."[27] Donors do not sign away their right to "control and oversight" over their sample, always retain the right to withdraw consent, and thus need a "constant flow of new information."[28]

On the other hand, respect for persons helps people protect their interests and avoid harm. Does keeping researchers from using archived data do that, given the almost invisible risk of harm? Doesn't respect for persons require honoring their preferences? Surveys repeatedly show strong majorities wanting to cooperate in (at least undemanding) research, so thwarting archival research defeats most people's wishes. Shouldn't respect for persons require the default assumption that people want to behave well, to help the larger research enterprise that benefits everyone, including them?

This leads Earnest Member to beneficence. Who must be beneficent to whom? The Report says that securing people's well-being "falls under the principle of beneficence." But isn't *everyone* ethically bound to be beneficent, including research subjects? And if government may promote beneficence, why may it not impose a duty on us all?

And which principles go with which issues? Is it unjust to use stored urine samples without permission or a failure of respect for persons to toss it away? Is it unjust to prevent a majority who want to participate in research from doing so to serve a tiny minority, or a failure of beneficence? Is it unjust to enjoy research's fruits but refuse to assist research efforts, or an autonomy right?

Finally, suppose Earnest Member thinks the principles conflict; that, for example, respect for persons requires defining the regulatory terms narrowly but justice requires a broad interpretation? The Belmont Report does not say which principle to prefer. Does a strong case for a weak principle overcome a weak case for a strong one? *Can* principles conflict? Can being beneficent be unjust? Can it be just to impair someone's autonomy?

In sum, the Belmont Report does not provide OHRP, IRB staffers and members, or researchers a legible ethics. The principles have no inherent meaning, nor can one be safely extracted from the Report. "[L]ike all general moral norms, they are abstract instruments offering vague advice, and are of little use in resolving profound and complex moral problems."[29] Predictably, "[s]cholars have already noted the tendency by ethics committees not to discuss overarching ethical principles," and one study "found that members 'did not normally discuss the relative merits of applications with overt reference to these principles' and that 'autonomy, beneficence and justice were not deployed as working models for decision-making.'"[30]

2.   "A LANGUAGE FOR DISCUSSING ETHICAL STANDARDS"

[It is] impossible to overestimate the importance of terminological precision and
conceptual clarity in satisfactory discussions of the ethics and regulation of research involving human subjects.
—Robert J. Levine, *Ethics and Regulation of Clinical Research*

Regulationists like Amdur try to rescue Belmont by saying that it's "much easier to evaluate the important IRB issues and to explain concerns to other IRB members if one has a language for discussing" ethics and that Belmont "gives IRB members the language they need to explain why they are concerned about a research procedure in a way that gets to the core ethical issues and is consistent from one discussion to another."[31]

But terms like "justice" mean wholly different things to different OHRP officials, IRB members and staffers, and researchers, as our effort to apply the principles to archival research showed. So does Amdur's own fumbling with the principles. For example, he says that to "implement" the "respect for persons" principle, "it is important to understand 'coercion.'" He explains:

Basically, coercion means that a person is to some degree forced, or at least strongly pushed, to do something that is not good for him or her to do. In discussions of research regulation the term "undue influence" is often used to describe the concept of coercion. Coercion is a concept that is impossible to define beyond a certain point. Like pornography, it is difficult to define but you know it when you see it. Does your salary coerce you into going to work? If you say no, then consider whether you would quit if you didn't get paid.[32]

First, notice that even coercion (a concept *far* simpler than the principles) is "impossible to define beyond a certain point." If words cannot be defined "beyond a certain point," how can they make language "consistent"? Amdur says you know coercion when you see it. But regulationists see a great jumble of things as coercion.

Second, when Amdur tries to explain coercion, he makes—it must be said—a pig's breakfast of it. His definition conflicts with the colloquial one. (A dictionary definition is "to compel by force, intimidation, or authority.") It conflicts with the legal understanding. (*Black's Law Dictionary* calls it "[c]ompulsion by physical force or threat of physical force.") It conflicts with the Belmont Report's usage ("[c]oercion occurs when an overt threat of harm is intentionally presented by one person to another in order to obtain compliance."). In *none* of these does coercion depend, as Amdur imagines, on whether coercion harms you. An operation may save your life, but if they tie you down and slip in the scalpel, you were coerced. Amdur thinks coercion means being "to some degree forced, or at least strongly pushed." But the colloquial, legal, and (apparently) Belmont definitions agree that coercion requires more, for they make physical force the core meaning and extend hardly further than its equivalents.

Amdur piles Ossa on Pelion by saying that "the term 'undue influence' is often used to describe coercion." I hope not, since undue influence is a related but distinct problem—the "improper use of power or trust in a way that deprives a person of free will and substitutes another's objective."

Amdur tries to clarify things by asking whether your salary coerces you to go to work and whether you would work if you were not paid. He apparently thinks your salary coercive. This doesn't even fit his own definition, since going to work need not harm you. But no matter. Your salary is part of a voluntary bargain—you work, they pay. That's not coercion, any more than a charitable contribution is coercion because it is tax deductible. Most behavior is motivated by *some* incentive, but motivation is not coercion.

Not only is Amdur's discussion of "coercion" incoherent, it conflicts with another IRB manual's. Mazur thinks "[c]oercion is the placing of pressure on an individual to do something for reasons other than his or her own." Like Amdur, Mazur does not see that coercion requires something near the threat of physical force. For Mazur, *any* pressure is coercive: "Coercion can be subtle: persuasion, argument, and personality can be used to compel an individual to act in a certain way."[33] But subtle is what coercion is not. Persuasion and argument are the *opposite* of coercion; they convince by reason, not force. And how can subtle things—persuasion, argument, "personality"—*compel* you to do anything?

How can the Belmont Report give IRB members a common language when instructors like Amdur and Mazur ignore words' meanings and cannot even agree with each other. When neither explain his definition but just announces it *ex cathedra*. On their evidence, the Report does not assist communication; it defeats it. No wonder IRBs are told that "'the word … is coercive.'"[34] No wonder commentators say that acronyms for research "may be subtly playing on the hopes or dreams of research subjects, a form of coercion." HELP and HOPE are "almost certainly coercive"; BOSS, CHEAPP, DRASTIC, and ICARUS are "possibly coercive."[35]

In sum, the IRB system depends on texts using ambiguous words to state incoherent principles. Those principles do not reflect disciplined thought and cannot guide IRBs to sensible decisions.

3.   IS A "HUMAN-SUBJECT RESEARCH" ETHICS POSSIBLE?

To see in more detail what happens when heavy-handed systems of regulation displace other normative systems, we turn to the example of [IRBs] and the regulation of research ethics.

—Carol A. Heimer, *The Unstable Alliance of Law and Morality*

If IRBs must seek guidance in an empty ethics, how can they avoid the wild variation in decisions that led NBAC to say that "the interpretation of the federal regulations can vary unpredictably"? That it is "almost impossible to develop consistent interpretations of the basic protections or those relevant to especially problematic research."[36] Regulationists' hopes lie in OHRP guidance about "the key regulatory terms—'minimal risk,' 'minor increase over minimal risk,' 'disorder or condition,' 'reasonably commensurate with those inherent in their actual or expected medical, dental, psychological, social, or educational situations,' and 'vital importance.'"[37] Yet NBAC concedes that guidance has "languished for decades in the face of bureaucratic hurdles" that will persist.[38]

Can OHRP write a coherent ethical code? Surely not. "Human-subject research" is not a meaningful category. It covers so many kinds of activities of so many kinds of researchers posing so many kinds of risks and benefits in so many kinds of settings with so many kinds of people that categorical rules will be bad rules. Biomedical research and social-science research comprise so many different disciplines asking such different questions using such different methods with such different relationships with research subjects that their ethical problems differ hopelessly. As Schrag reports, social scientists have long debated research ethics, and the "disciplines emerged with strikingly different conclusions about the proper relationship between researcher and research participant."[39] Nor does OHRP's definition of research as systematic and designed to develop generalizable knowledge help; that research is systematic or seeks generalizable knowledge is rarely the source of ethical problems.

The Sacred Texts, most regulationist writing, and much IRB thinking address biomedical, not human-subject, research, with notorious results. For example, IRB dogma is that the doctor/researcher is powerful and the patient/subject pitiful. But in ethnography the reverse is often truer, for researchers need the "goodwill and co-operation of their hosts."[40] Consent is often "negotiated and renegotiated"[41] and rests on subjects' trust, which depends on their "ongoing judgement."[42] When IRBs began regulating social science, they seemed blind to this difference. As IRBs gain authority over conflicts of interest, privacy, quality improvement, medical school curricula, and science fairs, the one-size-fits-all ethics looks ever stranger.

Despite the diversity of "human-subject research," regulationists seek a unified ethics. Elite commissions like NBAC believe an "independent, single federal office" must "promulgate a unified and comprehensive federal policy embodied in a single set of regulations and guidance that can be applied to all types of research involving human participants."[43] Yet despite much effort, attempts to write a legible code just for biomedical research have failed. Instead, principles narrower than Belmont's but far too broad to be useful for regulation emerge. Not for want of effort or intelligence. Ethical issues in research can be intricate and fact-specific and present irreconcilable conflicts among competing goods. Such issues are not easily reduced to a coherent ethics.

Even a coherent ethics for human-subject research would not suffice. Since IRBs are government agencies, their ethics must be legible *and* enforceable. IRBs and researchers must be able to tell what is required, and IRBs must be able to enforce the duty. This affects ethics, for, as I once wrote, "the law has goals that go beyond the immediate problems of bioethics, and those goals peculiarly shape the moral terms the law employs and specially alter the direction legal discourse takes. Furthermore, the law has limits that arise from its special social purpose, and those limits crimp the usefulness of law's language as a vehicle for bioethical discourse."[44] This is one reason lawyers' ethics are not announced in principles but in rules (much influenced by prolonged debate among lawyers themselves).

In short, *nobody* can write rules that cover all human-subject research and are bureaucratically workable and legally manageable. OHRP should particularly boggle. Its staff is far too small to represent the many relevant disciplines. Its directors have been an anesthesiologist, a veterinarian, a federal bureaucrat, and an MD/JD. None except the anesthesiologist seems to have done significant human subject research.

The IRB system both oversimplifies ethics and overcomplicates regulation. Having shrunken ethics to principles and swollen regulation to a Panopticon, some regulationists are surprised to find that legalization driving out personal, social, and professional norms. As Koski admits, trying "to regulate the implementation of ethical principles of conduct, is basically a failure."[45] As Kahn sees, "By overly focusing on making sure that rules are followed, we push researchers away from a real appreciation for issues and introducing whatever it takes to expedite the oversight process." Kahn quotes Koski: "We must move beyond the culture of compliance, to move to a culture of conscience and responsibility."[46]

But a culture of conscience and responsibility is just what IRBs replaced. In the bad old days, disciplines developed their own ethics through debates among specialists who understood their discipline's ethical problems. As ethics were regulated, nationalized, and legalized, this process eroded. Justification-by-scandal and distrust of scientists undermined disciplines as sources of ethics. But people subject to rules that they did not write and that violate their understanding of their situation and duties rarely embrace those rules.

4.   "MORTIFYINGLY STUPID": HOW IRBS DISCREDIT ETHICS

One of the IRB system's worst offenses has been teaching researchers contempt for ethics. It does so variously—not least by demonizing researchers and treating them unethically (as the next chapter argues)—but particularly by imposing the empty ethics I have described, an ethics that leads IRBs to treat identical cases differently. IRBs seem not to grasp how contingent and complex ethical problems are but "tend to feel that their own decisions are justified." Many think that they are "simply interpreting the regulations" and that their decisions are "inherently valid and essentially incontrovertible."[47] (They need to ponder Justice Jackson's remark: "We are not final because we are infallible, but we are infallible only because we are final.") Many scholarly disciplines have traditions of vigorous and informed ethical discussion. Simple-minded regulationist pronouncements contrast badly with such discussions.

Little discredits research ethics like the training in it. Many IRB chairs and members have scant or no "formal ethics training."[48] Much of the training they (and researchers) get comes from CITI. Schrag calls it the "most powerful engine of pseudo-expertise in the post 1995 IRB world," the "one-stop shop for universities to show that their faculty and students have had some training."[49] CITI's material is largely "written by administrators who value rote compliance over ethical reflection" and who get things wrong. For example, it says "scholars in the social sciences and humanities shouldn't claim that the regulations weren't written for them, because 'a close reading of the regulations will find mention of research methods and topics of inquiry relevant for researchers'" in those fields. But that close reading shows "no such thing," since the author "has confused a supplementary ruling from 1998 with the regulations."[50]

A sense of how far below academic standards ethics training sinks comes from Ronald Bayer, Professor and Co-Chair of the Center for the History and Ethics of Public Health at Columbia. He found it "the most insulting experience to sit in front of a screen, to download a text and then a series of questions to which there is only one right answer, and if God forbid you think that there may be an ambiguity or an uncertainty, you get the answer wrong." His colleagues discuss these tests "the way Russian social scientists used to talk about having to learn the right Marxist doxology in the old Soviet Union." People see "the entire process, not as something they feel proud about, but as something they experience as, in a way mortifyingly stupid, and stupefying—that is what it is, stupefying."[51] Schrag thinks "Bayer is right that many researchers hold ethics review in contempt. And he was right to trace much of that contempt to the terrible first impression made when smart researchers are compelled to complete an insulting, pathetic, mortifyingly stupid online tutorial."[52] (Sample CITI question: "Which of the following are the three principles discussed in the Belmont Report?" Your choices: (1) "Informed Consent, Institutional Assurance, Researcher responsibility"; (2) "Privacy, Confidentiality, Equitable selection of subjects"; (3) "Respect for Persons, Beneficence, Justice"; (4) "IRB review, Federal regulations, Declaration of Helsinki.")

Haskell calls academic disciplines "communities of the competent" that were "the seed crystals" for the modern university.[53] The "special authority and trustworthiness of community-sponsored opinions" arise from weathering "competition more severe" than "ordinary human communities" would tolerate.[54] The competent have "greater authority" than amateurs because they work in a "subculture of competing practitioners who expose and correct one another's errors."[55] Why should the competent respect a committee of amateurs who assert authority to evaluate the expert and reach the kinds of conclusions the "Vitamin A" case study and chapter 3 describe?

Were IRBs part of a community of the competent in research ethics, perhaps they could earn researchers' respect. But authoritative ethical debate is now done in secret by people with woeful claims to expertise even in regulationist ethics. And partly because regulationism is a movement and not a discipline, its literature—I have painfully learned—only sporadically reaches the standards Haskell's communities of the competent set. The IRB system was established to enforce ethics; too often is discredits them.

B. JUSTIFYING THE IRB SYSTEM

Central to the IRB ethos is its creation myth. That myth tells a story about how the IRB system arose and why it is necessary.

1. JUSTIFICATION BY SCANDAL

Rather than systematically gathering data, identifying problems, constructing an effective solution, and testing it, regulationists proffer justification-by-scandal. They invoke a few emblematic scandals and then proclaim the need not just for regulation, but for IRB regulation. Even as the key scandals of regulationist rhetoric recede into the past, even as IRBs assert authority over essentially scandal-free research, regulationists cling to justification-by-scandal. Genuine scandals rightly arouse indignation, but scandals justify regulation only if (1) they represent an evil that requires regulation and (2) regulation will do more good than harm. Several questions must be answered.

Is the scandal scandalous? Scandals can be initially misreported and then misremembered as they become political, ideological, and bureaucratic symbols. The lead-poisoning research in *Grimes v. Kennedy Krieger Institute* is often reviled, but the scandal was not the research—it was the judicial opinion calling it scandalous.[56] The leading modern scandal—Gelsinger—may be a scandal, a bad outcome, or an IRB failure; as Savulescu observes, "Other than a vague sense that the IRB should have done something more," there is "considerable confusion about where specifically the IRB members allegedly failed."[57]

The standard social-science scandals (Milgram, Zimbardo, and Humphreys) are dubiously scandalous. As Mueller observes, two "classic psychology studies seem to be regularly and selectively misrepresented" to show "widespread abuse in behavioral research." But there is "no systematic evidence on the extent, breadth and duration" of any distress Milgram's subjects may have suffered, "much less its severity relative to everyday experience."[58] And OHRP's *Guidebook* concedes that "Milgram's follow-up studies indicated that few if any subjects" had misgivings about participating. Zimbardo's research "was observed by parents, colleagues, a priest, and others," and there are "only anecdotal data about distressed prisoners."[59] Finally, Humphreys actually harmed no one, his ethics found both friends and enemies,[60] and his "critics disagreed among themselves about which elements of Humphreys's complex project design had crossed the line into abuse."[61]

Is the scandal accurately understood? Scandals are often misreported initially and distorted later. The media tend to prefer the lurid to the factual. To respond harshly to alleged harm to subjects.[62] To describe regulatory failings "without the benefit of historical perspective," a sense of the rate of misbehavior, or "a feeling for what is really possible."[63] Accusations and alarms sound loud and long; careful inquiry is slow and silent. So scandals slip from fact to myth. One IRB chair reprovingly told me Tuskegee researchers deliberately infected prisoners with syphilis. Fost and Levine think it undeniable that "the early history of research involving human subjects was dominated by scandals, including widespread egregiously unethical behavior by US physician investigators."[64] They cite only Beecher's 1966 article. Did his twenty-two (described) or fifty (attributed) instances of unethical research really "dominate" that history, were they really "widespread" among the many thousands of studies? Undeniably?

Is the scandal representative? Even scandals rightly reported and remembered must be representative to justify regulation. The emblematic research scandals occurred in particular parts of biomedical research and thus cannot justify regulating other parts of biomedical research, much less social science. They happened decades ago in deeply different circumstances and even foreign countries.

A principal problem with justification-by-scandal is that ethical opinions (like social mores) change. The past's culture is not the present's; ethical views and the world have so changed that past eras are poor guides for regulation. As a distinguished medical historian exclaimed to me, "Anybody who thinks an IRB in 1932 would have turned down Tuskegee is smoking heavy weed." Humphreys' adviser was a prominent sociologist who "encouraged him to look at so-called tearooms, places where men gathered for quick, anonymous sex." He was funded by the U.S. Public Health Service's National Institute of Mental Health.[65] His dissertation committee was "an eminent group of sociologists, some of whom had" written on research ethics. "He had tried to follow the few ethical precepts that had been taught him in graduate school." He won "a major award" and "rapid promotion and multiple job offers." So "[t]hose who considered his work an atrocity were up against not a single rogue researcher, but a good portion of an entire academic discipline."[66]

Humphreys' *Tearoom Trade* illustrates another problem with justification-by-scandal. IRB advocates use it to defend IRB review of social research. But it makes a bad exemplar, since the "deliberately covert and deceptive social research conducted by Humphreys was, and remains, quite rare."[67]

Can regulation solve the problem a scandal represents? Burris and Moss note that commentators invoke scandals to show regulatory failure "but do not seriously engage doubts about whether" IRBs actually "prevent or detect the sort of conduct that led to these harms."[68] IRB members and staffers, official and semi-official reports, and commentators simply assume that the IRB system works (or soon will).

If scandals justify the IRB system, it ought at least be structured to prevent them. But the crucial scandal—Tuskegee—was not the work of the people IRBs regulate; it was the work of the government that now uses its own misconduct to justify regulating private researchers. Furthermore, "some of the most notorious instances of unethical research in the midtwentieth century *were* reviewed by ethics committees." Willowbrook "had been reviewed by an ethics committee," and Tuskegee "apparently had also had such a review."[69]

2. PRESERVING PUBLIC TRUST

Moss states an adjuvant justification for IRBs: "maintain[ing] the public trust in the conduct of science."[70] Moss calls IRBs "necessary to maintain public trust in the research community."[71] This argument is solemnly advanced but seldom substantiated. Lacking evidence, regulationists usually just intimate that (1) confidence in research has fallen (2) because of research misconduct. Koski says public concern "is increasing, reflected in a rising tide of litigation, negative articles in the popular press, and other published commentaries."[72] He cites three articles. One says research-related litigation has increased, but in tiny numbers. The other two articles criticize research, but two articles do not a ripple make, much less a tide.

Actually, the "public approves of experimentation. An occasional catastrophe will touch off a public outcry with consequent overreaction, but on the whole the public continues to finance and to applaud medical experimentation and discovery."[73] Halpern notes that when the public-trust argument was most vigorously advanced, "[i]t was the federal policy community and not the public at large" that wished to expand IRB authority.[74] But assume research is less trusted than before. Is misconduct the reason? Regulationists offer no proofs and ignore contrary evidence. Americans distrust *all* their institutions more. Any increased distrust of research surely derives more from the factors increasing distrust generally than from scientific misbehavior.

Furthermore, do IRBs increase trust in research? Regulationists apparently reason that people (1) think research is dangerous, (2) know research is regulated, and (3) believe regulation makes research safe. I doubt people think much about (1). Regulationists themselves assume that because people don't know how dangerous research is government must protect them. If people really distrust research, they don't need IRBs to warn them against it. As to (2), I find that, far from being reassured, people (including many academics) are surprised that IRBs exist. I have yet to meet anyone outside the regulationist bubble who has heard of Gelsinger. Even well-educated people often don't know what happened at Tuskegee. And Harkness's search for "Belmont Report" in three major newspapers turned up only an obituary for the National Commission's chair. It found nothing for "Belmont principles."[75]

As to (3), is public trust enhanced when Congress passes a statute authorizing bureaucrats to regulate research? Congress is the least trusted public institution in Gallup's poll; the medical system is the fifth most trusted.[76] In 2011, doctors' "honesty and ethical standards" were rated very high or high by 70%, Congress's by 7%.[77] Who needs whose help with trust? HIPAA purports to increase trust by protecting privacy. Yet few "recognize, understand, or care about this complex law as it applies to research." Subjects ask about disclosure "exceedingly rarely." (One institution "received only 23 requests for accounting of disclosures," none from research.)[78]

If anything, regulationist rhetoric may *increase* public distrust. Regulationists dwell on scandals, denounce researchers, and declare that only IRBs keep subjects safe. Ominous legal forms and warnings about research and researchers also teach distrust. How does this sustain faith in research? Why not respond to any public distrust with the truth, which is largely reassuring?

In sum, the public-trust argument rests on assertion, not evidence or even argument. Regulationist speculation is implausible; contrary speculation is more convincing. This argument is a makeweight.

C. THE PERVERSITY OF THE IRB ETHOS

To respect autonomy is to give weight to autonomous persons' considered opinions and choices while refraining from obstructing their actions unless they are clearly detrimental to others.
—Belmont Report

While IRBs lack a legible ethics, they have a potent ethos. It betrays the autonomy that IRB ethics exalt, for the IRB system is instinct with paternalism. It assumes subjects cannot manage decisions but need governmental agencies to protect (OHRP says) their "rights, welfare, and well-being."[79] IRBs thus keep people from deciding whether to be research subjects and how to interact with researchers. As OHRP's director candidly admits, justifying IRBs "likely [*sic*] requires looking to true—hard—paternalism."[80]

1. THE RESURRECTION OF PATERNALISM

[B]ioethics has not come to terms with the deeply and pervasively paternalistic character of research ethics and thus has failed to adequately explore the soundness and limitations of its view.
—Franklin G. Miller and Alan Wertheimer, *Facing Up to Paternalism in Research Ethics*

Paternalism we have buried, but it still rules us from its grave. The IRB system's deep and pervasive paternalism rests on two mistakes: first, that people are not "capable of deliberation" about participating in research; second, that IRBs are.

Bioethics' fighting faith is that paternalism is the *summum malum*, that people manage their lives better than government, and that respect for persons requires honoring their choices. As Howard Brody says, medical ethics "views physician paternalism as a sin on a par with matricide and child abuse."[81] Autonomy is nominally the heart of research ethics. Yet what agency is as aggressively paternalistic as the IRB system? First,

IRBs decide whether the ratio of risk to benefit justifies participating in research. Second, IRBs minutely decide how researcher and subject may interact.

The first of these IRB functions infringes people's authority to decide what risks to take. That discretionary judgment IRBs make in ways many subjects would reject. For example, NBAC says that when subjects "incur risks with no personal potential benefit ..., there should be some limitation on the amount of social and physical risk that can be imposed, regardless of the participants' willingness."[82] This is doubly paternalistic. It decides for people that selfless acts are problematic (contrary to most Americans' beliefs) and assumes IRBs know better than subjects what risks to run and why.

The second IRB function—deciding how researcher and subject interact—is also paternalistic. When government tries to protect the weak, it ordinarily seeks ways less patronizing, as by requiring the strong to disclose information to the weak. But disclosures are usually narrow and few, disclosers usually formulate them, and disclosures are intended to *free* citizens to make their own decisions.

Miller and Wertheimer rightly say that bioethics has thought too little about its paternalism. Thus NBAC never explained *why* people can't decide whether "risks are reasonable."[83] Belmont advocates "refraining from obstructing" actions "unless they are clearly detrimental to others," but IRBs obstruct choices routinely. The voice is Jacob's voice, but the hands are the hands of Esau.

Miller and Wertheimer think it "easy to see why otherwise competent adults exhibit a variety of decisional defects that make it difficult for them to protect their own interests in assessing the risks and benefits of research." People "lack the requisite scientific and clinical knowledge," the sick succumb to the therapeutic misconception, and desperate patients "may well overestimate the benefits and underestimate the risks" of research.[84]

This is a poor reason to abandon the core principle of research ethics. It uses a slight fraction of human-subject research—the riskiest research with the sickest patients—to justify paternalism across all research. Most risk in social-science research arises from questions about people's own lives, a risk they manage daily. Even biomedical research generally poses such modest risks of serious harm that scientific and clinical knowledge is little needed. The therapeutic misconception affects only ill patients considering research offering *some* plausible chance of helping them. Finally, few research subjects are "desperate for the chance of medical benefit," and those who are may be the people *most* entitled to make their own assessments.

In addition, IRB paternalism goes *far* beyond "scientific and clinical" questions to, for example, questions about paying subjects to participate in research. In the rest of life, we pay people for work and risk, let them decide what work and risk are worth, and think people exploited if they are *not* paid. The IRB system turns compensation into exploitation. The OHRP *Guidebook* patronizingly thinks "offers that are too attractive may blind prospective subjects to the risks or impair their ability to exercise proper judgment." But why may people decide what pay to take for really dangerous jobs like lumbering or crab fishing but need IRB help evaluating payment for answering math questions?

Most IRB paternalism is not about big risks but about trumpery little things. IRBs pack consent forms with information sensible people ignore. Chapter 2 swarms with IRBs supervising microscopic risks of minuscule harms, like protecting people being practice-interviewed by relatives, lest they "feel coerced." Paternalism doesn't get much better than requiring government "approval before you may talk to your mother because she can't protect herself against you."[85] Or keeping a scholar from thanking by name the scientists and engineers he had interviewed, even though his interviewees regretted their anonymity.[86] Or telling a Canadian researcher not to "bother scientists" he wished to study because they were too busy.[87]

But even applied to Miller and Wertheimer's small category of decisions, their argument proves too much. It is *exactly* the old discredited justification of medical paternalism. Patients today routinely make—as of right—desperate decisions requiring genuinely arcane "scientific and clinical knowledge." Yet Levine describes a proposal to ask patients entering a coronary care unit with suspected or proved heart attacks for consent to "a complicated but rather harmless research maneuver." The IRB thought "the anxiety that might be produced in patients by subjecting them to the necessity to make such a decision might be substantial." It "might contribute" to "further damage to the heart or coronary care unit psychosis."[88] But as a seminal case warned, withholding "information for therapeutic reasons must be carefully circumscribed" lest it "devour" the autonomy principle.[89]

Not only do people make abstruse medical decisions, they daily navigate a sea of perils. They decide what to eat; yet bad diets kill. They decide whether to light up; yet smoking kills. They decide where to vacation; yet rafting kills. They decide what job to take; yet thousands die yearly at work. They buy cars; yet some are safer than others. They decide what sports to play; yet base-jumping, fishing (think boats and booze), hunting, and skiing kill. They decide what goods to buy; yet products-liability law is a carnival of death, dismemberment, and disaster. They invest their money and borrow other people's; yet credit-card debt and imprudent mortgages are roads to ruin.

Regulationists say subjects need special protection because researchers' interests diverge from theirs. This proves *far* too much. Divergence between doctors' and patients' interests underlay the argument for clinical informed consent. Journalists' commitment is to their story. Businesses exist to make money. Even devoted spouses do not have *entirely* interdependent utility functions. Among human interactions, those between researcher and subject have been among the less problematic, scandals notwithstanding. Subjects may not understand their choices as well as regulationists want. But they understand many graver choices—to borrow money, insure lives, buy houses, mortgage homes, pick a doctor, invest 401(k)s—no better.

In short, IRB licensing deviates far from the ways we usually regulate relationships in which the naive deal with the sophisticated. Where else could one find examples of such paternalistic intervention in people's decisions and dealings?

In evaluating the first argument against paternalism, I have argued that the standard presumption (that people generally should make their own decisions) fits most choices about research. What about the second argument—that government generally cannot make good decisions for its citizens? IRBs know too few research subjects to make good decisions for them. No committee could choose wisely for such diverse people making such varied choices. How could IRBs know what OHRP calls the subjective and hence "different feelings individuals may have about risks and benefits"?[90] As one regulationist says in a different context, only subjects "can weigh the severity of potential harms to themselves or to their communities, in terms of their own values, preferences, and concerns."[91]

IRBs tend to make decisions "on the basis of their own experience,"[92] which is atypical: IRB members are educated beyond the norm; their communities are often isolated culturally and even geographically. "Removed from the field, IRBs often find ... [some] potential dangers hard to assess—whether these will occur, and if so, which, to what degree, and with what effects, and how to weigh these against potential benefits."[93] People "too much confined to professional and faculty habits ... are rather disabled than qualified for whatever depends on the knowledge of mankind. ..."[94] And are not the regulationists who instruct IRBs "an order of men whose manners are remote from the present world, and whose eyes are dazzled by the light of philosophy"?[95] IRB members see through a glass darkly in another way—they have conflicts of interest. Their own status and funding can benefit from augmenting IRBs' authority. And IRBs are expected—and seem to expect—to protect their institutions, even though subjects might favor research that institutions fear.

These are reasons to expect what research confirms: IRBs are poor surrogates for subjects. Chapter 1 showed IRBs using stereotypes to predict reactions to questions about unhappy topics, a prediction people are better equipped to make personally. Similarly, in Gong's study, a few IRBs would not accept surrogate consent for research, and many restricted the pool of surrogates, "often excluding adult children." Yet in studies 68–96% favored using surrogate consent, and "[u]p to 72% of married and 96% of unmarried elderly" wanted their adult children as surrogates.[96]

In sum, IRB paternalism affronts basic principles of research ethics specifically and bioethics generally and betrays core norms of American culture and governance. Yet most choices most subjects make are easier and safer than choices patients specifically and citizens generally have an ethical, legal, even constitutional right to make.

2. PATERNALISM AND THE VULNERABLE

[The chair of Jackson State Prison's trustee committee said]: "Ladies and gentlemen, you are in a place where death at random is a way of life. We have noticed that the only place around here that people don't die is in the research unit. Now, just what is it you're here to protect us from?"
—Robert J. Levine, OHRP interview

IRBs are unembarrassed paternalists on behalf of even the sturdiest people. (A law professor interviewing partners in big-city law firms was told to broaden the survey "to better protect the participants.")[97] And "vulnerable" has become so capacious a category that it is another vehicle for paternalism, as this story suggests:

CASE STUDY: DOWN ON THE FARM[98]

Helene Cummins, a Canadian sociologist, knew that many farmers did not want their children to be farmers because the life was hard and the income poor. She wondered about "the meaning of farm life for farm children." She wanted to interview seven- to twelve-year-olds about their parents' farms, its importance to them, pleasant and unpleasant experiences, their use of farm machinery, whether they wanted to be farmers, and so on.

Cummins' REB first told her she needed consent from both parents. She eventually dissuaded them. They then wanted a neutral party at her interviews. A "family/child therapist" told the REB that "there would be an inability of young children to reply to some of the questions in a meaningful way," that it was unlikely that children would be able to avoid answering a question, and that the neutral party was needed to ensure [again] an ethical level of comfort for the child, and to act as a witness." Cummins had no money for an observer, thought one might discomfit the children, and worried about the observers' commitment to confidentiality. Nor could she find any basis for requiring an observer in regulations or practice. She gathered evidence and arguments and sought review by an institutional Appeal REB, which took a year. The Appeal REB eventually reversed the observer requirement.

Farm families were "overwhelmingly positive." Many children were eager and excited; siblings asked to be interviewed too. Children showed Cummins "some of their favorite places on the farm. I toured barns, petted cows, walked to ponds, sat on porches, and watched the children play with newborn kittens." Cummins concluded that perhaps "a humble researcher who respects the kids who host her as smart, sensible, and desirous of a good life" will treat them ethically.

Regulationists' most common questions about vulnerability are expanding IRB authority, "with the answer usually being 'yes.'"[99] The regulations already say that subjects "likely to be vulnerable to coercion or undue influence, such as children, prisoners, pregnant women, mentally disabled persons, or economically or educationally disadvantaged persons," require "additional safeguards" to protect their "rights and welfare."[100] IRBs can broaden their authority in two ways. First, "additional safeguards" and "rights and welfare" are undefined. Second, the list of vulnerable groups is open-ended and its criteria invitingly unspecified.

Who might not be vulnerable? Children are a quarter of the population. Most women become pregnant. Millions of people are mentally ill or disabled. "Economically and educationally disadvantaged" may comprise the half of the population below the mean, the three quarters of the adults who did not complete college, the quarter that is functionally illiterate, the other quarter that struggles with reading, or the huge majority who manage numbers badly. And it is easily argued, for example, that the sick and the dying are vulnerable.

The regulations speak only of vulnerability to "coercion or undue influence." Robert Levine says the vulnerable "are relatively (or absolutely) incapable of protecting their own interests" for want of the power, prowess, intelligence, resources, or strength to protect themselves "through negotiation for informed consent."[101] This is broad, but just the beginning, since regulationists and IRBs often seem to use vulnerability much more broadly than Levine does. Thus, the regulatory examples are uncertainly tied to the definitions: Prisoners are plainly vulnerable, but few pregnant women cannot make their own decisions. Carol Levine concludes that "vulnerable" is now so encompassing "that virtually all potential human subjects are included."[102] And NBAC says what many IRBs think: "Because most research involves uncertainty, all research participants are vulnerable in some sense."[103] This is the bottom of the slippery slope; nothing is certain, so everyone may (must?) be protected.

Calling children vulnerable is particularly problematic. In the American social and legal tradition, childhood generally does not justify governmental paternalism, for by statute and constitutional command, parents act for their children. But regulationists distrust parents almost as much as researchers.

Expanding the vulnerable category and consequently IRB paternalism also affronts the modern effort to *shrink* the number and size of categories of incompetence. Instead of treating patients as globally "competent" or "incompetent," the trend is to evaluate competence to make a given decision, thus increasing patients' authority. Similarly, minors' competence is increasingly evaluated choice by choice, not categorically. And law makes it elaborately hard to declare the mentally ill incompetent.

How should our two questions about paternalism be answered for vulnerable groups? IRBs are even less competent to understand the lives of the vulnerable than other lives. "Down on the Farm" suggests some garden-variety problems. The subjects already had protectors—parents who fed, clothed, housed, knew, and loved them and who did not become enemies because a researcher came calling. As one mother who had to get IRB approval to discuss her own family kept asking, why is there no assumption "that as a mother I would not want any harm to come to my children."[104]

Paternalism classically injures those it purports to protect. Recall the epigraph in which a prisoner asked "just what is it you're here to protect us from?" Regulationists answer—researchers. As chapter 2 showed, IRBs impede research with the sexually abused, minority groups, and the mortally ill. Are they protected, or silenced? Protected, or patronized? Protected, or obscured from public awareness and responsibility? Researchers who work with such groups "suggest that many IRB members, like the rest of society, are reluctant to confront abuse,"[105] and they adduce evidence that the nonabused are likelier to object to questions than the abused.[106] Bell and Salmon argue that conventional ideas about vulnerability "stereotype whole categories," like "drug users, who have generally been treated as a generic category despite important differences" based on factors like "gender, class and ethnicity."[107]

As Park and Grayson observe, clinic trials generally "offer free medication or free medical visits." Many regulationists fear these benefits might especially entice the needy. But Park and Grayson ask whether it is "better to receive some care" as a research subject or "none at all," and they answer that "if we strongly adhere to protecting the vulnerable, these populations would fail to receive this care simply because they have financial hardship."[108] And why should IRBs, rather than the vulnerable, decide?

Prisoners *are* vulnerable; prisons *are* brutal; researchers *have* abused prisoners. But it does not follow that IRBs know what is best for prisoners or should erect "very high barriers"[109] to prison research. McDonald, for instance, found that research can break prison's monotony and let the prisoner prove "that he can do something worthwhile." It requires risk, "sacrifice, perseverance, and altruistic ideals." This "improves his own self-esteem and elevates his status in the eyes of those who are important to him."[110] Inmates McDonald studied felt part of a group, most "expressed regret" when the research ended, and all "wished to be kept informed" about it.[111] In sum, IRBs have trouble seeing that "the inmate is not a neutral quantity" but "volunteers for certain advantages that are clear to him" and continues "because these desires are largely fulfilled."[112]

Similarly, none of Copes' prisoners thought their interview disturbing, almost 40% felt better afterwards, over half thought they were better placed "to help others increase their self-worth," 70% enjoyed "getting away" from ordinary life, a quarter were gladdened that somebody cared about their problems, and while IRBs don't consider pay a benefit, "inmates saw it as such," since "a lot of us don't get money" otherwise. None felt coerced into participating or mistook interviewers for prison employees (despite the regulationist belief that "[n]o matter how much they are assured otherwise," prisoners often associate researchers with "functionaries who can provide benefits or mete out punishment").[113]

IRBs' punishing paternalism also impedes research in poor countries, where disease proliferates and research is precious. Gilman and Hector say that IRBs tend to presume "investigators are intent on exploiting disadvantaged and poorly educated subjects." IRBs "are nearly always paternalistic" yet "have little (if any)" local experience. So IRBs protect poor countries by obstructing research in them. "Even the most benign study must navigate a maze of committees, setting the research process back months and even years. For example, a simple village survey study over a 5-year period could require 40 separate IRB approvals (or renewals)—at a high cost of time, effort and funding."[114]

IRB paternalism is deep and pervasive, but few regulationists justify it. IRBs make decisions for millions who could do better for themselves, thus flouting the preeminent regulationist principle—autonomy. Worse, IRBs select the vulnerable for intensified paternalism, degrading subjects by treating them as incompetent and perpetuating condescending stereotypes. Finally, IRBs exercise their paternalism by impeding research that might save and succor the lives of the people IRBs purport to protect.

3.   ETHICS WITH A HUMAN FACE

The free institutions which the inhabitants of the United States possess ... every instant impress ... the notion that it is the duty as well as the interest of men to make themselves useful to their fellow creatures. ...

—Alexis de Tocqueville, *Democracy in America*

The search for a legible IRB ethics having failed, I am examining the IRB ethos. It grows out of "a kind of consensus among people who call themselves bioethicists" and who have "become a kind of secular priesthood."[115] This priesthood exalts autonomy even while IRBs practice paternalism. But the IRB ethos sees autonomy and human obligations in controvertible and even repugnant ways. Handled crudely, autonomy notoriously degenerates into atomistic individualism. Fox and Swazey say that the "rights-oriented notion of rational, autonomous individualism" that typifies bioethics corrodes commitment "to responsibilities, duties, and obligations, to human dependency and interdependency, to trust, to a self-surpassing sense of solidarity with known and unknown persons, to community and society, and to qualities of the heart like sympathy, caring, and compassion—especially in response to the suffering of others."[116]

As we have seen, IRBs can hardly escape handling autonomy crudely, and an atomistic individualism thus animates the IRB ethos. It sees not only researchers, but also subjects, as narrowly self-interested. It assumes people do not (ought not?) want to participate in research. It doubts that altruism motivates people and mistrusts it. So Seelig and Dobelle say skeptically that it "may be true" that altruism is "something good." But "for whom is the good intended? If there is no obvious, direct potential benefit to the volunteer from volunteering, when are we justified in requesting participation in our project?"[117] Hellman and Hellman can imagine a "right to make a sacrifice for the general good" but think physicians cannot ask patients to make it.[118]

Most Americans admire altruism exactly because altruists help people without "obvious, direct potential benefit," and few will be as astonished as Seelig and Dobelle by the "unexpected finding" that helping research could be satisfying.[119] Seelig and Dobelle lovingly catalog altruism's pathologies. They admit that the chance to do good can be valuable "both for others, and the volunteer." But it is "clear" that this "benefit might prove to be the exception rather than the rule."[120]

The IRB ethos embodies a morally stunted view of human beings and their duties to each other and runs athwart the country's "whole moral and intellectual condition."[121] Tocqueville's America recognized that (as a later writer said) if communities depended only on "rational long-term self-interest, there would be little in the way of public spiritedness, self-sacrifice, pride, charity, or any of the other virtues that make communities livable."[122] Who would question helping, say, the children of famine because that help is not of "obvious" and "direct" benefit to donors? Many feel it a duty to donate blood and even organs—to give the gift of life.

Not just culture but law recognizes a duty of mutual aid. We pay taxes. Government regulation may regulate our property's value. We must proffer our presence, time, and efforts for jury duty. We may be drafted for military service and serve, suffer, and die. Some communities use volunteer fire departments. (When I called our rural fire department, my driveway overflowed with my neighbors' pickups.) We forfeit privacy to the census decennially. Some tax laws (like the charitable deduction) invite us to support social welfare. Public-health laws have long mandated intrusive surveillance. As early as 1891, health officials called this

a public duty in which "the people had consented" in the name of the common good to what might otherwise seem like an "arbitrary" or even "authoritarian" regime. Surveillance could demand limitations not only of privacy but even of liberty if the disease in question required mandatory treatment or isolation. At stake were questions of what individuals in a civil society owed to one another.[123]

The law's willingness to induce generosity has limits, yet some of them are regrettable, like the right not to save drowning babies. And social norms impose duties: "[V]erifiable non-rescues are extraordinarily rare, and verifiable rescues are exceedingly common," and often hazardous.[124]

The crabbed IRB ethos does not just affront the American moral tradition: "*Clinical research is a noble enterprise*" that is "*ethically required* on moral, cultural, religious, and humanitarian grounds." "No philosophical or religious tradition in the world ... does not support and require mutual aid among fellow-humans, solidarity with the weak and needy, and research for the improvement of support, help and care for those who are sick, suffering, or in pain."[125] The IRB ethos conflicts with a just morality of health care: Millions of subjects have assisted in research. Orentlicher suggests that "[i]n return for the benefits of earlier research, we might want to say that patients should be willing to participate in new trials."[126] And "with studies comparing different, well-accepted treatments, it would not be troublesome if patients felt some pressure to enroll," since they would be at no "greater risk of harm than if they did not."[127] This argument applies all the more where risk is realistically nil, as in archival research.

So, for example, an ethics of research that appreciates the personal, moral, and social interests at stake could reexamine IRB default rules.

Such rules ordinarily try to do for people what they would do themselves and to promote socially valued goals. (For example, intestacy statutes try to distribute intestates' property as they would want and to promote the social interest in helping families.) When research is little risky and when *some* default rule must be used—as in permission for archival research— rules should serve both the majority's wishes and social interests.

For example, people are massively willing to let researchers use information. In one "community-based primary care practice, only 3.6% of the patients refused to allow their medical records to be used in research."[128] Regulationists think biological samples from Africa "especially worrisome." Some "claim Africans believe that blood obtained ostensibly for research purposes will be used for sorcery," others that colonialism and slavery made Africans loath to share biological samples with Europeans or Americans.[129] But 95% of the Ugandans asked agreed to let samples of their children's blood be collected and stored. In short, the truncated morality of the IRB system is out of touch with the way most people think about their lives and their duties.

Put it in Belmont terms. Why does it show respect for persons to treat them as crudely selfish? To thwart their autonomous preferences? Why is it just to encourage people to receive research's benefits without assisting in its conduct? Why is beneficence required of researchers but suspect in subjects?

Or why does it show respect for persons for IRBs to depreciate ethical approaches to inquiry that seek to *increase* subjects' authority over the research? "Action research," for example, seeks to make researcher and "local stakeholders" a "collaborative team that determines the subject and methods of the work; learns and applies the methods together; analyses the outcomes; designs and implements the actions arising from the process; and together determine representations of that process." Its goals are "[d]emocratic collaboration, co-generation of knowledge, and a commitment to the democratization of human situations." Yet action research appears to alarm and repel IRBs, and some "have responded by denying permission for action research to be carried out at all."[130]

IRBs believe they serve research subjects. I doubt that subjects agree. I think they want what I found patients often sought from doctors— a human relationship of solicitude and consideration.[131] The IRB ethos trusts no researcher to treat subjects decently and substitutes legal for human relations. This takes two forms. First, the research enterprise is legalized. The self-regulation of scholars and disciplines is replaced by external rules. But people who distrust each other will cooperate "only under a system of formal rules and regulations, which have to be negotiated, agreed to, litigated, and enforced, sometimes by coercive means."[132] Gresham revised: bad law drives out good ethics. Second, the relationship between research and subject is legalized. Researchers must distribute legal forms rich in warnings against themselves and manifestly *in terrorem*. So researchers and subjects are taught to see themselves as legal actors and not human beings, as plain enemies and not possible friends.

How, then, can researcher and subject have the relationship they prefer? And how can subjects make good decisions about participating? IRBs expect subjects to make independent decisions on thorough information, but (as chapter 3 showed) this is rarely practical or necessarily wanted. In research as in clinical medicine, good decisions are often reached by working informally with the subject or patient to discover what quantum and kind of information helps. But anyone approached by the legal actor draped in warnings and forms and chained in IRB instructions is unlikely to feel comfortable. And the people we should worry about most—the poor and suffering—are especially likely to be intimidated, embarrassed, and alienated.

Researchers too should find such a relationship more rewarding and useful than the IRB world of distrust and constraints. As I once wrote,

[W]hen his studies let the scholar meet, talk with, and get to know the people the law regulates, he is blessed indeed. ... Americans are almost madly generous with their time and their intimacy. If the researcher cares about them, they will invite him into their lives, show him their world, and teach him their thoughts. The fortunate researcher finds in his work preceptors to heed, people to admire, and friends to cherish.[133]

Were IRBs abolished, researchers could treat subjects as people different from other people, differently circumstanced, needing different help, but sharing a need for concern and kindness. Researchers would not always rise to this opportunity and could abuse it. But they would not be unassisted, uninstructed, or ungoverned. Disciplines would debate the ethical issues they encounter, guide students in a human approach to human subjects, and sanction researchers deficient in humanity. And if this failed, the law's armory could punish the errant and protect the injured.

D. CONCLUSION

It is obvious that if one designs or regulates research in accord with the Belmont principles, the research will be valid science and also ethical science.
—Joan E. Sieber, *Using Our Best Judgment in Conducting Human Research*

The IRB system is a government agency that teaches researchers their duties and enforces its teachings with a confidence and stringency John Calvin might have admired. But it lacks an ethics to justify its authority. It promulgates an incoherent code for an incoherent category—human-subject research. It announces doctrines in a document—the Belmont Report—that is regulatorily useless. That Report is supposed to offer a "language for discussing ethical standards," but regulationists' use of it cruelly disproves the supposition.

The IRB ethos embraces what it denounces: paternalism. Paternalism is as damaging in IRB hands as regulationists say it is in researchers'. IRBs underestimate people's ability to understand their own lives and overestimate their own capacity to make decisions for others. So IRBs injure their wards, especially by impairing research that could help them.

In sum, IRBs demand that we treat as law the "thin gruel of smug answers," the "unquestioned formal procedures that are not open to revision" Bosk warns of.[134] This is, to return to our epigraph, "what happens when heavy-handed systems of regulation displace other normative systems."

5

The Rule of Law: The Lessons of Due Process

Due process is perhaps the most majestic concept in our whole constitutional system.
—*Joint Anti-Fascist Refugee Committee v. McGrath,* U.S. Supreme Court

Part II has been arguing that IRBs do less good and more harm than they might because regulatory choices have kept IRBs from making decisions well. Chapter 3 presented evidence that IRBs are poor decision makers and found some of the explanation in overworked committees operating beyond their competence. Chapter 4 found more of the explanation in the lack of an intelligible and intelligent ethics. Chapter 5 now argues that yet more of the explanation lies in the absence of the substantive and procedural rules agencies need.

In legal terms, this chapter investigates the system's rejection of "due process." Due process serves three crucial goals. First is "fundamental fairness," that "[p]rotection against Kafkaesque, unlimited discretion of officials [that] is the underlying goal of the due process clause."[1] That fairness includes telling citizens what the law is, letting them make their case, explaining decisions to them, and giving them recourse when government mistreats them. The second goal is better decisions, since good decisions grow out of good rules, both substantive and procedural. Ad hoc decisions are haphazard and inconsistent; poor procedures produce ill-considered results. The third goal is persuading the regulated to promote the agency's ends. Due process obliges agencies to treat people in ways that lead them to see the agency as legitimate, accept its judgments, and even make its goals their own.

To put the point differently, due process is crucial because making well-considered and well-founded decisions is hard for everyone, even experts guided by rules, and because lawless government is illegitimate. When agencies lack substantive rules, prudent procedures, and meaningful accountability, their decisions are likely to be unexplained and inexplicable, to be unfair, unreliable, and alienating.

A. IRBS AND THE RULE OF LAW

Yet, designation has been made without notice, without disclosure of any reasons justifying it, without opportunity to meet the undisclosed evidence or suspicion on which designation may have been based, and without opportunity to establish affirmatively that the aims and acts of the organization are innocent.

—*Joint Anti-Fascist Refugee Committee v. McGrath,* U.S. Supreme Court

American government "has been emphatically termed a government of laws, and not of men."[2] This ideal is made concrete by the principles of due process. It traditionally has two components. One is rules that tell both the agency and those it regulates what is required of them. The other is procedures that shape the agency's work. IRBs, however, might as well be told, "Decide what you like as you like." IRBs *may* constrain themselves substantively or procedurally. But they need not, and the system's structure and ethos discourage it. If IRBs violate their own rules and procedures, researchers have no remedy. This would be problematic in any agency. But agencies like IRBs that both make law and prosecute and judge offenders especially need the rule of law, for they tend "to act more arbitrarily, to use ad hoc solutions and sanctions rather than solutions and sanctions formally prescribed by standing laws." They have incentives to judge people unfairly and undervalue their liberties.[3] All this makes real what Kafka imagined.

Regulationists rarely recognize such concerns explicitly and answer them badly implicitly. Mazur's IRB manual warns that even after debating and voting, "members may hold different perspectives on what the decision making was about and even on what decision was made." So before answering questions, members may need "to reflect on the discussion."[4] Jaeger actually describes an IRB making decisions without knowing what it has done.[5] If after studying, debating, and voting IRB members do not even know what was decided, the decision cannot have been made properly or well.

All this matters. It matters because lawless government is illegitimate. Because governments have a duty of "fundamental fairness"—to tell citizens what the law is, to let them make their case, to explain decisions affecting them, and to give them recourse when they are mistreated. Because good government is impossible without good law: Ad hoc decisions are erratic and ill-considered, poor procedures produce poor results, and agencies that are not accountable abuse their authority. This chapter, then, argues that an IRB system that flaunts the rule of law—or norms, procedures, and accountability—cannot act justly, deliberate wisely, or merit respect.

B. THE FAILURE TO ACHIEVE RULES AT ALL

That a conclusion satisfies one's private conscience does not attest its reliability. The validity and moral authority of a conclusion largely depend on the mode by which it was reached. Secrecy is not congenial to truth-seeking and self-righteousness gives too slender an assurance of rightness.

—*Joint Anti-Fascist Refugee Committee v. McGrath*, U.S. Supreme Court

A government of laws must *have* laws—rules telling citizens and government what government may, may not, or must do. Freedom, Locke said, "is, to have a standing rule to live by" and not be subject "to the inconstant, uncertain, unknown, arbitrary will of another man."[6] So laws must give anyone "of ordinary intelligence a reasonable opportunity to know what is prohibited." Nor may laws be so vague that they delegate "basic policy matters to policemen, judges, and juries" for "*ad hoc* and subjective resolution."[7] Yet the IRB system rules are so incomplete, ambiguous, open-ended, and optional that it is pursuing Lon Fuller's "most obvious" route to disaster in creating and maintaining a system of legal rules—"a failure to achieve rules at all."[8]

Consider a garden-variety case. Ceci and Bruck wanted to assess children's testimony, especially in child-abuse cases. They planned to show six- to ten-year-olds a tape of a fireman telling a child not to play with his hat and of the child answering "gentle suggestive questioning" by falsely saying the fireman had hit him. They wanted to see how children explained the falsehood. Calling it "unethical to show children public servants in a negative light," the IRB said no even though (a) the NSF and NIH had reviewed the proposal and the NSF had funded it, (b) experts thought the video harmless and said children often saw much worse on TV, (c) experts saw no risk of "negative impressions of police or firemen," and (d) two other IRBs had said yes.[9]

What law governed this IRB? The HHS regulations ignore so much and speak so vaguely "that men of common intelligence must necessarily guess at [their] meaning and differ as to [their] application."[10] For example, § 46.111 says risks must be reasonable in relation to benefits and to the importance of knowledge gained. Risk, harm, and injury connote serious consequences, yet regulationists can treat as harms "depression, altered self-concept, increased anxiety, decreased confidence in others, guilt, shame, fear, embarrassment, boredom, frustration, receiving information about oneself that is unpleasant, and inconvenience."[11] What can "risk" mean if it includes Mengele's barbarism and the inconvenience of describing your admiration for Congress? Is "decreased confidence in others" bad? Does it depend on whether you are Pangloss or Calvin? On what confidence you started with? Is boredom a research risk or a subject's failing? Is frustration a harm or just a challenge? How do you measure risk? Is it a terror or thrill to climb Everest? How do you assess knowledge's importance? Since the regulations suggest no way to do so, IRBs are forced back on what one manual calls "the vagaries of intuition."[12]

Much of § 46.111 is no clearer. Risk must be "minimized" by methods "consistent with sound research design" that "do not unnecessarily expose subjects to risk." But "risks," "minimized," "consistent," "sound," and "unnecessarily" all lack the "terminological precision and conceptual clarity" whose importance Levine cannot overestimate. As a great judge said, "'Reasonable,' 'duly,' 'malice,' are all double-faced 'weasel' words, capable of treachery."[13] Yet "reasonable" or "reasonably" appears twenty times in these shortish regulations and some form of "appropriate" thirty times.

As Beauchamp argues, the regulations also leave "research" ill-defined. First, the term research is used to define research, "creating problems of circular definition." Second, the regulations don't explain key parts of their definition, like "systematic investigation," "testing," and "generalizable knowledge." Third, "the definition is vague and overly broad because it is not clearly confined to biomedical research, clinical research and behavioural research—or even to *scientific* research, more generally." Finally, and crucially, "it does not preclude 'research' from having a very close tie to 'practice.'"[14]

IRB members and staffers Klitzman interviewed reported that federal agencies disagreed with each other. Some interviewees cited conflicts over "whether to exclude women who are of childbearing age and pregnant, but seriously ill and with no other options." One interviewee lamented that "NIH keeps saying, 'You need to include women, and can't discriminate against them.' But FDA is pretty clear: most trials exclude women of childbearing potential, unless they are sterilized, and have quadruple birth-control methods—pretty nutty stuff."[15]

Not only are the regulations a Great Grimpen Mire of ambiguity, they often leave IRBs simply uninstructed. When subjects are "vulnerable," IRBs must require unspecified "additional safeguards."[16] IRBs may impose unspecified extra disclosure requirements when it "would meaningfully add" to protecting subjects.[17] The emergency-research regulations require "[a]dditional protections, including" but not confined to a list.[18]

Furthermore, their ethos invites IRBs to ignore even clear rules. An OHRP letter says that regulations "provide a floor, not a ceiling," and that institutions can impose "additional restrictions."[19] One manual says IRBs may require protections exceeding the regulations.[20] Another says § 46.116(a)(6) "outlines only a minimum federal standard" and that "federal policy" lets IRBs exceed it "as they deem appropriate."[21] The CEO of "a consulting firm in human research protections" writes that "to say, 'This is what it says in the regulations and that's what you should do,' ignores best practice and the need for higher standards. And, once you get into the area of best practice, you leave the realm of right and wrong."[22] So IRB members, for example, demand "that the benefit either to myself or the benefit to the community and to knowledge that's gained far outweigh the pain or the difficulty of laborious telephone interviews or whatever it might be."[23] "Far outweighs" is *not* the regulatory standard, nor a good one. The regulations, in short, are too ambiguous, incomplete, and discretionary to be law.

Schrag finds lawlessness compounded by "false claims" about the "regulations flitting from university to university, without citation." The University of Iowa says that the federal regulations prohibit researchers from deciding whether their "study meets the definition of human subjects research." Schrag writes that the "regulations say no such thing, but you can find the same falsehood at the University of Southern California." Schrag describes "various mechanisms by which such falsehoods spread."

In the IRB Forum, for example, "most queries are answered by IRB staffers explaining how they believe a situation ought to be handled" with no authority "beyond the Belmont Report and the federal regulations."[24]

IRBs not only are unconstrained within their jurisdiction, they cannot be kept within jurisdictional limits. Without visible authority, probably many, and possibly most, IRBs seek to protect their institution. Some IRBs "protect" researchers: "'You don't understand what was at stake. We did it to protect you.'"[25] Moss calls protecting investigators an "important function."[26] Manuals can ignore even OHRP guidance about jurisdictional limits: When people in sensitive positions are interviewed for oral histories "it is appropriate" to require informed consent, OHRP "reinterpretation of oral history practice under the Common Rule notwithstanding."[27] Similarly, an IRB manual reports that some "institutions acknowledge that, although some undergraduate ethnography research may not meet the federal definition of research," IRB review is "educational" and prepares students to be ethical researchers.[28]

OHRP's *Guidebook* aggravates this failure to achieve rules. Schrag says that "federal officials boast" of the regulations' "flexibility,"[29] but the *Guidebook* far exceeds flexibility. Thus after calling "the risk/benefit ratio" an IRB's major ethical judgment, the *Guidebook* says that that judgment is not "a technical one valid under all circumstances" but "often depends upon prevailing community standards and subjective determinations of risk and benefit."[30] To escape lawlessness, judgments need *some* basis in rules, not "subjective determinations."

The system's lawlessness is reflected in the unpredictable decisions IRBs make. Chapter 3 listed many examples, so a few suffice here. Two elite organizations say of Subpart D (on vulnerable subjects) that key terms like "'minimal risk,' 'minor increase over minimal risk,' and 'disorder or condition'" are "interpreted in widely varying ways."[31] And one study found confusion over HIPAA "common among all players, from research participants to privacy boards to institutions and even states."[32]

Regulationists beg OHRP for clarification. The IOM laments IRBs' "extreme variability in the regulatory interpretations and approval decisions." IRBs "conflate the Common Rule and Privacy Rule, or apply the research provisions of the Privacy Rule to activities for which they are not applicable."[33] The HIPAA criteria that IRBs use "are complex and very subjective." To issue a waiver, IRBs must interpret "adequate" three times and "practicable" twice. IOM observes that "adequate" is "highly subjective," that OHRP has not defined "practicable," and that "institutions apply varying definitions."[34]

OHRP repeatedly promises to clarify regulations. But Schrag tells a typical story. The OHRP director Bernard Schwetz "conceded that his office had failed to offer clear guidelines for the review of nonmedical research." He "promised 'a lot of examples' and said the OHRP 'will give more guidance on how to make the decision on what is research and what is not.'" He later reiterated the promise, "pledging that the 'OHRP will seek public comment on a draft version of the guidance document before it is finalized.' But Schwetz retired that September, and no document appeared by his promised year-end deadline—or by the end of the following year." This "broken promise continued a tradition, dating back to 1966, of empty assurances."[35]

For example, one IRB administrator cited prison research, where an IRB must choose one of four categories. They "just don't really fit a lot of research," so the IRB must "always kind of *stretch it a little bit* to fit the research" into a category. "*It's almost a wink and a nod*," since both the IRB and OHRP know "this stuff stinks to work with."[36] When OHRP does respond, it "may not do so in writing, or may say that the clarification does not apply more generally." One interviewee said OHRP has "not been forthcoming." It is "very difficult to get any kind of opinion from them, which is very disturbing." If you ask about "a very specific situation, they make it very clear that their opinion is relevant to this very specific question, at this specific time, for this particular institution, for this particular subject—they are not providing any general rules or guidance or algorithms." One IRB administrator reported that OHRP had just accepted "our changes from *two years ago!* I have not gotten anything back from more recent reports." But not everything takes "two years. We have not gotten back things from *three* years ago!" And interviewees "felt that OHRP staff frequently won't even discuss perceived reluctance in responding."[37]

Some of OHRP's motives are frankly described by Gary Ellis, the director of OHRP's predecessor (OPRR):

"[I]t's not ever going to be exempt, if you call me on the phone and ask me that." He conceded that such decisions left more work for the researcher, but they would not expose the OPRR to a charge of letting a dangerous project through. "At some level," he explained, "I've taken care of the human subject. That's the highest priority. The second priority is self-preservation of the bureaucrat. And the third priority is the researcher."[38]

Freed from law, IRBs can consult flatly illegitimate factors. Klitzman writes that instead of "careful 'ethical analysis,'" many chairs and members "draw on their 'gut feelings' and 'intuition,' seeking 'peace of mind'" about a study. They "vary in how much they weigh their anxiety. Interviewees occasionally use 'the sniff test' to sense whether a protocol seems ethically sound."[39]

In sum, IRBs' most authoritative law—the federal regulations—is effectively lawless, a failure manifest in the regulation's opacity, the *Guidebook's* refusal to clarify them, regulationists' complaints about regulatory obscurity, and IRBs' incompatible treatment of identical protocols. But regulationists seem unperturbed. An IRB manual, for example, cites a two-institution study. Institution A's IRB agreed with the investigators that the research's findings lacked clinical utility and might worry parents. So it approved the study, "provided that parents were not given its results." Institution B's IRB agreed "with experts who believed the research results might have potential predictive value and/or clinical relevance." So it approved the study, "provided that parents were given the results." The manual finds both decisions correct. "Both IRBs acted on their views" of the research's information and clinical usefulness.[40]

Similarly, three IRB luminaries at an excellent institution say their two IRBs "vary in methodology and approach." One "tends to approve protocols with minor reservations while the other tends to review more critically," but it cannot be said which is right.[41] Thus what Frankel said of pre-reform sentencing is true of IRBs: "With a delegation of power so unchanneled," judges have "the greatest degree of uncontrolled power over the liberty of human beings that one can find in the legal system" and wield it in a way that is "totally unruly."

"[A]bsolute and uncontrolled discretion in a government agency that runs a vast program" is "an intolerable invitation to abuse."[42] But IRBs receive that invitation. OHRP proffers it by endorsing "subjective" and "community" standards. The IRB consultant proffered it when he saw no "'right' answers to questions in our field. Nothing in human research protections is black or white; it is all gray."[43] If all is gray, why prefer an IRB's opinion to a researcher's? If all are blind, can anyone be king?

C. A PROCEDURAL WASTELAND IN THE LAW

The heart of the matter is that democracy implies respect for the elementary rights of men, however suspect or unworthy; a democratic government must therefore practice fairness; and fairness can rarely be obtained by secret, one-sided determination of facts decisive of rights.
—*Joint Anti-Fascist Refugee Committee v. McGrath*, U.S. Supreme Court

IRBs are as poor in procedural as in substantive law. The system assures researchers *none* of the basic elements of due process in Judge Henry Friendly's classic catalog.[44] Due process's goals—fundamental fairness and good decisions—can often be met without using all those elements, but they cannot be met without using any of them. Stefan Timmermans' experience of thesis research in a hospital introduces this world without due process. Like many ethnographers, Timmermans (now a UCLA sociologist) believes neither "in absolute truth" nor "objective finding" and does not worry "about the generalizability or reliability of my study."

CASE STUDY: THE DEGRADATION[45]

Timmermans is writing his Ph.D. thesis and appears with his supervisor before an IRB. They prepared what they wanted to say but are unprepared for what happens. Timmermans is stopped from reading his statement. "For the 35 minutes that Professor Star and I are in the room, we are able to talk for approximately four minutes. Each time we try to say something we are interrupted or ignored. We both feel we are part of a Goffmanian public degradation ceremony." The IRB members loathe Timmermans' initial paper and "vent their anger in a continuous outpouring of hostile criticisms."

His IRB is incensed, Timmermans concludes, because of its "rigid definition of 'objective science.'" Timmermans tries to explain himself. A doctor/IRB member "interrupts fiercely: 'You did NOT do theory, only hypotheses. [He yells and waves his hands violently.] If you write something, we should know HOW MANY PEOPLE said WHAT, there should be NUMBERS in here. There is [*sic*] NO DATA in this paper.'" Timmermans' IRB is also furious at his "representation of the medical profession" and the hospital. Members say Timmermans is "evaluating the emergency department staff" and making "'jerks' out of them. One physician even accuses me of straight-out lying because 'they (emergency personnel) cannot have said that.'"

Timmermans concluded that "the IRB members were mainly concerned with the promotion of a positivistic research paradigm and with shielding the medical profession from outside criticism. They perceived my writing as a threat to the reputation of their institution and the medical profession."

1. FAIR HEARINGS

Sentencing is today a wasteland in the law. ... There is an excess of discretion given to officials whose entitlement to such power is established by neither professional credentials nor performance.

—Marvin E. Frankel, *Lawlessness in Sentencing*

Judge Friendly's first element of due process is a neutral arbiter. IRBs are not neutral: Their ethos is not neutral, nor is their incentive structure. Members are not selected for neutrality and usually work in the researcher's institution. Regulationists insist that researchers' situation distorts their judgment and unfits them to work unsupervised. By that logic, as Nelson writes, IRB members' conflicts of interest look disqualifying. Yet in "contrast to the enormous attention paid to investigator conflicts of interest in recent years, very little has been paid to similar conflicts on the part of IRBs."[46]

IRBs' neutrality is further compromised by the common belief that "[p]rotecting the university goes without saying."[47] To Moss, long chair of an IRB at Chicago, private universities are "largely corporations" that "are sensitive to political influences that compromise their corporate interest" and that will do anything to protect that interest. IRBs help by weeding out "politically sensitive studies."[48] And an IRB member told Rambo: "'I don't give a tanker's damn [*sic*] about your human subject. This is all about liability. The University doesn't like lawsuits or anything that could tarnish its image. ... No one gives a god damn about the truth, it's about liability.'"[49]

Courts and agencies seek neutrality by isolating judges from the judged, but IRB members may be researchers' competitors and even enemies, and IRBs can rely "on their personal impressions of PIs."[50] As one respondent wrote, there is "quite some show of 'muscle' and if a member has a score to settle with an investigator, woe to the whole study." He has seen researchers who "dare not speak out lest the committees sit on their studies for ever (with a what-can-you-do attitude)."[51] Interviews and "documented experiences" convince van den Hoonaard "that decisions in some ethics committees are guided by jealousies and sometimes even vendettas."[52]

Unfettered authority corrodes arbitral neutrality. Bakunin saw nothing "more dangerous for man's private morality than the habit of command. The best man, the most intelligent, disinterested, generous, pure, will infallibly and always be spoiled at this trade." So "power and the habit of command become for even the most intelligent and virtuous men, a source of aberration, both intellectual and moral."[53] Even judges in criminal trials are therefore admonished to "suppress personal predilections," control their "temper and emotions, and be patient, respectful, and courteous."[54]

IRB authority, however, is ill constrained, perilously clad in righteousness, and insensitive to its own strength. Klitzman found "IRB chairs, directors, administrators, and members" generally denying having power or thinking it "minimal or justified, because they were 'merely following the regulations,' had an 'open,' impersonal, and unbiased process, and were themselves subject to higher administrative agencies." They thought their authority "legitimate because it is based on 'the community's values' and overriding goals."[55] Little here induces humility or respect for persons.

Demonizing researchers exacerbates arbitral arrogance. Amdur thinks researchers who criticize IRBs for demanding "clarification or justification" show "a lack of respect" that "is an important finding that should be taken into account when making IRB determinations."[56] When Rambo awaits IRB trial, she is offered no chair but sits "on the floor in the hall, outside the conference room, in a black jacket, skirt, hose, and heels, waiting my turn. A loud male voice booms, 'Rambo? Rambo? Good God, what a name for this one.'" Later, an IRB member tells her, "'You can't publish that manuscript anywhere. I don't care if you submit it to *Vogue*, *Cosmopolitan*, *Ladies Home Journal*, *Soldier of Fortune*, or *Field and Stream*, you can't publish that anywhere. ... If I thought bitch slapping you would bring you to your senses, I'd do it.'"[57]

Agencies try to temper arbitral bias; IRBs generally do not. Agency arbiters are often a separate and isolated class; IRB members are often colleagues. Arbiters are chosen to be neutral; no one knows how IRB members are chosen. Arbiters are socialized to recognize biases and subjectivity; IRB training is generally superficial and unlikely to moderate bias. Arbiters are hemmed in by procedures and substantive rules; IRB members roam free. Arbiters explain decisions, exposing biases to themselves, onlookers, and the judged; IRBs need explain only a rare refusal to permit research. Arbiters are subject to review, which detects and discourages bias; IRBs are immune.

A neutral arbiter means little without a fair hearing,[58] but hearings are an act of IRB grace. Fitzgerald found that grace was not abounding, that procedures rarely assured researchers real hearings or IRBs good evidence. Most applicants were allowed "a short, plain-language description of the project" too short for "a truly informative narrative." One IRB member usually summarized applications, thus directing "members' thoughts and discussion."[59] Chapter 2 describes the confused and erratic choices that can ensue.

Notice of the evidence is also critical to due process. Unlike courts and agencies, IRBs are not given orderly ways to receive and analyze evidence. Members and staffers introduce evidence (often conjecture and anecdote) into discussions unawares. Fitzgerald found IRBs evaluating risk through a "*personal experience* narrative." These "urban myths or contemporary legends" were "told as true."[60] Lacking notice, researchers could not correct them. Relatedly, researchers need to know what an IRB plans to do and why—what rules it thinks govern, how it interprets them, how it sees the research, and what doubts it has. Fitzgerald found that even if researchers attended meetings, it was after "members had already heard and discussed the reviewers' narratives." So researchers spoke "in the context" of narratives researchers hadn't heard.[61] Due process can also include the right to call witnesses to educate fact-finders. Expert witnesses might analyze research's significance or subjects' vulnerability, explain a standard treatment's inadequacy, review the evidence that discussing sensitive topics is not dangerous, or explore the informed-consent literature. Similarly, questions of method in specialized fields are outside IRB ken and within an expert's.

Finally, due process can require public proceedings. Criminal defendants are constitutionally entitled to them, partly to restrain judicial power.[62] Menikoff says transparency produces "substantial benefits at relatively little cost."[63] But much "IRB work occurs behind closed doors," with IRBs keeping minutes, correspondence, and decisions private.[64] Noting that "IRB meetings are closed to the public" and confidential, Elliott says that secrecy may be the system's most dangerous flaw.[65] Van den Hoonaard says no ethics committee "has made its consultations and decisions a matter of public record" and that even IRB membership "is often unknown or not published."[66] Klitzman's interviews with IRB officials convinced him that IRBs may like the secrecy because it can "reduce questions about their processes and decisions."[67]

2. SOUND DECISIONS

[Sentencing] is by and large a bizarre "nonsystem" of extravagant powers confided to variable and essentially unregulated judges, keepers, and parole officials.
—Marvin E. Frankel, *Lawlessness in Sentencing*

The quality of IRB decisions turns partly on another element of due process—a decision on the evidence. But the failures in due process we have just cataloged make such a decision unlikely, as the erratic decisions the multisite studies confirm. The occasional peeks into IRB meetings suggest that IRBs do not understand how harmful this is. For example, Stark "observed misbehavior" in three IRBs. They understood research methods poorly, overestimated risks, and relied "on personal experience rather than scholarly research. All three committees judged proposals based on the proportion of spelling and typographical errors in the proposal."[68]

A decision on the evidence is unlikely unless another element of due process is required—a statement of the reasons for a decision. As Judge Frankel testified, this helps arbiters "be fair and rational." When they can be "casual about explanations, and free of any obligation to account," it is "easy to hand out inaccurate or incomplete information,"[69] and the arbiter is unlikely to "organize a full and coherent explanation even for himself."[70] (This may explain how Mazur expects IRB members to vote without knowing what they are deciding or why.)[71] So judges "must explain themselves when they rule whether a postal truck driver was at fault in crumpling a fender and, if so, how much must be paid to right the wrong."[72]

Finally, as Judge Frankel writes, "Decisions based upon secret reasons bear no credentials of care or legitimacy."[73] They lend "a quality of baleful mystery rather than open justice" and leave unquelled suspicions of unfairness that are exacerbated when researchers learn how erratic IRB decisions are.[74] Yet "the world of ethics committees hides behind a shroud of mystery that hovers over their proceedings."[75]

No agency is inerrant, so due process includes ways to correct bad decisions. Those ways depend on a record of proceedings. Extensive paperwork rarely reveals IRBs' thinking. But without such a record, the right to an appeal and to judicial review are empty. You can't appeal an error unless you know it was made. And without a right of appeal and judicial review the other due process elements are empty. Appeals and judicial review hold agencies to their rules and the law's. They move agencies to anticipate and answer criticisms. As Judge Frankel said, they deter the trial judge from seeing "himself as the final authority," thus "sinking deeper each year the footings of premises" untested "by detached scrutiny or by open debate."[76]

Appeals and judicial review serve yet another purpose. No rules are entirely comprehensive or comprehensible and so gain meaning through the accretion of precedents that generate broader principles. This is how for two centuries the Supreme Court has given meaning to the Constitution's Delphic provisions and the state courts have nurtured the "common law" of torts, property, and contracts. But since IRBs do not write opinions and since their decisions cannot be appealed within the agency nor reviewed by courts, IRBs cannot benefit from this way of developing and refining rules.

A last element of due process serves the others—counsel. Researchers are ill-placed to tell what the law is or to interpret it. Lawyers specialize in this. They also learn the implicit rules, practices, and assumptions that supplement formal rules. They assemble evidence, build cases, and present arguments. Law "renders men acute, inquisitive, dexterous, prompt in attack, ready in defense, full of resources,"[77] and researchers and IRBs alike can benefit. Yet IRBs seem to treat researchers' attempts to get legal help as acts of war.

Finally, OHRP could better supervise IRBs if it accorded IRBs due process. For example, when OHRP made findings in "basically a routine audit" of an IRB, the IRB responded but "never even heard back" until "we got the letter that basically we were being shut down." Klitzman's interviewees could not tell what standards OHRP applies but report a "'focus on seemingly minor matters.'" Klitzman says that "audit citations can seem 'ridiculous,'" like the criticism that "the number of IRB members voting doesn't match the number in the room 'because someone went to the bathroom.'" Worse, one IRB chair reported "OHRP's perceived vindictiveness to nail people." And despite "frustrations with audits, interviewees felt that individuals had to be careful not to respond resentfully."[78]

3. DUE PROCESS IN CONTEXT

But in an assembly possessed of the almost immeasurable powers that belong to this House, and in an assembly with regard to which appeal against its proceedings is a thing totally unknown ... excess of jurisdiction is the greatest fault the House can possibly commit. ...

—William E. Gladstone, Debate on the Parliamentary Oath (Mr. Bradlaugh)

The IRB rejection of the rule of law is so complete that even convicts are better treated than researchers. Parolees are convicted criminals with only conditional liberty, but when accused of violating parole conditions they get a prompt inquiry near the scene by an uninvolved arbiter. They must be told of the hearing, its purpose, and its charges. Parolees "may appear and speak" and "bring letters, documents, or individuals." Ordinarily, witnesses must be "available for questioning" in the parolee's presence. A hearing summary is made; decisions must rest on the evidence and be explained.

Then parolees are entitled to a *second* hearing in a reasonable time to determine what the facts are and whether they justify revoking parole. Parolees must be allowed to show that parole was not violated or should not be revoked. Again they receive written notice of charges, disclosure of evidence, a chance to be heard in person, to cross-examine adverse witnesses, "neutral and detached" arbiters, and a written statement of the "evidence relied on and reasons for revoking parole."[79]

This chapter's first section criticized IRBs' lawlessness. The second section criticized their procedural anarchy. These faults exacerbate each other. For example, IRB rules prefer "reasonable" to definitions. "Reasonable" can work *if* its use is disciplined procedurally. The reasonable-person standard accommodates the broad range of delicts that tort law covers because it has been refined by centuries of decisions that clarify general rules with concrete examples. Both sides have lawyers who have studied the term. They present arguments for its interpretation in the circumstances of the case and introduce evidence according to rules and supervised by the judge. The judge defines reasonable for the jury, after hearing both sides' views. A jointly chosen jury deliberates as long as necessary. The judge may override improvident verdicts, and the judge's rulings may be appealed.

We have just seen that IRBs use few of the procedures government agencies use to discipline decisions. Nor could they afford to. The system is already crushingly cumbersome and costly, and good procedures would make it much more so. Event licensing of all human-subject research and IRB imperialism already overload IRBs. Costs and delays would multiply if, for example, IRBs had to tell researchers how they perceived the issues, specify the evidence they accepted and let researchers introduce theirs, rest decisions on evidence, explain decisions, allow appeals, and accept judicial review. The IRB system's structure, in short, makes fair procedures and sound decisions unaffordable.

D. RESEARCHERS AND PROCEDURAL JUSTICE

No better instrument has been devised for arriving at truth than to give a person in jeopardy of serious loss notice of the case against him and opportunity to meet it. Nor has a better way been found for generating the feeling, so important to a popular government, that justice has been done.

—*Joint Anti-Fascist Refugee Committee v. McGrath,* U.S. Supreme Court

I have argued that without due process agencies can neither be fair nor wise. Nor can they be effective, for obedience to law is better won by "procedural justice" than by "command and control" regulation. "Literally hundreds of studies have shown that people's perceptions of whether they have been treated fairly matter a great deal" to their willingness to cooperate with authorities.[80] This is true of those dealing "not only with the police and the courts but also with managers at work, teachers in school, and parents in families." People under regulation tend to "place the greatest weight on whether the procedure through which the decision was made was fair" and "the least weight on the actual content of those decisions." That is, they primarily ask how "they are treated during the procedure: whether their views are listened to and considered; whether they and their rights are respected; whether they are treated with courtesy and dignity."[81] Thus "studies link the fairness of workplace procedures to employee's willing-ness to voluntarily help their work groups, to their intention to stay with their company, and to the quality of their job performance."[82]

Worse, command-and-control regulation can "communicate a message of mistrust in employees, conveying a sense that the organization is an ad-versarial force to the employee," a sense likely to alienate employees from the organization and its goals. And "interpersonal dynamics may often be affected, as employees that maintain surveillance systems are pit against those being scrutinized."[83] Thus "people may experience surveillance-related intrusions into their lives as procedurally unfair, leading them to experience anger and other negative emotions" that injustice engenders. So "surveillance leads to a loss of cooperation between communities and law enforcement, thus only compounding the need for—and therefore cost of—surveillance."[84]

Frey's broad version of this argument uncannily describes the regu-lationist contempt for researchers we have so often encountered (recall Koski's scorn for them in the Introduction). Frey speaks of the distrust that government manifests for citizens when people have "little room" to act. Bureaucratic controls "are then extensive, and no citizen is taken to be trustworthy. The burden of the proof to have acted correctly lies with the individual citizen while the public authority is considered to be correct *a priori*." This distrust "undermines the citizens' civic virtue," and they break "laws whenever they expect to do so at low cost." Thus a "vi-cious cycle of progressively lower civic virtue and increasing distrust by the rulers may lead to general cynicism."[85]

In short, procedural justice comprises fair decision making and fair treatment, "treatment involving respect for people; respect for their rights; treatment with dignity and courtesy; care and concern from au-thorities."[86] But we have repeatedly seen an agency that is instinct with bias, ignores regulations, mishandles decisions, acts arbitrarily, and treats researchers scornfully. Neither OHRP nor regulationist orthodoxy en-courage IRBs to consider, much less practice, procedural justice. From "The Degradation" on, this chapter has profusely described procedural injustice and harsh distrust.

Many researchers think IRB regulation formalistic and unrelated to ethics.[87] Said one, "I do not need an ignorant and self-righteous bureau-crat telling me what to do, especially when such people set themselves up as the ultimate arbiters of ethics and professional conduct."[88] (Recall the description of ethics education as "mortifyingly stupid.") People subjected to "negotiating informed consent for every trivial intervention" begin to see all IRB rules as trivial and bureaucratic,[89] as onerous requirements imposed for petty and even foolish reasons: "Getting protocols approved gets worse each year because you have to document more and more and more USELESS stuff. For most of my work I receive coded samples devoid of patient identifiers, yet I have to fill in all sorts of crap and REPEAT OVER AND OVER AND OVER AGAIN that I couldn't track down these subjects if I tried."[90]

Regulationists' inability to show that IRBs protect subjects also undermines researchers' respect. "REBs are perceived as bureaucratic gate keepers," which is "unsurprising if ethics review lacks the credibility of a solid evidential base."[91] A director of OHRP's predecessor frankly admitted that his "'second priority is self-preservation of the bureaucrat. And the third priority is the researcher.'"[92] IRBs preach respect but practice contempt.[93] Bosk rightly says, "The presumption of prospective review— that our subjects are in need of protection—has embedded within it an insulting distrust of our integrity and motives."[94] One student of bureaucracy criticizes regulation that makes "two percent of a group 'behave' at the expense of the other 98 percent," that implies "that 'the Government has a deep and abiding distrust of citizens generally' and 'assumes every citizen is automatically a crook.'"[95] As a "high-profile researcher" put it, "Any set of rules that makes you kiss arse is probably a bad thing."[96]

The "mystical" IRB process alienates researchers: "Protocols are submitted, months pass, and requests for changes are made, justified by institutional policies and federal regulations that are unfamiliar to most researchers. Few IRBs offer substantial help in preparing protocols for review." Researchers have "little understanding" of "what will pass scrutiny," partly because many researchers think IRB review is arbitrary.[97]

Much in the IRB structure and ethos, in short, discredits IRB ethics and regulation. As Emanuel acknowledges, many researchers think review a "barrier," not "a constructive process." Gunsalus finds "considerable anecdotal evidence" of IRBs seen not "as helpful ethical advisors, but instead as barriers."[98] Bledsoe says many scholars "appear to lead lives either of resentful compliance with IRB or of fearful avoidance of it," dreading the process and resenting the way it chills and distorts research.[99]

Some alienation manifests itself in contempt for the IRB system and its dogmas. Some leads researchers toward noncooperation and even civil disobedience. Like aggressive taxpayers, some researchers test the line between avoidance and evasion. This may mean exploiting the regulations' impressive imprecision and can shade into disingenuous rationalizations. HHS's Inspector General concluded that "IRB shopping, in which research sponsors seek out the IRB they choose to work with, places considerable pressure on IRBs and their institutions."[100] And "ethics overregulation" may prompt institutions "to outsource clinical trials through 'contract research organizations'" working abroad or among undocumented immigrants.[101]

The alienated obey regulations only where necessary. If an IRB asks what questions you plan to pose, answer acceptably but act as you think proper. The sociologist Ann Swidler says IRBs "'turn everyone into a low-level cheater.'" One scholar doubts "'there is much relationship between what people' tell IRBs and 'do in the field.'"[102] Half the researchers in one study "self-reported 'illegal' behavior."[103] Another study found people "submitting incomplete protocols, submitting partially false protocols, conducting research prior to IRB approval, never submitting protocols to the IRB, and ignoring all or some IRB decisions and required changes."[104] At one ethics symposium, an audience member said "'IRBs don't want to hear about inductive research; thus, strategy involves deception or being disingenuous.'" Another member suggested hiding "'anything that might be controversial.'" Another advised saying "anything to make the IRB happy," including inventing "'possible research findings,'" recycling "'bureaucratic language,'" and using "'the same protocol as someone else.'"[105]

Some fields specially provoke alienation. Katz contends that IRBs "have forced participant-observation field researchers underground."[106] Because they "commonly appreciate that their field interactions were research only in retrospect," they must "abandon their methodology or gather data in the uneasy awareness that they might be charged with violating ethics rules."[107] So IRB jurisdiction over "nonfunded research inevitably leads to the development of an uncomfortable culture of dishonor."[108]

This is part of the broader problem of political pressure on research. Thus, for fear of Congress's reaction, half those surveyed deleted from NIH grant applications alarming words like "gay; lesbian; bisexual; sexual intercourse; anal sex; homosexual; homophobia; AIDS; bare backing; bathhouses; sex workers; needle-exchange; and harm-reduction." They study not sex workers but "women at risk."[109]

A few people announce their contempt for contemptible rules with brio. When the distinguished sociologist Howard Becker was told that his graduate students needed IRB approval "to hang out at a bus station and talk to passengers," he said go ahead and report me. He planned "to claim the projects are not research but conceptual art," since universities "don't hassle artists."[110]

Some regulationists hope IRBs might command respect as colleagues. But colleagues do not operate *de haut en bas*. Colleagues do not dictate research methods to each other. Collegial deference must be earned, and civility is expected. Collegial accountability is mutual and informal.

In sum, when an agency flouts the rule of law, the regulated tend to resent the agency, its commands, and its authority. They comply grudgingly, partially, or not at all.

E. CONCLUSION

Representing a profound attitude of fairness between man and man, and more particularly between the individual and government, "due process" is compounded of history, reason, the past course of decisions, and stout confidence in the strength of the democratic faith which we profess.

—*Joint Anti-Fascist Refugee Committee v. McGrath,* U.S. Supreme Court

The IRB system is lawless and unaccountable. It is constrained by neither substantive nor procedural rules. IRBs need *some* discretion, and nobody loves a rule-stricken bureaucracy. The new sentencing guidelines (to return to our analogy) are legitimately criticized for keeping punishments from fitting crimes and criminals. But the IRB system is far outside the tolerable range of discretion. Even in McCarthyite loyalty investigations, "the 'suspect' could appear before the loyalty board, consult with counsel, and present witnesses in his 'defense.'" Researchers are assured none of these protections. Like McCarthyite suspects, researchers have no "right to confront witnesses against him or, more important, even to learn their identity," and charges are "often vague and almost impossible to rebut."[111]

Chapter 3 found IRBs making decisions so arbitrarily and capriciously that they cannot have followed rules nor been accountable. Chapter 4 searched for law-like rules in IRB ethics and found them not. This chapter's search for law-like rules in law-like places found IRBs following

Fuller's "first and most obvious" route to disaster—"a failure to achieve rules at all." Nor are *any* of the elements of due process so crucial to fair and prudent decisions required. No committee makes good decisions about complex and arcane questions without substantive standards and sound procedures.

Could IRBs comply with the duties of due process and the dictates of good decision-making? Substantively, IRBs would need sensible standards to apply and members competent to apply them. Chapter 4 doubted the possibility of a meaningful research ethics that fit all human-subject research. And chapter 3 argued that—particularly given the range of issues IRBs handle—IRBs cannot have enough people with enough specialized expertise to evaluate all the issues they face.

What procedures would IRBs need to be fair and sensible? Any of the standard elements of due process would improve both fairness and decisions but strain an already broken system. A genuine explanation of an IRB's decisions would oblige IRBs to consider problems thoughtfully, guide researchers in responding to decisions, and build a common law of decisions. This would intolerably increase IRB workloads. The curse of universal event licensing created a system that cannot adequately handle all the decisions the IRB system has arrogated to itself. How could it tolerate the burden of making those decisions fair and wise?

All this is not a failure in legal technicalities. It is a failure to provide fundamental fairness, sound decisions, and recourse against injustice.[112] It is government power exercised without law or accountability, thus dooming agencies—agencies of amateurs evaluating complex and unfamiliar questions—to err too often and too harmfully.

6

Censorship in a System of Free Expression

It is offensive ... to the very notion of a free society ... that in the context of everyday public discourse a citizen must first inform the government of her desire to speak to her neighbors and then obtain a permit to do so.

—*Watchtower Bible & Tract Society v. Stratton,* 536 US 150 (2001)

The introduction to part II suggested that regulation is a challenging enterprise, that its success depends on profiting from the law's experience with it, and that the IRB system has largely been built and run in apparent ignorance of that experience. Thus in explaining why IRBs inescapably err too often, the last three chapters have examined several standard regulatory issues, including the kind and quality of work IRBs do and the lack of substantive and procedural guidance they receive. This chapter investigates another standard regulatory problem—taking on work agencies do badly. Here, that work is censorship. Censorship is so inimical to democracy that the first amendment and the Supreme Court's interpretation of it assume that censors are inherently dangerous and must be rigorously constrained.

Respect for persons requires free expression. The Declaration of the Rights of Man said it in 1789, the Universal Declaration of Human Rights in 1948. In 1791 our Constitution prohibited any law "abridging the freedom of speech, or of the press." But researchers may not seek, receive, or impart information and ideas without a license from an agency the government mandates and supervises. IRB censorship violates the principle of free expression extensively and intensively: No American censorship in living memory has covered so many aspects of so many people's engagement with so many topics of so much importance so intrusively.

Americans principally understand free expression through the Supreme Court's first-amendment jurisprudence and its long-tested categories and principles.[1] It is fundamental in that jurisprudence that "requiring a permit to engage" in speech betrays "our national heritage and constitutional tradition."[2] Government cannot stop you from asking your neighbors whether they favor a third party. But become a scholar and government does just that. Yet scholars are "entitled to the same rights as other citizens," and the Supreme Court has frequently said free expression "is particularly necessary in the academic context if the university is to perform its function."[3]

The IRB system violates almost every doctrine the Supreme Court has created to protect free expression. I briefly count the ways and then ask how IRB censorship damages universities and the free inquiry to which they are dedicated.

A. THE SYSTEM OF FREE EXPRESSION

The journalist has a mandate from society to document contemporary reality. ... Social scientists have no such mandate; we document reality to explain it. Our audience is professional, and society gives us no protection in the First Amendment.
—Stuart Plattner (former NSF human-subjects research officer), Comment on IRB Regulation of Ethnographic Research

CASE STUDY: VALUES?[4]

"Because of the seriousness of allegations made against the IRB process— for example, that oblique sociopolitical values influence their decisions," Stephen Ceci asked 157 IRBs to evaluate hypothetical protocols dealing with discrimination in hiring by Fortune 500 firms. Each IRB got one of nine protocols which "were similar in their wording and identical in their treatment" of the subjects—personnel officers. Protocols varied in ethical difficulty and social sensitivity. There were three levels of ethical problems: those involving only "deception (which is technically permissible in certain circumstances)," those involving deception and failure to debrief subjects "(which is impermissible under the DHHS general requirements)," and "those involving no technical violations." The three levels of social sensitivity were proposals "to examine discrimination against minorities and women," "reverse-discrimination proposals to document discrimination against white males," and "nonsensitive proposals to examine discrimination against obese and short" people.

IRBs withheld approval from 63% of the reverse-discrimination proposals, 51% of the discrimination proposals, but only 26% of the height/

weight proposals. The presence of ethical problems potently predicted whether height/weight studies would be approved, but "the socially sensitive proposals' outcomes were not reliably influenced" by their presence. So "sensitive proposals containing neither deception nor a failure to debrief were rejected as often as proposals that did contain such violations." In short, IRBs were "reluctant to approve any socially sensitive proposal, vis-à-vis the same proposed treatment of human subjects couched in a politically neutral context."

Furthermore, IRBs' discussions of nonsensitive protocol were "uniformly approving." But discussions of sensitive protocols "frequently contained types of complaints that were not listed in the other cases, though the alleged problems should have pertained to all of the proposals, for example, methodological weaknesses in the design."

1.　"OUR NATIONAL HERITAGE" AND IRB CENSORSHIP

The first amendment protects not just "speech" but a "system of freedom of expression" comprising "the right to form and hold beliefs and opinions on any subject, and to communicate ideas, opinions, and information." It encompasses "the right to hear the views of others" and to listen to their version of the facts, to "inquire and, to a degree, the right of access to information." The system is "essential" to "self-fulfillment," to "advancing knowledge and discovering truth," and to permitting "participation in decision making by all members of society."[5]

When regulationists contemplate these freedoms, they deny that researchers have them, as Plattner bizarrely asserts in our epigraph. Research (an IRB manual says) "is a *privilege* and not a *right*," a "privilege given by the institution to individuals who have assured their willingness to work within the federal guidelines."[6] One regulationist thinks "the 'property rights' question has been asked and answered: Researchers do not have an inalienable right to conduct research with human subjects." Just "as we have no inalienable right to force *Evaluation Review* to publish our work or compel NSF to award us taxpayer money, we have no inalienable right to research others [*sic*]." That scientists accommodate peer reviewers and editors "but squawk and flap loudly when IRBs require the same is astonishing."[7] An American Psychological Association working group calls research "a privilege" granted by the researchers' institution, the federal government, and funders. This "is made most clear when the privilege is revoked, as it has been."[8] And Moss (the former Chicago IRB chair) says that while constitutional arguments "may have theoretical merit, in practice these arguments are moot." Universities "are sensitive to political influences that compromise their corporate interest." Were IRBs "found unconstitutional," the replacement might be "far more limiting."[9]

These assertions blend *ipse dixit* and error. The idea that you have no right because the government infringes it misunderstands what rights are. (A right is exactly what government may not take away.) The manual that thinks free expression is a property interest is mistaken (it is a liberty interest), and the manual misunderstands how such issues are properly "asked and answered" (through judicial decisions). The argument that researchers have no right to speak because they cannot compel government to give them money or journals to publish articles is just wrong. (It is a right to speak without government interference, not a right to government funds or to the resources of private bodies.) It says much about the intellectual quality of regulationism that these arguments are so ignorant.

Hamburger answers the suggestion that the citizen's right is a researcher's "privilege" by imagining a "Newspaper Review Board" that compelled journalists to disclose their identity, warn interviewees of the risks of talking, get signed consent, foreswear deceit, honor privacy, "and otherwise cause no harm." The board would keep journalists from causing "upset," "worry," social "stigma," "moral harm," legal risk, or economic loss. This is risibly unconstitutional yet, because journalists inflict far more harm than researchers, makes more sense than an IRB.

2.   CENSORING WORDS, SUPPRESSING IDEAS

To justify suppression of free speech there must be reasonable ground to fear that serious evil will result if free speech is practiced.
—*Whitney v. California*, 274 US 357, 376 (1926) (Brandeis, concurring)

Perhaps regulationists do not see that IRBs censor because they assume that research is always "conduct" and never "expression" and that conduct can be regulated even if speech cannot be. The line between conduct and expression *can* be uncertain, and some aspects of some research are surely regulable conduct. But IRBs censor expression in even the narrowest sense: They decide when, where, and how citizens may speak, write, publish, or read words. They decide who may speak to whom, when, and how. They decide whether prospective subjects may be addressed. They specify who may be addressed. They stop researchers from addressing people because of their status or because it would be "inequitable." They require some people to be addressed. They compel researchers to speak and listen even to people who are not potential subjects. They dictate how people are approached. By letter? After potential subjects respond? By phone? In person? IRBs decide what words researchers may, may not, and must use in contacting subjects. IRBs discourage researchers from speaking to people and people to researchers. As one manual says, "body language, credentials, and speech influence decisions," so "IRBs generally prefer indirect (e.g., telephone and letter) to direct interpersonal recruitment strategies."[10]

IRBs decide whether a researcher needs consent and whether it must be written or oral. IRBs decide how a researcher may solicit consent, even prescribing thousands of words. IRBs decide what questions a researcher may ask and their wording. IRBs insist that language never be varied. IRBs prescribe how researchers record information (e.g., banning notes). IRBs require that researchers report what they have read and minutely report progress. IRBs specify what researchers may, may not, or must publish. They oblige researchers to report findings to particular people. They decide how data are presented and even keep researchers from presenting "results in a way that does not respect (or agree with) the subjects' interests."[11] One manual says that "although there are few legal restrictions on observing public activities or tabulating public records, doing so without informed consent stretches our ethical imperatives and may further erode the public's trust in social research."[12]

In these ways and more, IRBs censor in the core sense of regulating speech. But censorship's wrong is not just regulating words; it is also regulating the development, examination, expression, and use of ideas. As Spece and Weinzierl stipulate, "certain 'harmful' forms of experimentation, even if obviously communicative, are *not* covered by the First Amendment." But while not "all experimentation is itself 'speech' or 'communication'" it is still "protected as a central and unique part of a highly favored process imbued with direct communicative processes as well as conduct that can properly be considered expressive because of its essential part in the enterprise of searching for the truth."[13] IRBs regulate the development of information and ideas in unprecedented detail.

"IRB involvement may start early" when researchers generate and refine hypotheses. IRBs do not just talk to researchers, but to "study sponsors and medical product manufacturers. Often, there are multiple exchanges of information and discussions, with the IRB asking a host of questions and receiving a host of answers, and inevitably some answers generate new questions."[14]

B. THE ORTHODOXY REVIEW BOARD

A long line of cases in this Court makes it clear that a State or municipality cannot "require all who wish to disseminate ideas to present them first to police authorities for their consideration and approval. ..."
—*Cox v. Louisiana*, 379 US 536, 557 (1964)

CASE STUDY: VOICES[15]

Matt Bradley, a Master's degree candidate, envisioned a 48-minute documentary with "'at-risk' youth," all working class, mostly black, presenting their perceptions and experiences "of home, neighborhood, and community." The youths would be primarily responsible for what they portrayed. The IRB staff often told him "they had never encountered research like mine." They thought it might be journalism, which "was not bound by the same IRB requirements because a journalist does not interpret data, she only collects and presents it." But they suggested IRB approval "just to be safe."

Bradley could not describe his methods fully because the youth were to be "largely responsible" for them. He said videotaping would be central and listed other possibilities, "including interviewing, participant-observation, cognitive mapping, journaling and drawing." The IRB demanded "a list of the range of procedures that might be chosen by the subjects" and their risks. Bradley acknowledged that "illegal activities might be revealed" and that "photos, audio-taped interviews, and video-tapes" might show "behavior that is not deemed socially acceptable." He described elaborate procedures for preventing this and warning his collaborators about risks.

The IRB said that confidentiality was poorly protected and that the subjects' risks outweighed the study's benefits. In addition, "people in the community might be upset about the portrait." Bradley saw benefits in the youths' chance "to become involved in community activities and discussions, and reflect on and share their past experiences in a way that can be productive and helpful both for them and for the larger community." The IRB never told Bradley what a benefit was or how to measure it against risks. He vainly said "that the project would provide insight into perceptions about those who are labeled 'at-risk' or 'delinquent' and would create public awareness" about the youths. He concluded that the IRB was not interested in benefits to them or the community.

Bradley also said that while he labored "to explain our collaborative process, the IRB did not value or take the time to understand it" or the direct influence the "subjects" would have in "planning, filming, editing, and presenting the documentary." Because they "didn't have credentials (i.e. degrees, formal training in filmmaking, etc.)," the IRB treated them "only as 'subjects'—the objects of my study, not partners in my research," thus keeping them from choosing how to present "themselves and their world" and from getting "credit for their work on the videotape."

Bradley asks if it is right to silence "'at-risk' youth or a group of young black men living in a predominantly white town" because they might upset people. He says the IRB's attempt to protect "the 'human subjects,' and—let's not kid ourselves—the university's ass as well" could "make research benign and meaningless and sustain the marginalization of people by relegating them to the status of anonymous objects of study." Can the "participatory researcher" work "with vulnerable and marginalized populations in a way that acknowledges their knowledge and experiences" and amplifies "their voice and self-determination"?

1.   IRBS AND THE PRINCIPLES OF THE FIRST AMENDMENT

[T]he impious presumption of legislators and rulers ... who being themselves but fallible and uninspired men, have assumed dominion over the faith of others ... hath established and maintained false religions ... through all time . ...
—John Milton, *Areopagitica*

Regulationists' attitude toward research reverses the Supreme Court's attitude toward free expression. For them, researchers are the danger, should presumptively be restrained, and bear the burden of proof. For the Court, government is the danger, should presumptively be restrained, and bears the burden of proof. Blasi calls abusing official power "an especially serious evil"[16] because it is "so antithetical to the entire political arrangement, is so harmful to individual people, and also is so likely to occur, that its prevention and containment" dominate the political system's other goals.[17] The Court so distrusts regulation of public debate[18] that it more willingly trusts government "where race is concerned, than where speech is concerned."[19]

It is basic that that speech cannot be restricted "because of its message, ideas, subject matter, or content.[20] So no statute can create "broad discretionary licensing power" that lets officials decide "which expressions of view will be permitted."[21] The law must *prevent* officials "from encouraging some views and discouraging others" by exercising arbitrary authority.[22] And the standard is not: "Did an official discriminate?" It is: "*Could* an official discriminate?" It is also basic that "officials and judges tend to overestimate the dangers of controversial speech."[23] Furthermore, officials "may well be less responsive than a court" to free expression.[24] Thus a judicial, not an administrative, assessment of the speech is necessary.[25]

Because expression is "vulnerable to gravely damaging yet barely visible encroachments" it "must be ringed about with adequate bulwarks."[26] First, the Court relaxes procedural principles to make claims simpler to bring and win. It is unusually easy for people to challenge and courts to overturn laws limiting speech. Against ordinary practice, litigants may challenge laws limiting expression even without applying for the license to which they object.[27] Litigants may challenge a vague or overbroad law even if it is unobjectionable applied to them.[28] And the Court discards "ordinary rules against appellate factfinding" and against "second guess[ing] lower-level decisionmakers."[29] (To lawyers, this is all a Big Deal.)

The second bulwark is judicial hostility to agencies "charged particularly with reviewing speech, or conduct commonly associated with it," for that "breed[s] an 'expertise' tending to favor censorship over speech."[30] The hostility peaks when the agency licenses speech: "Any system of prior restraints of expression comes to this Court bearing a heavy presumption against its constitutional validity."[31] Decades of cases hold that government "cannot 'require all who wish to disseminate ideas to present them first to police authorities'" when the police can "'say some ideas may, while others may not,'" be disseminated.[32]

In short, the IRB method—event licensing—is at the apex of threats to free expression. The First Amendment's "chief purpose" is "to prevent previous restraints upon publication."[33] Law can limit *post*-publication defamation but may not license speech to prevent it.[34] Speech might injure reputations, but government cannot create a Reputation Review Board. Loathing of prior restraint dates to Milton and Locke. Blackstone said that liberty of the press means "laying no previous restraints upon publications, and not in freedom from censure for criminal matter when published," for licensing makes one person "the arbitrary and infallible judge of all controverted points in learning, religion, and government."[35]

Why is prior restraint worse than subsequent restraint, even criminal prosecution? Because it is more inhibiting.[36] Licensing exposes more expression to regulation than post-publication sanctions do. IRBs subject all human-subject research to review. Censors' decisions "may in practice be final."[37] Prosecutions occur only if "a public prosecutor, who cannot be single-minded, as can an administrative agency,"[38] decides to act. And defendants get "the safeguards of the criminal process."[39] Criminal trials are public; prior restraints generally provide "less opportunity for public appraisal and criticism."[40]

For such reasons, prior licensing must pass so many tests that even an abbreviation of Tribe's summary is wearying:

(1) The burden of proof must rest on government to justify any restraint on free expression ... and on government to demonstrate the particular facts necessary to sustain a limitation on expressive behavior; (2) [A censor] ... must act within a specified brief period of time; (3) [A censor must either] ... issue a license or ... go to court to restrain unlicensed expressive acts; mere denial of the license cannot create an enforceable legal bar to expressive activities; ... (6) A scheme of censorship or licensing must assure a "prompt final judicial decision" reviewing any "interim and possibly erroneous denial of a license." ...[41]

Prior licensing faces still *more* special requirements. Like precision. *Any* law not giving someone "of ordinary intelligence fair notice that his contemplated conduct is forbidden"[42] is "void for vagueness." But laws impairing expression must be *especially* clear. Clearer yet must be laws subjecting expression to prior restraint. They "must contain 'narrow, objective, and definite standards to guide the licensing authority'" so that the law does not permit "appraisal of facts, the exercise of judgment, and the formation of an opinion."[43]

Furthermore, vague statutes that "'abut upon sensitive areas of basic First Amendment freedoms'" can inhibit their exercise.[44] Unfettered discretion and prior licensing "intimidate[] parties into censoring their own speech."[45] And in a loyalty-oath case, the regulation's intricacy and uncertainty made "it a highly efficient *in terrorem* mechanism" frightening a teacher into shunning anything that "might jeopardize his living by enmeshing him in this intricate machinery."[46] So as Kellum says, speech is chilled even "by the highly-involved and intimidating process of approaching a government official and filling out the necessary paperwork."[47]

The third bulwark is that when expression is at stake, people are entitled not just to due process, but to "the most rigorous procedural safeguards"[48] that reflect "'the necessary sensitivity to freedom of expression.'"[49] The Court said, "[S]ince only considerations of the greatest urgency can justify restrictions on speech, and since the validity of a restraint on speech in each case depends on careful analysis of the particular circumstances," procedures are crucial, and regulation's validity may turn on their safeguards.[50]

Fourth, speech *may* be suppressed when a truly exigent danger justifies it, most famously when words "create a clear and present danger" of causing evils Congress may suppress.[51] More recently, the Court forbade government to proscribe advocating force or illegal conduct unless it is "directed to inciting or producing imminent lawless action" and likely to do so.[52]

The Court's fifth bulwark is that regulation interfering with a fundamental right like free speech must be "strictly scrutinized." That is, it must be "necessary" to serve a "compelling state interest." This is the highest standard of justification the Court knows. "Necessary" means truly essential; "compelling" means maximally needed.

Sixth, the equal-protection clause requires treating similarly situated people similarly. Journalists do freely what researchers cannot. The saga of gutter journalism and the yellow press is fabulously longer and lusher than the history of research scandal. Journalists' assaults on privacy are legion. Journalists try to humiliate subjects, expel them from office, get them jailed, and squeeze secrets from them. Why may not researchers do what journalists are entitled to do and even praised for?

The IRB system ignores all these bulwarks. It uses the most disfavored means of regulating speech—prior restraint—but flouts the safeguards the Court imposes on it. The last two chapters described the lack of "narrow, objective, and definite standards." Chapter 3 (about decisions) said this "permitted and encouraged" IRBs to make "arbitrary and discriminatory" decisions, discriminatory because similarly situated people are treated differently (doctors and clinical researchers; journalists and social scientists) *and* because boards discriminate on prohibited grounds.

Finally, however slight research's risk, every project must be licensed. And this

overinclusive regulation of the mere risk of injury is all the more distant from a lawful prohibition on injury because it includes the risk of harms—such as "upset," social "stigma," and "moral harm"—that are the ordinary consequence of free discussion and publication. If legally cognizable harms were its sole concern, the government could rely upon the general rules against negligence or could adopt rules against specific, substantive types of injury.[53]

2. IRBS AND THE PRINCIPLES OF RESEARCH

[A licenser's office] enjoins him to let pass nothing but what is vulgarly received already.
—John Milton, *Areopagitica*

CASE STUDY: TRUTH AND POWER[54]

Joan Sieber is a former acting director of an NSF program who chairs IRBs, visits sites for IRB accreditation, and edits the *Journal of Empirical Research on Human Ethics*. She describes four cases in which social scientists studied academically powerful people who made the scholars pay "a high price."

In 1978 Peters and Ceci wanted to see whether psychology journals were influenced in selecting articles by the prestige of authors' institutions. They took thirteen articles with an author from a prestigious place, altered the names and affiliations, and resubmitted them to the journals that had published them, with permission from the papers' authors and publishers. They planned to debrief the editors and through them the reviewers. They consulted senior colleagues (including two editors) and (unofficially) the co-chair of the American Psychological Association's ethics office. None demurred.

Three journals recognized the articles. All but one of the remaining journals "resoundingly rejected" them. Their reasons "were overwhelmingly methodological ones, with additional criticisms of poor writing style. In most cases, the style of criticism was extremely harsh."

Two editors who recognized the articles "responded with threats and insults." One "threatened legal action and professional censure, sent a copy of his irate letter to the authors' department chair," and said that manuscripts from that university "might receive well-deserved rejection for their assumed complicity in this deceptive study." That "editor regularly published deception research," yet Sieber says that Peters and Ceci's research was deemed highly unethical, apparently because "busy and important people" were deceived. Two editors wrote letters to Peters and Ceci "notable for their lack of subtlety, their overt bullying, their degree of over-reaction, and their angrily paternalistic style of insulting young investigators." Peters and Ceci's department chair "withdrew all departmental support (e.g., use of duplicating machines, postage, etc.) from the study until the time that all editorial boards were informed of the research and the deception involved." On the chair's recommendation, Peters was denied tenure. He received it on appeal only after an American Psychological Association accreditation committee commented on his case in its report.

Sieber suggests that social scientists are better placed than journalists to study the powerful and "that the only reason university administrations and IRBs would condone deception research on the powerless and prohibit it on the powerful is fear of reprisal." But what does she conclude from the fact that "the powerful typically have powerful institutions that will close ranks around them, while the social science investigator is typically left to fend for herself"? That since the powerful hardly need protection, IRB review is otiose? No. That it should be intensified.

First, Sieber seems to think social scientists should not identify powerful malefactors. "Social scientists are not investigative journalists. Their role is to generate generalizable and valid knowledge—to examine what happens, and how it happens." She does not say why social scientists cannot also be "investigative journalists," or why generalizable knowledge is inconsistent with naming names, or why examining what happens and how does not require specificity. Sieber continues, "A 'gotcha' response to the discovery of faltering stewardship is not becoming to the scientist and is especially likely to engender vengeful behavior on the part of the powerful persons studied." What is a "gotcha" response? Why is naming names such a response? Why is it unbecoming to describe Auschwitz, Tuskegee, Watergate, or Enron?

So Sieber argues that, because the powerful felt "entitled to greater protection from intrusion" and thus "to damage the researcher and to create turmoil within the researchers' institution," researchers need "more than adequate methodological and ethical review by as many appropriate reviewing bodies as one can muster," especially "the approval of one's department chair, and IRB." Even if research is exempt because the powerful are public figures, "the IRB owes it to the investigator, to the institution, and to the idea of scientific freedom and responsibility to carefully review protocols for research on the powerful."

The IRB system's structure and ethos make IRBs guardians of intellectual, institutional, and ideological orthodoxy. Members tend to be orthodox because they are drawn from a pool in which orthodoxy (virtually by definition) swamps heterodoxy. And what committee wants disruptive members? Also, orthodox usually looks safer than unorthodox research, since unconventional hypotheses, novel methods, and touchy topics incite IRBs' fears of trouble.

Further, scientific judgment is biased toward "the known and accepted rather than the unconventional and contrarian," toward "the liked, in-group, high-status investigator against the unappealing, dissenting, lone-wolf, challenging, out-group, low-status investigator."[55] This may help explain why Lincoln and Tierney see a change from protecting subjects "toward monitoring, censuring, and outright disapproval of projects that use qualitative research, phenomenological approaches, and other alternative frameworks."[56] IRBs objected to "nonquantitative or experimental research methods (i.e., qualitative methods), new paradigms for inquiry (e.g., phenomenological, feminist, post-modern, Foucauldian, and/or constructivist), and lack of fit with traditional rigor criteria (e.g., generalizability, replicability, objectivity)."[57]

Furthermore, economics disadvantages the unorthodox. Drug company trials, NIH-funded studies, and other large projects can ordinarily afford the IRB gauntlet; unorthodox research sometimes cannot. For example, observational health research and academic translational research are marginally funded and thus vulnerable to IRB costs.

IRBs tend to favor orthodoxy in ideology as well as methodology. The regulations tell IRBs to ignore "possible long-range effects of applying knowledge" from research, like "the possible effects of the research on public policy." But the IRB ethos virtually invites members to promote their political, ideological, and cultural agendas. For example, the justice principle seems to tell IRBs to consult their own sense of right. As Justice

Holmes wrote, if you don't doubt your premises or power, "you naturally express your wishes in law."[58] As Fleischman found, "The regulation notwithstanding," some "members consider ethical issues well beyond those related to the specific risks to participants."[59] And Klitzman's "data suggest that, at times, committees *do* take these risks into account."[60]

A cavalier approach to regulations exacerbates this problem. One manual admits that despite regulations prohibiting IRBs from considering long-term consequences of findings, "when research deals with controversial topics," discussion of such risks "will inevitably surface at IRB meetings, and members may feel strongly that legitimate knowledge to be gained from a study could be interpreted wrongly or be publicized with mischievous intent." So "it may be appropriate for one of the investigator's colleagues on the IRB to mention, offline, the concerns that were raised."[61]

Another manual warns that because merely asking questions "may unintentionally reinforce undesirable characteristics of research subjects," IRBs may need "to help narrow the gap between strict scientific objectivity and responsible social values."[62] So IRBs decide what political, social, and moral characteristics are "undesirable" and what social values are "responsible." Similar problems are posed by the advice to examine "comprehensively the emotional, social, and political ramifications of asking questions, reporting observations, and sharing conclusions with others outside of the research population."[63] In "Whose Values?" IRB members who knew they were being studied openly made ideological arguments and voted their ideological preferences. Robert Levine—an experienced observer—finds this "in harmony" with his observations.[64]

Other aspects of the IRB system's structure and ethos make ideological judgments routine. For instance, the core IRB question—whether benefits outweigh risks—can require ideological calculations. One IRB manual advises members that when a study involving risk asks "a question that is not important," the risk is likely to outweigh the benefit.[65] But importance rests on opinions about social values. Before the Second World War, "the dominant story both Indians and ethnographers told was one in which the past was glorified, the present disorganized, and the future promised assimilation." After the war, the past was "exploitation, the present resistance, and the future ethnic resurgence."[66] Which story should an IRB approve? How should it treat ethnographers who want to give voice to the voiceless or who think that that corrupts objectivity?

Ideological and cultural beliefs also shape method. Like a willingness that would appall any court to accept racial classifications. One IRB told a white Ph.D. student interested in ethnicity's effect on career expectations not to interview black Ph.D. students "because it might be traumatic for them."[67] Another IRB told a physician that white researchers could not interview black patients, nor black interviewers white patients. And a black scholar reports having "to fight—not once but many times—to defend her research," as when an IRB "asked her point-blank, 'what I thought could be learned by talking only to Black women.' After a nine-month struggle with the board and her sense of scholarly integrity," she yielded.[68]

IRBs routinely make value-laden judgments about people. Stark says:

sound decisions about human subjects came to be represented in *the characteristics of decision-makers* rather than in *the actual substance of decisions*: the involvement of scientists conducting the studies under review came to be seen as a contaminant of sound judgment, lay people were ultimately regarded as having privileged moral sensibilities, and individuals from certain demographics were believed to bring special perspectives to deliberative groups.[69]

IRBs' ideological judgments are likely to protect the social, political, and economic status quo. The IRB ethos inhibits research, and when inhibited research questions the status quo, restricting it suppresses those questions. Research that reveals abused power or oppression is hampered and halted. However unintentionally, regulationism, like "many other moral entrepreneurial campaigns," favors "dominant classes over the weaker. Powerful, elite groups can now better hide their mechanisms of control, while weak and powerless groups" cannot "tell their stories from their own perspective."[70]

For example, a UCLA study was "a centerpiece" of union efforts to organize casino workers. It found the workers badly off. The UCLA Office for Protection of Research Subjects said that the absence of IRB review forced it to "prohibit researchers from disseminating any of the data." A UCLA official explained that "there was no university check on whether the study was partisan," as though an IRB had any basis for deciding what was "partisan" (and as though research must, or even could, be "nonpartisan").[71]

Murphy and Dingwall observe that "[e]thnographers often study powerful people in publicly funded settings where informed consent" protects "the *status quo* from interrogation and powerful members from scrutiny." This deters ethnography from promoting "public accountability for the use of public resources or the impact of private interests on the public sphere."[72] Feeley too thinks IRBs discourage "a socially relevant and critical sociology."[73] He describes the influential sociologist who "explores conditions under which American lawyers, judges, and other officials embrace torture" and who "would be delighted if what he wrote tarnished reputations and forced resignations."[74] Few IRBs would understand that delight.

Jack Katz finds "advocacy research" nationally "under fire." The UC-San Francisco IRB "severely compromised" a public-health study of bathhouses by insisting that their managers be told the study's objectives and consent to it. The same IRB blocked Malone when she and "community co-investigators" wanted to study "illegal single-stick cigarette sales in a low-income, predominantly minority neighborhood." Although prosecutors acquiesced, "the IRB, after consulting with university 'risk management' and legal counsel, blocked the study" because stores "might break the law." These IRBs protected the bathhouse and store personnel "as members of business groups whose profits might be hurt." Katz finds IRBs' constraints on "critical social research" a "significant turning point" in impeding "progressive inquiry and expression."

Orthodoxy is shielded when IRBs stop "controversial" research. Moss, recall, expects IRBs to "protect the institutional interest" by "weeding out politically sensitive studies." Whittaker thinks "[p]rotecting the university goes without saying."[75] And "Florida State's standard consent form asks, 'Is the research area controversial and is there a possibility your project will generate public concern?'"[76] What might not provoke "controversy"? For one IRB, smoking-related research was "too politically hot."[77] Since IRB deliberations are not public, consider an analogy—research that attracts legislative attention. The NIH receives about one Congressional inquiry a week about grants, like one about 200 grants listed by the "Traditional Values Coalition," which questions studies of "behavior in so-called at-risk groups."[78] Research provokes controversy by affecting commercial interests. Federal programs to punish research misconduct have given corporations a "weapon against unwelcome environmental research—the unsupported allegation of research misconduct."[79] Since 1892, for example, the lead industry has assailed research on lead poisoning.[80]

Ideology also enters decisions when "community" opinion must be consulted. That opinion can be ignorant and oppressive even when the community is the country and its voice the Congress. One study concluded that most people sexually abused as children "fall in the normal or superior range of adjustment" and that few "have clinically significant disorders."[81] After "months of attacks by therapists, child advocates, talk show hosts, journalists, religious organizations, and politicians," both the House and Senate condemned the study.[82] Tom DeLay, the House Majority Leader, falsely claimed the article advocated "normalizing pedophilia," which froze "thoughtful scientific exchange" because defending the article's scholarship became "an indictment of one's moral character."[83]

3. IRBS AND THE PRINCIPLES OF THE UNIVERSITY

[T]he university is a traditional sphere of free expression so fundamental ... that the Government's ability to control speech within that sphere by means of conditions attached to the expenditure of Government funds is restricted by the vagueness and overbreadth doctrines of the First Amendment.

—*Rust v. Sullivan*, 500 US 173 (1991)

The Court has "long recognized" universities' "special niche in our constitutional tradition" and "the expansive freedoms of speech and thought associated" with them.[84] During an earlier era of repression, Chief Justice Warren wrote that university teachers and students must be "free to inquire, to study and to evaluate."[85] Yet academic freedom is frail; external attacks and internal ideology lead universities to repress research. What in living memory has compromised academic freedom and fettered inquiry like the IRB system? In the '50s, universities harassed and fired "subversives." Today, it subjects research to review by officials free to suppress any of it for reasons they need not state. Yet few regulationists think academic freedom is at stake, much less degraded. O'Brien observes that OHRP pays "little attention" to it (e.g., one mention in the *Guidebook*).[86] Van den Hoonaard finds it taking "a distant seat" to IRB members' "subjective opinions."[87]

Moderate regulationists ignore academic freedom; others denounce it. Whittaker sneers at "the freedom claimants" who "bristled defensively" in those "early days when research boards were seen as an affront to the liberties of scholarly self-direction." The "certitude about knowledge and the sacred dictums of academic freedom have permitted the belief that every scholar has the right to pursue individually chosen projects, unfettered, uninterrupted and uncriticized." These ideas "now belong to the dreamtime of university and research life," and "eyebrows would be raised at any serious claim of 'knowledge for its own sake.'"[88] Moss says contemptuously, "The 'Art Bell'-like hypothesis" that an IRB "conspires to stifle academic freedom is a myth largely disseminated by individuals who have never been substantively involved" with IRBs.[89] Nobody imagines a right to be uncriticized. But it was Moss who said that "[p]rivate universities are largely corporations" where respect for academic freedom "is desirable, but not indispensable."[90] And Moss (the weeder-out of "politically sensitive studies") dispenses with it. You don't have to conspire if you are proud to advertise.

At academic freedom's core is classically the principle that "[t]eachers are entitled to full freedom in research and in the publication of the results." Universities depend "upon the free search for truth and its free exposition. Academic freedom is essential to these purposes and applies to both teaching and research."[91] Two ideas are crucial to academic freedom. First, that faculty members are not servants of the university but have independent authority in teaching and research. Second, that the university should shield faculty from community pressure.

Regulationists see researchers as employees like any others. But faculty, the AAUP says, are "members of a learned profession, and officers of an educational institution." They are "the appointees, but not in any proper sense the employees," of universities. They have "professional functions" the institution is neither competent nor entitled to direct. In "independence of thought and utterance," professors' relationship to the university is like that of federal judges and the President (who appointed them).[92] As Curran put it, loyalty to a university is part of a scholar's "general responsibility to his discipline, to teaching, and to research." But "freedom to pursue these objectives as he sees fit is probably the value he places highest and guards most tenaciously."[93] OHRP, however, says, "Insistence upon well-conceived and -conducted research should be evident both in written policies and in actions of institutional officials. ... Approval procedures should be devised such that the institution supports only well-designed and properly executed research."[94]

The university is also damaged by IRB distrust of researchers. Robert Levine fears "that presumptions of distrust are alien" to universities' "most fundamental presumptions." Research is crippled if colleagues "police and harass each other because they think there is a high likelihood" of dishonesty. Argument and dialogue wither "in an atmosphere of distrust."[95] But IRBs are taught distrust, and researchers fear it. One scholar finds it hard "to forget being the object of a certain kind of investigative gaze." His "IRB, following standard administrative intimidation tactics," planned "to put an untenured faculty member on the spot and extract his compliance."[96] And one respondent wondered if a survey about IRBs was wise, since "[a]ll of our emails may be monitored."[97] An "especially insidious effect" of IRB authority is that it insulates them "from criticism by deterring researchers from airing their grievances." IRB attention might bring "'more restrictions on their work.'"[98] And Amdur's manual tells IRBs that researchers who criticize them show a lack of respect which is "an important finding" for "IRB determinations."[99]

The Supreme Court calls the university "a traditional sphere of free expression."[100] That sphere should protect scholars from community pressure to stop research, tailor results to its taste, and avoid offense, but IRBs expose scholars to communities in novel and noxious ways. As Feeley says, IRBs have "the form and function of censorship boards," and "universities that embrace them uncritically indulge community standards rather than" serving the traditional function of shielding researchers against them.[101] The regulations want members who promote "sensitivity to such issues as community attitudes." The *Guidebook* says that IRB risk-benefit decisions often turn on "prevailing community standards."[102] IRBs may waive consent in emergency research only if the community is elaborately consulted.

Elite commissions too would open scholars to outside pressure. The NRC and IOM want "appropriate community involvement in housing health hazards research [*sic*] involving children" so that "protocols are responsive to any community concerns." And consent reflecting "appropriate community input." And "meaningful and ongoing dialogue" on research design, including "the research question," the risks, the knowledge sought, and its "relevance and importance to the community." This "will ensure" (again) that the community vets "potentially controversial research."[103] Similarly, one IRB manual wants researchers to review questions with "representative community members" to "reveal sensitive or problem areas."[104]

The problems with this are plain. First, it gives communities a heckler's veto, even though expression cannot be burdened, "punished or banned, simply because it might offend a hostile mob."[105] Yet as Becker writes, good studies of community social structure "will make somebody angry."[106]

Second, "community" is an empty term. (Even some regulationists admit "it may be difficult to define."[107]) Is it the country? The state (in one study all Mississippi)? The university town? The town in which research is done? People with an illness? An ethnic group? If a sociologist studies Catholic parishes in Boston, what is the community? People brought up Catholic who live in the parish but don't go to mass? People who call themselves Catholic but reject basic church doctrines? Excommunicates?

Third, what does a community "think"? Researchers must "recognize the community as a unit of identity."[108] Is it? Communities are said to have "concerns, needs, values, and priorities."[109] Indeed, but usually many conflicting ones. How can community priorities be identified? Should the sociologist studying Catholic parishes ask the cardinal? Parish priests? Parishioners? These questions being unanswerable, IRBs demand meetings to which many are called but few will come.

Fourth, why should a community's opinion matter? If subjects and communities disagree, why should the subject yield to the community? Communities bind us by coercion (governments) or agreement (churches or clubs), but respect for persons surely frees us from bondage to a community an IRB assigns. Researchers must persuade people to participate in research, but why may a community stop a willing subject from participating?

IRBs subject every scholar engaged in human-subject research to whatever scrutiny a board of censors inflicts. Their orders cannot be challenged, however ignorant or idiosyncratic or imprudent or improper. Little could more betray the tradition of academic freedom and the ideals of the university.

C. CONCLUSION

Academic freedom is not exhausted in the right to express opinion. … Influences that gradually sap and undermine the conditions of free work are more ominous than those which attack the individual in the open.

—John Dewey, *The Middle Works*

Disciplined learning, academic freedom, democratic government, and human progress all require the free flow of ideas. The IRB system impairs it. It not only limits the expression of ideas; it aborts them. It prevents discovery of the knowledge on which ideas are based. It arrests ideas' development. It drives scholars away from risky topics, socially essential fields, and controversial ideas. IRBs can censor with impunity. IRB standards are too vague and IRB procedures too loose to restrain censorship. IRBs are structured to impose orthodoxy in substance and methods. IRBs are told to censor thought when they decide that research's risks outweighs its value. IRBs are asked to corrode academic freedom when they are told to give communities power over research. This is truly "offensive—not only to the values protected by the First Amendment, but to the very notion of a free society."

In this part, I have asked why IRBs err too often. I said that IRBs make kinds and quantities of decisions no agency could make well. They do so without the rules—substantive and procedural—that ordinarily discipline agencies' decisions. Finally, this chapter shows that censors' work is so at odds with a free society that it can be done properly only if it is aggressively limited in ways that IRBs are not.

Conclusion: The Imperial IRB

[M]ankind are more disposed to suffer, while evils are sufferable, than to right themselves by abolishing the forms to which they are accustomed. But when a long train of abuses and usurpations, ... evinces a design to reduce them under absolute Despotism, it is their right, it is their duty, to throw off such Government ... such is now the necessity. ...
—Declaration of Independence

Researchers have been disposed to suffer accustomed evils, but the lawless and unaccountable IRB system's long train of abuses and usurpations has grown despotic and destructive. It cannot show it does good, but it demonstrably costs lives, health, and welfare. It is built to err: Its method is improvident. It gives amateurs tasks beyond their competence and workloads beyond their capacity. It lacks a legible and convincing ethics, cogent and convincing regulations, and effective and fair procedures. It overtaxes informed consent. It corrodes free expression and academic inquiry. A system so fundamentally misconceived creates evils that can only be righted by abolishing the forms to which we are accustomed.

On hearing my arguments, regulationists ask: "But what would replace IRBs?" This is the wrong question. The argument against the IRB system depends not on its replacement but rather on the fact that it is fundamentally structured to do more harm than good. If there is little reason to think IRBs achieve their purpose and much reason to think that whatever good they do must cost too much, the agency itself is the problem to be solved. Bloodletting was long doctors' most common treatment. When its inefficacy and injuries became clear, most ailments it "treated" could not be cured. But that was no reason to keep on doing more harm than good.

This is not to say that human-subject research ought not be regulated. "[I]n wishing to put an end to pernicious experiments, I do not mean to preclude the fullest inquiry. Far from it. ... I would patiently go round and round the subject, and survey it minutely in every possible aspect."[1] In other words, we need—at last—the investigation and thought that should have *preceded* the IRB system's creation, thought to identify the actual problems to be solved, find cost-effective solutions, and make regulation law-abiding and accountable.

A. THE IMPERIAL IRB

Upon what meat doth this our Caesar feed,
That he is grown so great?

—William Shakespeare, *Julius Caesar*

Despite the regulationist conviction that the IRB system is incontrovertibly necessary, many of its aspects are widely criticized. Even OHRP's advanced notice of proposed rule-making seems implicitly to acknowledge many problems with the system. But despite the number and gravity of these criticisms, they inspire primarily proposals only for modest reforms. The most plausible reforms would make the system less destructive by pruning it—ending multiple review of multisite studies, sparing harmless research IRB scrutiny, making review faster and smarter, and so on. Such reforms could make IRBs less damaging, but for the reasons I have surveyed, they could not create a system worth its costs.

Furthermore, the greater the reform, the more opposition it would provoke. Even if a serious reform were implemented, I doubt it would last. Reforms that truly reduced the IRB system's costs would usually bring it nearer its original (relatively modest) ideal. But the same forces that caused that ideal to collapse would gradually corrode serious reforms. To put it differently, the IRB system achieved its authority through the power of its imperialism, and no meaningful reform could long resist that power. Just sketching the history of IRB imperialism suggests how hard it would be to tame it and to institute and preserve genuine reform.

1. IRB IMPERIALISM

The IRB system was born imperial, its jurisdiction broad and its constraints slight. It has colonized new lands and occupied them in battalions. A system born primarily to keep government from conducting another

Tuskegee irrepressibly finds more research to regulate, more duties to enforce, and harsher standards to impose. In 1978, Albert Jonsen used "the term *ethical imperialism* to describe the imposition of one field's rules onto another discipline." He thought "amateurs in ethics" practiced "'imperialism, which is constituted by establishing a rule and applying it ruthlessly.'"[2] In 1980, Sola Pool attacked "bureaucratic elephantiasis."[3] In 2007, Zywicki said IRBs' "defining feature" may be the IRB system's "tendency to expand well beyond" their original purpose.[4]

From the start, the regulations defined "research" and "human subject" capaciously. The latter, for example, encompasses chemotherapy patients and captains of industry. Neither definition is tied to risks, seeking generalizable knowledge is not inherently dangerous, and many subjects protect themselves better than IRBs do. Second, IRB rules were defined loosely, and IRBs were unconstrained by appeals, judicial review, or hierarchy. Event licensing allowed IRBs to regulate research minutely. And OHRP, IRBs, and regulationists have swollen this authority, as a short review shows.

Jurisdiction over People   IRBs regulate ever more kinds of people. It was a short step from supervising federal research to regulating federally funded research. It was a big step to governing all university and hospital research, but one taken early and easily.

Initially, IRBs supervised scholars. Graduate students were added, though they were overseen by faculty. Adding undergraduates was puzzling, for their papers are rarely published, "systematic," or contributions to "generalizable knowledge." They are pedagogic exercises, not research. Yet odder is IRBs' "penetration into high schools, middle schools, elementary schools" and science fairs.[5] The Society for Science and the Public has rules "to help pre-college student researchers follow federal guidelines," since IRBs must protect "the rights and welfare" of anyone studied. Sheela Chandrashekar's high-school science-fair project asked if meditation or exercise helps mental acuity more. Her subjects exercised (a few minutes of walking, jumping jacks, and running in place), so her project posed "more than a minimal risk" and needed approval from the state Science and Engineering Fair's Scientific Review Committee. Only after "numerous forms" and "several phone calls" could the dangerous Sheela proceed.[6]

IRB authority has for decades reached outside the United States. Scholars working abroad must submit to IRB review. And other countries must create IRBs to help regulate American research abroad (however little a poor country might want to). Even the limitation of IRB authority to people working at institutions receiving federal funds is weak, since in many fields, journals will not publish unlicensed research.

The IRB is part of a larger change in universities. Academic freedom classically meant that responsibility for research was the scholar's, not the university's. This is being replaced by universities that hire faculty and supervise their work. So even parts of the university that were once understood to be helping scholars in the work they chose to do—like colleges and support units—universities now think part of a regulatory system.[7] So too in the IRB, where universities have "shifted power and responsibility away from researchers and IRB members and toward full-time administrators."[8]

Jurisdiction over Subject Matter   Second, IRB jurisdiction burgeons because IRBs regulate more activities. The justificatory scandals, the Belmont Report, and the HHS regulations all concerned biomedical research, but IRBs now regulate social-science research and are edging toward the humanities. Some regulationists are eying journalism: When people are "data sources, in oral history, journalism, etc., somebody has to ensure (again) that" they get "the right sort of information."[9] Van den Hoonaard finds IRBs "easily inclined" to take on new activities like "in-classroom student work, quality assessment, autobiographies, ethnographies, pedagogical exercises, and the work of student interns."[10] And "over the horizon for research-ethics review are cultural geography, civil engineering, film studies, research in the new media, art, and theatre."[11]

IRB jurisdiction is reaching into hospital and university administration, like quality improvement. Hospitals have a legal and ethical duty to organize care well, a duty enforced by agencies public and private. But "the growing consensus" is that QI is research requiring IRB approval.[12] And we earlier saw an IRB asserting authority over medical school curriculum.

The category "harm" balloons toward panphobia:[13] financial, social, dignitary, and psychological harm, even discomfort and inconvenience. Within such categories, ever smaller risks of ever smaller injury are treated gravely. Confidentiality is elaborately covered by HIPAA, which IRBs often enforce. In one two-stage inquiry, IRB demands for a conflict of interest or financial statement went from 10% in 2002 to over a third in 2008.[14] IRB sensitivity intensifies when the "vulnerable"—an always expanding category—are studied.

IRBs move beyond protecting subjects to protecting, for example, third parties. So an elite commission wants researchers studying children's housing hazards (like lead paint) to tell IRBs about "legal and ethical obligations to potential third parties."[15] Some IRBs and regulationists postulate communities IRBs should protect. IRBs are said to protect research itself by promoting trust. IRBs protect their institutions from liability and even controversy and protect researchers against subjects. And regulationists speak of preventing "unethical" research.

IRBs not only review more risks; they assess more aspects of research, especially its quality. As early as 1974, Cowan wrote that "all agree" that research that cannot produce "scientific facts" is unethical. A Canadian REB chair said that "[i]f 'ethics creep' means improving the quality of research" his REB would "run, not creep" toward ethics "imperialism."[16] IRBs aspire to "improve the quality of the data."[17] More, the standard seems to be moving from "no invalid research" to "methodologically optimal research."[18] IRBs evaluate researchers' scholarly capacity. And some IRBs evaluate researchers' ethics and character (including their deference to the IRB).

IRBs not only license research, they "exercise ongoing oversight, reviewing even minor changes and re-reviewing every protocol annually."[19] They train and test researchers. They "ensure [again] that institution, IRBs, and investigators" behave properly. "Annual reviews are now widely practised," and "other monitoring" is discussed: supervision of consent, checking adherence to protocols, and "monitoring for data integrity."[20] IRB "supervision continues as data are analyzed and findings are discovered."[21]

Paperwork   Forty years ago, Cowan called the "increasing volume" of paper documenting "safety, benefits, and risks"[22] a "major problem" and warned that "even more reports, memoranda, and the like will so overburden" researchers "that some, perhaps many," would stop working with human subjects.[23] Today, applications lengthen. Trivial changes require troublesome paperwork. An accreditation agency wants a nonscientific member's presence "documented for every action item."[24] Dr. Coe yearly lists the number of patients studied, "all measurements in blood and urine in our data banks," and papers published. Yearly he supplies a bibliography and a summary of recent literature (with search-engine criteria), summarizes "changes to the risk-benefit ratio," answers sporadic IRB questions, and more. In multisite studies, paperwork stupefies (for one nine-site project, over 15,000 pages).

Bureaucratization and Professionalization   Organizations gain authority by bureaucratizing and professionalizing. IRB administrators and staff members proliferate, creating a class that benefits from increasing the budgets, elevating the status, and extending the domain of IRBs. They organize to achieve these goals and claim authority from the credentials Big Ethics issues.[25]

New Worlds to Conquer   Regulationists are abubble with hopes for new authority. "[E]thical regulation is flowing towards ever-stricter rules." The IOM would extend IRBs' reach "to the entire private sector,"[26] NBAC to "the entire private sector," domestic *and* international.[27] OHRP apparently concurs.[28] One regulationist wants "a compendium of best ethical practices" for accrediting all IRBs, more "government control of regulations for all institutions," stiffer IRB training, fees for IRB review, and payment for all research subjects.[29] Another regulationist thinks it "clear" that IRBs "promote patient safety and good technical standards" and sees "further candidate roles" like protecting public health.[30] Gray thinks disclosing "intrinsic" conflicts of interest—career advancement, professional recognition, and getting grants—is part of informed consent.[31] Committees increasingly want interviewees to approve transcripts.[32] Shore says that community- and institution-based review "may be the ideal."[33]

2.   REFORM AND THE IMPERIAL IMPERATIVE

As this sketch suggests, attempts to reform the system must overcome an imperialism that serves what I have wryly called Big Ethics—the strategically situated people who and institutions that believe in and benefit from the IRB system. I have spoken of justification-by-scandal, but (Heimer and Petty say) while scandals "may supply the energy for creating regulatory regimes" and "shore up commitment," bureaucracies "take on a life of their own." Much of the "lush growth of new regulatory bureaucracy" is the self-aggrandizement that is natural when bureaucracies attract people committed to their work and dependent on their success and who thus fight to preserve and extend its authority.[34]

Schrag, for instance, says the principal factor in the system's seizure of authority over social-science research "was simple bureaucratic turf-grabbing." Public Health Service bureaucrats were the "most powerful, determined players" in drafting regulations. They "designed rules primarily for health research" and resisted "challenges from their parent department, Congress, the White House, and outside critics." This turf fight inspired 1974's rush "to publish regulations before Congress could pass a law" and 1981's rush to keep the new administration from reexamining the issue.[35]

When Congress debated legislation, its sponsor feared "medical research, not research in general,"[36] and the National Research Act "limited its scope to 'biomedical and behavioral research.'" Nevertheless, HEW's regulations applied to all department-funded "'research, development, and related activities in which human subjects are involved.'"[37] The President's Commission "failed to investigate what harms and wrongs, if any, social scientists were committing, how IRBs already handled various types of social science research, and what alternative remedies existed."[38] The Commission's conclusions about IRBs "were unsupported, or even contradicted, by the evidence" gathered.[39] The Belmont Report's progenitors "were willing neither to listen to social scientists nor to leave them alone."[40] What social scientists had done or said was "irrelevant." As Beauchamp (a principal author) wrote, it was "out and out" a "paternalistic commission."[41]

When Reagan was elected, Charles McCarthy was Director of the Office of Protection from Research Risks (OHRP's predecessor). As he "later recalled, 'everybody knew that this was not a time to try to propose a new regulation.'" So he described jurisdiction over social-science research "as a *reduction* of regulation." To do this, "he had to distort the effects of both the 1974 regulations and their proposed replacements."[42] He "exaggerated the existing extent of" regulation of behavioral research and "then claimed that the new rules were more lenient, stating that the 'proposed new rules would exempt risk-free behavioral and social science research resulting in deregulation of about 80% of research.'"[43] Schrag writes,

McCarthy later admitted that his arguments had been deceptive. As he explained in 2004, he told the Reagan transition team that the new regulations were less stringent than the old ones. "Of course, they weren't, but they looked like they were because we wrote some exceptions." He pulled a similar ruse with the lame-duck secretary, packaging the new rules as "Diminished Regulations for the Protection of Human Subjects" while trusting "nobody down there in the last weeks of the Harris administration ... would actually read it."[44]

Bureaucrats not only believe in their mission, they benefit from imperialism. Becker describes research regulation as "an ambitious bureaucracy with interests to protect, a mission to promote, and an ideology to explain why it's all necessary."[45] Zywicki says that the incentives of "academic bureaucracy generally tend toward an assertion by IRBs of enlarged influence," which "tends to increase the director's power" and salary and to "feed the growth of the IRB industry."[46] And as Heimer and Petty say of staffers, IRBs are "their livelihood, a secure niche on the edges of the research and scholarly world."[47] Hence professionalization, certificates, degrees, and accreditation.[48] As one manual says frankly, "certification can provide a sense of professional accomplishment, enhancement of professional standing, and peer recognition." And be "a valuable career tool by confirming value to current employers and by making one's resume more appealing."[49]

Another part of Big Ethics benefits from the IRB system—people whose careers depend on it. This includes those who sell IRBs services (like training and accreditation) and those who write about research ethics. The latter want a discipline with a secure place in hospitals and universities—departments, degree programs, certificates, conferences, and the rest.

The actors in Big Ethics are not cynically self-seeking; they truly believe in the IRB ideology and ethos. The sociology and psychology of Big Ethics sustain them. Big Ethics moves (van den Hoonaard says) "in a bubble of compliance,"[50] virtually without the "critical self-reflection" and "voices of dissent" of serious academic disciplines. Thus "so many people are professionally invested in the current oversight system that they cannot imagine replacing it, only tinkering with it."[51] (Upton Sinclair said it was hard "to get a man to understand something when his salary depends upon his not understanding it.")[52] And there is Becker's moral entrepreneur—the "crusading reformer" who is "profoundly disturbed" by "some evil" and who "feels that nothing can be right in the world until rules are made to correct it." His ethic is absolute; "what he sees is truly and totally evil with no qualification. Any means is justified to do away with it. The crusader is fervent and righteous, often self-righteous."[53]

Van den Hoonaard sees a regulationist moral panic. A moral panic is a "sudden eruption of measured concern shared by a significant segment of the population, with disproportional claims about the potential harm moral deviants" can inflict. Moral panics "involve exaggeration of harm and risk, orchestration of the panic by elites or powerful special-interest groups, the construction of imaginary deviants, and reliance on diagnostic instruments."[54] And "[f]or a moral panic to be effective, it is essential to seize on highly publicized, ethically dubious cases."[55] This overstates things (no "significant segment of the population" obsesses over research wrongs) but catches crucial features of regulationism, like its caricature of researchers, its exaggeration of trivial risks, its embrace of the paternalism it denounces, and its minute regulation of activities that law otherwise hardly notices.

IRB incentives amplify the pressures the IRB ethos encourages. In the IRB world, broader, stricter regulation seems to obviate threats from OHRP and prospective litigants. Meanwhile, IRBs (being unaccountable) freely extend their authority. And since regulation's costs fall largely on researchers, subjects, and research's beneficiaries, IRBs are little subdued by ordinary budgetary constraints.

Furthermore, from its bubble, Big Ethics has little reason to doubt its competence and rightness. This is human enough. For example, Kahneman says that while scholars agree that stock picking is essentially "a game of chance," stock pickers think themselves skillful and resist facts that challenge their belief, livelihood, and self-esteem. Their "illusions of validity and skill are supported by a powerful professional culture," and "people can maintain an unshakable faith in any proposition, however absurd, when they are sustained by a community of like-minded believers."[56]

Nor does life in the bubble cultivate a humility to temper imperialism. Researchers bear the stain of Auschwitz and Tuskegee; IRBs subdue them. IRBs have ethical insight; researchers are blind. As one "Research Compliance Services Director and Research Integrity Officer" said, unless the IRB "actively advocates for research participants, those responsible for harming participants are unlikely to be held to account," for researchers are unlikely to see subjects "as 'us,' but more likely as 'them.'"[57] Having unaccountable power over people confirms IRBs' moral confidence. They find the malefactors they seek and have few mechanisms to correct their misconceptions (like their exaggeration of the risks of asking people questions). Working unchallenged in a bubble means never having to say you're sorry.

How, in short, can Big Ethics—bureaucrats, IRBs, and commentators—want real reform enough to demand, or even tolerate, it? It has not: "Bioethicists and a succession of expert investigations have identified the regulatory defects of the IRB, but defined the remedy as more of the same—more review, more documentation, more training." The IRB system was crucially shaped by moral entrepreneurs in a moral panic who were not "thinking about regulatory technique"[58] and who "devised a labyrinthine network of regulatory bodies and an arcane and sometimes inconsistent patchwork of rules."[59] The assumptions and norms that have flourished within the regulationist bubble confirm the rightness of their imperialism. How can they tolerate serious challenges to it?

B. REGULATING RESEARCH WITHOUT IRBS

[A] law [that] depends upon the initiative of officials in detecting violations and in prosecuting ... will almost certainly be difficult to enforce.
—Walter Lippmann, *A Preface to Morals*

The IRB system's existence and ideology have preempted the "fullest inquiry," the minute survey of the subject that should be the basis for regulating research. This is work law routinely undertakes. For example, scientific misconduct is regulated by "trusting scholars to behave and then punishing offenders."[60] Doctors and journalists may be sued in tort to compensate victims and deter malefactors. Suits against researchers are rare, but lawyers specializing in them yearn for plaintiffs,[61] so the rarity of suits probably reflects the paucity of serious wrongs, not judicial indifference to researchers' misdeeds. If anything, the most famous case—*Grimes v. Kennedy-Krieger Institute*[62]—betrays judicial contempt for researchers.[63] Tort law has important limits, partly because damages must be sufficient to repay litigation expenses. But class actions are possible when damages are individually small, agencies can be allowed to sue on behalf of subjects, damages can be statutorily multiplied, and lawyers' fees can be authorized.[64] Even the threat of suits matters, for "[m]ost up-per- and middle-class professionals react viscerally to the prospects" of being sued or investigated.[65] (Thus doctors wildly overestimate the risk of malpractice suits.)

Where researchers truly sin, harsh, even criminal, sanctions may be appropriate. Such sanctions already punish some kinds of research mis-conduct. Eric Poehlman, for example, "pleaded guilty to lying on a federal grant application" and fabricating data on obesity, menopause, and ag-ing. He was made to pay restitution, barred from receiving public funds, professionally ruined, and sentenced to a year in prison and two years probation.[66]

Ultimately, however, law's success turns on its ability to command the cooperation of those it regulates. As Lippmann wrote, "The amount of law is relatively small which a modern legislature can successfully im-pose," since "unless the enforcement of the law is taken in hand by the citizenry, the officials as such are quite helpless."[67] Citizens are likeliest to cooperate when they believe they have a duty to obey the law and when they believe the law is morally right. Here considerable research has es-tablished the weakness of the "command and control" regulation and "alternative approaches, based on social motivations."[68] As Tyler puts it, "values shape rule-following. In particular, values lead to voluntary behavior, including both voluntary decision acceptance and cooperation with legal authorities."[69]

How does government inculcate the right values? First, as chapter 5 said, by according people "procedural justice." Tyler writes, "If authority is exercised fairly, the law and legal authorities are viewed as legitimate and seen as entitled to be obeyed."[70] Tyler asks if procedural justice leads "people to voluntarily accept the decisions made by legal authorities" and answers, "Studies across a wide range of issues suggest that they do" in both criminal and administrative settings.[71] Yet as we have seen, the IRB system's structure, practices, and ethos little encourage IRBs to accord researchers the respect for persons it wants researchers to accord subjects.

The second way government inculcates right values is by adopting regulations that make moral sense to the people it regulates. The failure to do so has helped cause what Stewart calls "an acute problem of grow-ing regulatory fatigue" in which agencies are asked to do more but seem "less and less capable" responding efficiently and effectively. "Regulatory results often fall short of expectations" even while regulation grows "ever more burdensome."[72] Stewart primarily blames "excessive reliance on command-and-control" regulation which tries "to dictate the conduct of millions of actors in a quickly changing and very complex economy and society throughout a large and diverse nation." Stewart describes a trend toward alternatives like promoting "self-regulating measures by nongovernmental entities."[73] Similarly, Tyler writes, "In recent decades, the recognition that self-regulation has value has been a widespread one within the law."[74]

Part of the value of such self-regulation is that without it, the federal regulations, the system's research ethics, and IRBs' actions too often reflect judgments researchers can neither understand nor respect. When regulating professions, the law has ordinarily resolved such problems with the principle that self-regulation is a defining feature of professions. This is essentially true even of doctors and lawyers—so often so able to harm patients and clients. Why are researchers different? Not because of research scandals. Scandals not only mar all professions, but they can be part of self-regulation, like Beecher's article. Beecher was an elite physician writing in an elite medical journal. As intended, he evoked discussion and change. Similarly, Milgram, Humphreys, and Zimbardo inspired a rewarding professional debate about the ethical questions their research raised. As Schrag comments, "The problems with Humphreys' work stemmed not from a lack of oversight, or from a scofflaw's flouting established ethics, but rather from the novelty of his questions and methods. By taking his critics seriously, Humphreys became an earnest participant in the hard work of defining the ethics of sociology."[75] More generally, the years before the IRB system's rise were remarkably fruitful "for the social and behavioral scientists eager to debate and codify the ethics of their disciplines."[76] And in 1964, before Beecher's article, "the NIH had appointed an internal study group to investigate the ethics of clinical research."[77]

Professional regulation is better suited than OHRP and IRBs to develop the ethics disciplines need. Disciplines need specificity, not Belmont principles. They need debate by people who know a discipline's ethical problems and how to manage them well. Whether studying drug users on mean streets or Muncie's bourgeoisie, ethnographers know the risks and how to reduce them better than IRB members who have never seen meth, visited the Midwest, or read ethnography. Disciplines need open, contentious national and international debate among proficients, not insular, ill-informed, unpublished deliberations of individual IRBs or the recurring pattern of "writing policies for social scientists without meaningful input" from them.[78]

Furthermore, IRBs act prospectively, but ethics often turns on developing circumstances. Recall the elite report telling researchers to "anticipate and define their legal and ethical obligations" to third parties and to plan for them.[79] Nobody can "anticipate," much less "define" both "legal and ethical obligations" to uncertain "others" in unknowable conditions. Scholars consult colleagues about ethical problems and report them in their journals so that researchers can better manage the novel and complex ethical problems they meet. As Petit realizes, "[t]here is no regulation like self-regulation." Facing ethical dilemmas, researchers need to "identify strongly with" their ethical code.[80] And, Halpern argues, good regulation builds "on core features and strengths of scientists' informal morality. Where formal oversight stints or obstructs scientists' longstanding traditions," regulation falters.[81] As we have seen, governance that researchers find ignorant and perverse discredits ethics and breeds resistance.

Disciplines are not only better suited than OHRP and IRBs to write professional norms; they also have ways to enforce those norms. This cannot "ensure" faultless behavior. *Nothing* can. But it builds on "the historical record" of designing "oversight structures that deploy the strengths of the colleague network and avoid some of its shortcomings." For example, in the mid-twentieth century, funders "created scientific advisory panels that quite effectively monitored the hazards of clinical trials." This "drew on researchers' informal traditions, adding a straightforward means—control over funding—for delaying or stopping clinical experiments judged to be too hazardous."[82]

Furthermore, legal scholars argue that "socially understood standards" and "loss of reputation, censure, ostracism, and disruption of community relationships" work better than "incentives and restraints established through direct law and regulation."[83] Halpern says scientists "conform to group norms to maintain the esteem of their colleagues" and avoid ostracism.[43] This hardly assures good conduct, but, Haskell writes, "our reliance upon it is far-reaching and by no means misplaced," for professions are markets whose members value reputations.[85] There are scofflaws in professions as elsewhere, but as Veblen said, only those of "aberrant temperament can in the long run retain their self-esteem in the face of the disesteem of their fellows."[86] In sum, professional opinion—often superior to IRB ethics both in formulation and application—bears hard on researchers. The willful and wicked can flout it, but with other constraints it shapes researchers' choices.

Social factors also restrain researchers. They must respect "public tolerance for investigatory risk."[87] Disliking unethical research and unpleasant publicity, funders impose "written consent statements, insurance that would compensate injured subjects, and review of research protocols by panels of scientific advisors."[88] If anything, funders are more exigent and fearful now than before. And professional journals work to exclude unethical studies. Medical journals decline to publish research lacking IRB approval.[89] The International Committee of Medical Journal Editors wants conformance with the Declaration of Helsinki in addition to IRB approval, and journals are obliging.[90] Not least, universities and hospitals have procedures for punishing unethical research.

Regulationists say "[r]esearchers have always prided themselves on their methodological problem-solving skills" but particularly before "the rise of federal regulations" gave ethics little thought.[91] Halpern's account of twentieth-century research ethics rebukes this ignorance. She cites Lederer's investigation of the early twentieth century, which concluded that American investigators were never "'free to do whatever they pleased with their human subjects,'" since scientists and the public would have rejected "reckless experimentation." Halpern shows that concern for both consent and subjects has "long been at the center of scientists' moral traditions."[92] As Schrag observes, "Anthropologists, sociologists, historians, folklorists, and others have long recognized" that studying people may impose special ethical challenges and long "debated the exact nature of their ethical obligations."[93]

Regulationists seem to assume that only law can tame researchers. But, for example, the Nazi experience "reveals the insufficiency of formal rules," for "Germany regulated experimentation in considerable detail"[94] by 1931, before the Nazis and the Nuremberg Code. Generally, good behavior depends more on the regulated than the regulators. Hamburger says that IRBs are not "the primary obstacle to research harms and that researchers themselves have been."[95] Studied, researchers "almost uniformly expressed an understanding of and an appreciation for" protecting subjects that seemed genuine and reflected "internalization of a strong social ethical norm."[96] Even Robert Levine thinks "the most important reason that the record is so good and that there have been so few injuries is that most researchers are keenly aware of the potential for injury and take great care to avoid it."[97]

After all, researchers are no worse than the rest of us and have little wish to harm those they work with. Indeed, research can stimulate in researchers appreciation of, affection for, and gratitude toward the people who help them. Read the dedications and acknowledgments in researchers' books to find these sentiments warmly expressed. Thus Beecher, whose article regulationists eagerly invoke, opposed "formal, codified rules" for research and thought "an 'intelligent, informed, conscientious, compassionate and responsible investigator offered the best protection for human research subjects.'"[98]

Why, then, have researchers tolerated IRB abuses and usurpations? Partly because they react to scandals as regulationists do—with horror. Partly out of ignorance: They are told that only IRBs can prevent Tuskegees and understand research ethics. Partly because regulationists have seized the high ground and cast on doubters the taint of Tuskegee and Auschwitz. Researchers also have a collective action problem: They do not know the breadth and depth of damage IRBs inflict, since IRB secrecy relegates them to personal experience and colleagues' anecdotes. And while they may think IRBs pernicious in their own discipline, how can they evaluate IRBs in other disciplines? Nor can researchers individually resist IRBs: Universities fear offending the Great Funder and getting bad publicity. IRBs treat researchers as creatures of the university, a view university administrations tend to like. Worst, researchers know IRBs can cripple their work and their career.

In addition, most researchers know too little about regulation to see the system's perversity. They do not recognize how wasteful event licensing is. How lawless and unaccountable IRBs are. How empty IRB ethics are. How little similar activities are regulated. How much IRBs offend the system of free expression. Many researchers assume that no government agency can be abolished. Many dream of exempting their corner of research from review. Many propose measures—like centralized IRBs—that might lighten their burden. Many imagine educating IRBs. They persist in hope even as IRB imperialism triumphs.

Nevertheless, many researchers feel a deep, justified anger at the unreasonable restraints IRBs have placed on rewarding inquiries. They have moving stories to tell and reasons to tell them. I hope this book convinces them to do so. IRB imperialism can also be challenged judicially. I have argued the unwisdom, not the illegality, of IRB regulation. But the IRB system is a *vade mecum* of ways to affront the first amendment and the due process clause. Litigation's path is long, but a decision holding IRBs unconstitutional would oblige government to devise a constitutional IRB system, something probably beyond human ingenuity.

C. CONCLUSION

And who can doubt that it will lead to the worst disorders when ... people devoid of whatsoever competence are made judges over experts and are granted authority to treat them as they please?
—Galileo Galilei

All government agencies are flawed. But which is so fundamentally misconceived in so many costly ways as the IRB system? It is a compound of deadly regulatory errors. The first was not asking what problem IRBs solve, the problem's dimensions, and how best to solve it. So regulationists exaggerate the problem's severity and IRBs' benefits. The second error was event licensing. It is gruesomely inefficient. Better to punish malefactors harshly than condemn both regulators and the regulated to the torment of licensing.

The third regulatory error was ignoring costs. It is always bad to pay more for things than they are worth, but when the cost is lives, health, and welfare, it is disastrous. The fourth error was using amateurs for work professionals hardly do well. Evaluating scholarship and ethics in specialized disciplines is complex and controvertible. Amateurs—however earnest and admirable—must be overwhelmed. The fifth error was thinking "human-subject research" is a coherent ethical category and supposing that the Belmont principles could do more than give IRBs a kindergarten ethics. The sixth error was ignoring IRBs' paternalism and their inconsistency with regulationist doctrine.

The seventh regulatory error was tolerating lawlessness. Law guides agencies' decisions and constrains government power. An agency with neither substantive nor procedural rules is foolhardy and illegitimate. The eighth error was courting the rigidity, pettiness, arrogance, and prudishness that plague censors. The error trebled when censorship was imposed where it is least appropriate—the university. The ninth error was relying so centrally on a mechanism as unreliable as mandated disclosure. Finally, the tenth error was making IRBs unaccountable. It is wrong in a democracy for agencies to answer only to themselves. And because IRBs are unaccountable, they need not acknowledge their errors. "Such is now the necessity which constrains us to alter our former Systems of Government."

Research was regulated before IRBs proliferated; it would be regulated were IRBs abolished. But the IRB system is a bad tool. Event licensing squanders resources. Overworked amateurs cannot assess what they do not understand. An agency without due process can be neither wise nor fair. A primitive ethics and a perverse ethos mislead regulators and researchers. Mandated disclosure is a triumph of hope over experience. Censorship is presumptively wrong in a free society and intolerable in universities. So a lawless and unaccountable agency deters researchers from helping to preserve human life, protect human health, and promote human welfare. It is time to throw off the forms to which we are accustomed.

Notes

INTRODUCTION

1. Sydney A. Halpern, *Lesser Harms: The Morality of Risk in Medical Research* 3 (University of Chicago Press, 2004).

2. 42 USC § 289(a).

3. 45 CFR 46.

4. Sydney Halpern, *Hybrid Design, Systematic Rigidity: Institutional Dynamics in Human Research Oversight*, 2 Regulation & Governance 85, 88–89 (2008).

5. 45 CFR 46.102(d).

6. 45 CFR 46.102(f).

7. 45 CFR 46.111.

8. NBAC, *Ethical and Policy Issues in Research Involving Human Participants: Report and Recommendations* 25 (2001).

9. Susan M. Labott & Timothy P. Johnson, *Psychological and Social Risks of Behavioral Research*, 26 IRB 11, 12 (2004).

10. Carol A. Heimer & JuLeigh Petty, *Bureaucratic Ethics: IRBs and the Legal Regulation of Human Subjects Research*, 6 Annual Review of Law & Social Science 601, 616–617 (2010) (doi: 10.1146/annurev.lawsocsci.093008.131454).

11. Will C. van den Hoonaard, *Seduction of Ethics: Transforming the Social Sciences* 26–27 (University of Toronto Press, 2011).

12. Ibid at 285.

13. Because official sources are obscure and training is generally primitive (see chapters 4 and 5) and because the manuals—principally Amdur, *Handbook*, Bankert & Amdur, and Mazur, *Guide* (see the Preface's short forms)—intend to help IRB members make decisions, these manuals are influential and offer a rare insight into the IRB world. Amdur's 2011 manual has five Amazon reviews, all five stars and all like this: "As an IRB member I love this book, nice compact resource that makes me a better reviewer and helps to focus our IRB meetings. A must have for any IRB committee members, or any applicants wanting a better understanding of the IRB process. I love this book so much I'm reluctant to lend it out for fear I won't get it back!"

14. Koski refers to Henry K. Beecher, *Ethics and Clinical Research*, 274 NEJM 1354 (1966).

15. Greg Koski, *Research, Regulations, and Responsibility: Confronting the Compliance Myth—A Reaction to Professor Gatter*, 52 Emory L J, 403 (2003).

16. I am indebted to Zachary Schrag for these categories.

17. 45 CFR Parts 46, 160, and 164 (2011).

18. Heimer & Petty, 6 Annual Review of Law & Social Science at 615 (cited in note 10).

19. Lura Abbott & Christine Grady, *A Systematic Review of the Empirical Literature Evaluating IRBs: What We Know and What We Still Need to Learn*, 6 JERHRE 3 (2011) (doi: 10.1525/jer.2011.6.1.3).

20. Scott Burris & Kathryn Moss, *U.S. Health Researchers Review Their Ethics Review Boards: A Qualitative Study*, 1 JERHRE 39, 39 (2006).

21. Philip Hamburger, *The New Censorship: Institutional Review Boards*, 2004 Supreme Court Review 271, 335–336.

22. Carol A. Heimer, *The Unstable Alliance of Law and Morality*, in Steven Hitlin and Stephen Vaisey, eds., *Handbook of the Sociology of Morality* 196 (Springer Science & Business Media, 2010) (doi: 10.1007/978-1-4419-6896-8_10).

23. Jerry Goldman & Martin D. Katz, *Inconsistency and Institutional Review Boards*, 248 JAMA 197, 198 & 202 (1982).

24. Omri Ben-Shahar & Carl E. Schneider, *More than You Wanted to Know: The Failure of Mandated Disclosure* (Princeton University Press, 2014).

25. Heimer, *Unstable Alliance* at 198 (cited in note 22).

26. Heimer & Petty, 6 Annual Review of Law & Social Science at 622 (cited in note 10).

27. Franklin G. Miller & Alan Wertheimer, *Facing Up to Paternalism in Research Ethics*, 37 HCR 24, 25 (2007).

28. Mazur, *Guide*, at 6.

29. Todd Zywicki, *Institutional Review Boards as Academic Bureaucracies: An Economic and Experiential Analysis*, NwS 861, 881.

CHAPTER 1

1. Drawn from S. M. Berenholtz et al., *Eliminating Catheter-Related Bloodstream Infections in the Intensive Care Unit*, 32 Critical Care Medicine 2014 (2004), and Bridget M. Kuehn, *DHHS Halts Quality Improvement Study: Policy May Hamper Tests of Methods to Improve Care*, 299 JAMA 1005 (2008).

2. NBAC, *Ethical and Policy Issues in Research Involving Human Participants: Report and Recommendations* 26 (2001).

3. IOM, *Responsible Research: A Systems Approach to Protecting Research Participants* viii (NAP, 2003).

4. Robert J. Levine, *Ethics and Regulation of Clinical Research* (Yale University Press, 1988) (2nd ed.).

5. Ibid at xvi. Levine is too modest to say that he was such a resource—a consultant to the former commission and one of the "advisors and consultants" for the latter's IRB *Guidebook*.

6. Greg Koski, *Research, Regulations, and Responsibility: Confronting the Compliance Myth—A Reaction to Professor Gatter*, 52 Emory L Rev 403, 406 (2003).

7. Carol A. Heimer, *The Unstable Alliance of Law and Morality*, in Steven Hitlin & Stephen Vaisey, eds., *Handbook of the Sociology of Morality* 195, 196 (Springer Science & Business Media, 2010) (doi: 10.1007/978-1-4419-6896-8_10).

8. Levine, *Ethics and Regulation* at 39 (cited in note 4).

9. National Commission for the Protection of Human Subjects of Biomedical and Behavioral Research, *Report and Recommendations: Institutional Review Boards, Appendix* (HEW, 1977), quoted in Edward L. Pattullo, *Governmental Regulation of the Investigation of Human Subjects in Social Research*, 23 Minerva 521, 530 (1985).

10. Levine, *Ethics and Regulation* at 40 (cited in note 4).

11. Scott Burris & Kathryn Moss, *U.S. Health Researchers Review Their Ethics Review Boards: A Qualitative Study*, 1 JRHRE 39, 40 (2006).

12. Richard S. Saver, *Medical Research and Intangible Harm*, 74 U Cincinnati L Rev 941, 947 (2006).

13. Scott C. Burris & Jen Welsh, *Regulatory Paradox in the Protection of Human Research Subjects: A Review of OHRP Enforcement Letters*, NwS 643, 651 (2007).

14. Sarah J. L. Edwards et al., *Ethical Issues in the Design and Conduct of Randomized Controlled Trials*, 2 Health Technology Assessment 29, 30 (1998).

15. Ibid at 35.

16. David A. Braunholtz et al., *Are Randomized Clinical Trials Good for Us (in the Short Term)? Evidence for a "Trial Effect,"* 54 J Clinical Epidemiology 217 (2001).

17. Jeffrey M. Peppercorn et al., *Comparison of Outcomes in Cancer Patients Treated Within and Outside Clinical Trials: Conceptual Framework and Structured Review*, 363 Lancet 263 (2004).

18. Gunn E. Vist et al., *Outcomes of Patients Who Participate in Randomized Controlled Trials Compared to Similar Patients Receiving Similar Interventions Who Do Not Participate*, Cochrane Database of Systematic Reviews 2008, Issue 3. Art. No.: MR000009 (doi: 10.1002/14651858.MR000009.pub4).

19. Levine, *Ethics and Regulation* at 39 (cited in note 4).

20. Drawn from Susan H. Wootton et al., *Unproven Therapies in Clinical Research and Practice: The Necessity to Change the Regulatory Paradigm*, 132 Pediatrics 599 (2013) (doi: 10.1542/peds.2013-0778).

21. Jon Tyson, *Dubious Distinctions between Research and Clinical Practice Using Experimental Therapies: Have Patients Been Well Served?*, in A. Goldworth et al., eds., *Ethics and Perinatology* 214, 217 (Oxford University Press, 1995).

22. Sam Horng, *Descriptions of Benefits and Risks in Consent Forms for Phase 1 Oncology Trials*, 347 NEJM 2134, 2134 (2002).

23. J.A. DiMasi et al., *The Price of Innovation: New Estimates of Drug Development Costs*, 22 J Health Economics 151 (2003).

24. Jerry Menikoff with Edward P. Richards, *What the Doctor Didn't Say: The Hidden Truth about Medical Research* (Oxford University Press, 2006).

25. Charles W. Lidz et al., *Therapeutic Misconception and the Appreciation of Risks in Clinical Trials*, 58 SSM 1689 (2004).

26. Ibid at 1690.

27. Charles L. Bosk, *Occupational Rituals in Patient Management*, 303 NEJM 71, 72 (1980).

28. Jay Katz, *The Silent World of Doctor and Patient* 166 (Free Press, 1984).

29. Eric J. Cassell, *The Changing Concept of the Ideal Physician*, 115 Daedalus 185, 186 (Spring 1986).

30. Ibid at 191.

31. Carl E. Schneider, *The Practice of Autonomy: Patients, Doctors, and Medical Decisions* 52 (Oxford University Press, 1998).

32. Lidz et al., 58 SSM at 1690 (cited in note 25).

33. Dan Ariely, *Predictably Irrational: The Hidden Forces That Shape Our Decisions* 178 (Harper Collins, 2008).

34. Joye K. Willcox et al., *Antioxidants and Prevention of Chronic Disease*, 44 Critical Reviews in Food Science & Nutrition 275 (2004) (doi: 10.1080/10408690490468489).

35. Goran Bjelakovic et al., *Mortality in Randomized Trials of Antioxidant Supplements for Primary and Secondary Prevention: Systematic Review and Meta-Analysis*, 297 JAMA 842 (2007) (doi:10.1001/jama.297.8.842) (emphasis added).

36. Debra S. Echt et al., *Mortality and Morbidity in Patients Receiving Encainide, Flecainide, or Placebo: The Cardiac Arrhythmia Suppression Trial*, 324 NEJM 781 (1991).

37. Lidz et al., 58 SSM at 1690 (cited in note 25).

38. Charles Fried, *Medical Experimentation: Personal Integrity and Social Policy* (North-Holland, 1974).

39. Sarah J. L. Edwards et al., *Ethical Issues in the Design and Conduct of Randomised Controlled Trials*, 2 Health Technology Assessment 19 (1998).

40. Daniel Kahneman, *Thinking, Fast and Slow* 223 (Farrar, Straus & Giroux, 2011).

41. Ibid at 224.

42. Ibid at 224–225.

43. Jerry Menikoff with Edward P. Richards, *What the Doctor Didn't Say: The Hidden Truth about Medical Research* 34 (Oxford University Press, 2006).

44. Ibid at 263, n26.

45. Samuel Hellman & Deborah S. Hellman, *Of Mice but Not Men: Problems of the Randomized Clinical Trial*, 324 NEJM 1585, 1588 (1991).

46. Ryan E. Lawrence et al., *Competing Commitments in Psychiatric Research: An Examination of Psychiatric Researchers' Perspectives*, 35 International J Law & Psychiatry 380, 385 (2012) (doi: 10.1016/j.ijlp.2012.09.003).

47. Ibid.

48. OHRP *Guidebook*, chapter 3.

49. NBAC, *Ethical and Policy Issues* at 72 (cited in note 2).

50. Ibid.

51. Zachary M. Schrag, *How Talking Became Human Subjects Research: The Federal Regulation of the Social Sciences, 1965–1991*, 21 J Policy History 3, 6 (2009).

52. Patricia Cohen, *As Ethics Panels Expand Grip, No Field Is Off Limits*, New York Times (February 28, 2007), http://www.nytimes.com/2007/02/28/arts/28board.html.

53. J. Michael Oakes, *Survey Research*, in Bankert & Amdur at 418.

54. Saver, 74 U Cincinnati L Rev at 946–47 (cited in note 12).

55. Ibid at 945–946.

56. Katinka De Wet, *The Importance of Ethical Appraisal in Social Science Research: Reviewing a Faculty of Humanities' Research Ethics Committee*, 8 J of Academic Ethics 301, 302 (2010) (doi: 10.1007/s10805-010-9118-8).

57. Ibid at 312.

58. Drawn from Thomas Hadjistavropoulos & William E. Smythe, *Elements of Risk in Qualitative Research*, 11 Ethics & Behavior 163 (2001).

59. J. Michael Oakes, *Risks and Wrongs in Social Science Research: An Evaluator's Guide to the IRB*, 26 Evaluation Review 443, 449 (2002) (doi: 10.1177/019384102236520).

60. AAUP, *Research on Human Subjects: Academic Freedom and the Institutional Review Board* 1, 4 (Judith Jarvis Thompson et al., AAUP, 2006).

61. Schrag, 21 J Policy History at 13 (cited in note 51).

62. Richard T. Campbell, *Risk and Harm Issues in Social Science Research*, Human Subjects Policy Conference at 7–8 (April 2003).

63. Lee A. Green et al., *IRB and Methodological Issues: Impact of Institutional Review Board Practice Variation on Observational Health Services Research*, 41 HSR: Health Services Research 214, 225 (2006).

64. William Burman & Robert Daum, *Grinding to a Halt: The Effects of the Increasing Regulatory Burden on Research and Quality Improvement Efforts*, 49 Clinical Infectious Diseases 328, 329 (2009) (doi: 10.1086/605454).

65. AAUP, *Research on Human Subjects* at 4 (cited in note 60).

66. Association of Academic Health Centers Press Release, *HIPAA Creating Barriers to Research and Discovery: HIPAA Problems Widespread and Unresolved since 2003*, Association of Academic Health Centers 1, 6 (June 16, 2008).

67. Ibid at 2.

68. Richard A. Epstein, *HIPAA on Privacy: Its Unintended and Intended Consequences*, 22 Cato J 13, 23 (2002).

69. Academy of Medical Sciences, *Personal Data for Public Good: Using Health Information in Medical Research* 41 (January 2006), http://www.acmedsci.ac.uk/viewFile/publicationDownloads/Personal.pdf.

70. Mark A. Hall & Stephen S. Rich, *Laws Restricting Health Insurers' Use of Genetic Information: Impact on Genetic Discrimination*, 66 American J Human Genetics 293, 305 (2000).

71. Ibid at 302.

72. Karen J. Wingrove et al., *Experiences and Attitudes Concerning Genetic Testing and Insurance in a Colorado Population: A Survey of Families Diagnosed with Fragile X Syndrome*, 64 American J Medical Genetics 378, 380 (1996).

73. Mark D. West, *Secrets, Sex, and Spectacle: The Rules of Scandal in Japan and the United States* 84 (University of Chicago Press, 2006).

74. C. K. Gunsalus, *Rethinking Protections for Human Subjects*, 49 Chronicle of Higher Education B24, B24 (2002).

75. Susan M. Labott & Timothy P. Johnson, *Psychological and Social Risks of Behavioral Research*, 26 BMJ 11, 12 (2004).

76. *Guidebook*, chapter 3A, http://www.hhs.gov/ohrp/archive/irb/irb_chapter3.htm#e1.

77. AAUP, *Research on Human Subjects* at 97 (cited in note 60).

78. Mazur, *Guide* at 19.

79. John H. Mueller, *Ignorance Is Neither Bliss Nor Ethical*, NwS 809, 813–814 (2007).

80. Drawn from Wendy Terry et al., *Hospice Patients' Views on Research in Palliative Care*, 36 Internal Medicine J 406, 406 (2006) (doi: 10.1111j.1445-5994.2006.01078.x), and Susan Jane Alexander, *'As Long as It Helps Somebody': Why Vulnerable People Participate in Research*, 16 Intl J Palliative Nursing 173, 174 (2010).

81. Eleanor Singer & Felice J. Levine, *Protection of Human Subjects of Research: Recent Developments and Future Prospects for the Social Sciences*, 67 Public Opinion Quarterly 148, 163 (2003).

82. Elana Newman & Danny G. Kaloupek, *The Risks and Benefits of Participating in Trauma-Focused Research Studies*, 17 J Traumatic Stress 383, 383 (2004).

83. Kirsten Bell & Amy Salmon, *Good Intentions and Dangerous Assumptions: Research Ethics Committees and Illicit Drug Use Research*, 8 Research Ethics 191, 192 (2012) (doi: 10.1177/1747016112461731).

84. Campbell, Human Subjects Policy Conference at 9 (cited in note 62).

85. Newman & Kaloupek, 17 J Traumatic Stress at 390 (cited in note 82).

86. Zachary Schrag, *Ignorance Is Strength: Pseudo-Expertise and the Regulation of Human Subjects Research*, Keynote Talk for "Outside Authority," Science & Technology in Society (STS) Conference, Virginia Tech, 2011, at 8.

87. Kathryn A. Becker-Blease & Jennifer J. Freyd, *Research Participants Telling the Truth About Their Lives: The Ethics of Asking and Not Asking About Abuse*, 61 American Psychologist 218, 223 (2006).

88. John D. Lantos, *Should Institutional Review Board Decisions Be Evidence-Based?*, 161 Archives of Pediatrics & Adolescent Medicine 516, 516 (2007).

89. Becker-Blease & Freyd, 61 American Psychologist at 221 (cited in note 87).

90. Ibid.

91. Newman & Kaloupek, 17 J Traumatic Stress at 390–391 (cited in note 82).

92. Becker-Blease & Freyd, 61 American Psychologist at 221 (cited in note 87).

93. Ibid.

94. Ibid at 222.

95. Ibid at 221.

96. Newman & Kaloupek, 17 J Traumatic Stress at 383 (cited in note 82).

97. Ibid at 385–390.

98. Ibid.

99. NBAC, *Ethical and Policy Issues* at 83–84 (cited in note 2).

100. Larry Gostin, *Hospitals, Health Care Professionals, and AIDS: The "Right to Know" the Health Status of Professionals and Patients*, 48 Maryland L Rev 12, 38 & 39 (1989).

101. Jeffrey M. Moulton et al., *Results of a One Year Longitudinal Study of HIV Antibody Test Notification from the San Francisco General Hospital Cohort*, 4 J Acquired Immune Deficiency Syndromes 787, 791 (1991).

102. Elaine M. Sieff et al., *Anticipated versus Actual Reaction to HIV Test Results*, 112 Am J Psychology 297, 299 (1999) (emphasis added).

103. Amy R. Sheon et al., *Preventing Discrimination Against Volunteers in Prophylactic HIV Vaccine Trials: Lessons from a Phase II Trial*, 19 J Acquired Immune Deficiency Syndromes & Human Retrovirology 519, 523 (1998).

104. Roxanna Alcaraz et al., *The Effects on Children of Participating in Studies of Minors' Access to Tobacco*, 26 Preventative Medicine 236, 240 (1997).

105. Scott D. Halpern et al., *Empirical Assessment of Whether Moderate Payments Are Undue or Unjust Inducements for Participation in Clinical Trials*, 164 ArIM 801, 803 (2004) (emphasis added).

106. Laurie Sloane & Jay Hull, *Deception of Research Subjects*, in Bankert & Amdur 213–214.

107. IOM, *Responsible Research* at 61 (cited in note 3).

108. Mazur, *Guide* at 15.

109. Labott & Johnson, 26 BMJ at 12 (cited in note 75).

110. Elisabeth Smith Parrott, *Ethnographic Research*, in Bankert & Amdur 404.

111. Levine, *Ethics and Regulation* at 48 (cited in note 4).

112. Hadjistavropoulos & Smythe, 11 Ethics & Behavior at 165 (cited in note 58).

113. NBAC, *Ethical and Policy Issues* at 72 (cited in note 2).

114. R. A. Laud Humphreys, *Tearoom Trade: Impersonal Sex in Public Places* (Aldine Transaction, 2007).

115. Zachary M. Schrag, *Ethical Imperialism: Institutional Review Boards and the Social Sciences, 1965–2009* 14 (Johns Hopkins University Press, 2010).

116. William D. Schlaff et al., *Increasing Burden of Institutional Review in Multicenter Clinical Trials of Infertility: The Reproductive Medicine Network Experience with the Pregnancy in Polycystic Ovary Syndrome (PPCOS) I and II Studies*, 96 Fertility & Sterility 15, 17 (2011) (doi: 10.1016/j.fertnstert.2011.05.069).

117. Schneider, *The Practice of Autonomy* (cited in note 31).

118. Bayless Manning, *The Purity Potlatch: An Essay on Conflicts of Interest, American Government, and Moral Escalation*, 24 Federal Bar J 239, 253 (1964).

119. Frank Anechiarico & James B. Jacobs, *The Pursuit of Absolute Integrity: How Corruption Control Makes Government Ineffective* 23 (University of Chicago Press, 1996).

120. Greg Koski, *Tipping Point, Over the Top, or Just Noncompliance as Usual?*, 38 HCR 27, 29 (2008).

121. Greg Koski, *Research Ethics and the Intensive Care Unit: Getting Behind the Wheel*, 31 Critical Care Medicine S119, S120 (2003).

122. Greg Koski, *Beyond Compliance … Is It Too Much to Ask?*, 25 IRB 5, 6 (2003).

123. Laurence B. McCullough, review of Jerry Menikoff & Edward P. Richards, *What the Doctor Didn't Say: The Hidden Truth about Medical Research*, 297 JAMA 1496, 1497 (2007).

124. Mazur, *Guide* at 30.

125. Ibid at 3.

126. Norman Fost, *Fusing and Confusing Ethics and Regulations*, in Paula Knudson et al., eds., *1974–2005 PRIM&R Through the Years: Three Decades of Protecting Human Subjects* 457 (PRIM&R Boston, 2006).

127. Edward L. Pattullo, *Governmental Regulation of the Investigation of Human Subjects in Social Research*, 23 Minerva 521, 531 (1985).

128. Will C. van den Hoonaard, *Is Research Ethics Review a Moral Panic?*, 38 Canadian Review of Sociology & Anthropology 19, 30 (2001).

129. Carol A. Heimer, *Thinking About How to Avoid Thought: Deep Norms, Shallow Rules, and the Structure of Attention*, 2 Regulation & Governance 30, 43–44 (2008).

130. Ronald F. White, *Institutional Review Board Mission Creep: The Common Rule, Social Science, and the Nanny State*, 11 Independent Review 547, 554 (2007).

131. Donna Shalala, *Protecting Research Subjects—What Must Be Done*, 343 NEJM 808, 809–810 (2000).

132. IOM, *Responsible Research* at 5 (cited in note 3). Emphases in this paragraph and the next two are added.

133. NRC & IOM, *Ethical Considerations for Research on Housing-Related Health Hazards Involving Children* 8 (NAP, 2005).

134. Robert Klitzman, *The Myth of Community Differences as the Cause of Variations Among IRBs*, 2 AJOB Primary Research 24, 29 (2011) (doi: 10.1080/21507716.2011.601284).

135. David Hyman, *Institutional Review Boards: Is This the Least Worst We Can Do?*, 101 NwS 749, 768 (2007).

136. E. L. Pattullo, *Reconciling Risk and Regulation*, 18 Society 34, 35 (1980).

137. Philip Hamburger, *The New Censorship: Institutional Review Boards*, 2004 Supreme Court Review 271, 341.

138. ALI, Restatement (Second) of Torts § 46(1) (emphasis added).

139. Ibid § 46 Comment (d).

140. 562 US ___, ___ (2011); 131 S.Ct. 1207, 1211 (2011).

141. *Watchtower Bible & Tract Society of New York v. Village of Stratton*, 536 US 150, 160 (2001).

142. *Memphis Community School District v. Stachura*, 477 US 299, 308 (1986).

143. ALI, Restatement (Second) of Torts, § 46, Comment (b).

144. *Memphis*, 477 US at 310 (cited in note 142).

145. ALI, Restatement (Second) of Torts, § 46, Comment (d).

146. 45 CFR 46.102(I).

147. Mattathias Schwartz, *The Trolls Among Us*, New York Times Sunday Magazine (August 3, 2008) (available at www.nytimes.com/2008/08/03/magazine/03trools-t.html?pagewanted=all&_5=O).

148. The husband of one of the *Real Housewives of Beverly Hills*, apparently despairing over financial and marital woes, killed himself partly because he feared the show's vilification (http://www.nytimes.com/2011/09/07/arts/television/beverly-hills-housewives-goes-on-after-a-suicide.html, accessed January 10, 2012). A Jenny Jones show guest later murdered another male guest who had said he was attracted to him (http://en.wikipedia.org/wiki/The_Jenny_Jones_Show, accessed January 10, 2012).

149. Levine, *Ethics and Regulation* at 46 (cited in note 4).

150. E.L. Pattullo, *Who Risks What in Social Research?*, 2 IRB: A Review of Human Subjects Research 1, 12 (1980).

151. Caroline H. Bledsoe et al., *Regulating Creativity: Research and Survival in the IRB Iron Cage*, NwS 593, 604 (2007).

152. Sydney A. Halpern, *Lesser Harms: The Morality of Risk in Medical Research* (University of Chicago Press, 2004).

CHAPTER 2

1. Adil E. Shamoo & Felix A. Khin-Maung-Gyi, *Ethics of the Use of Human Subjects in Research* 58 (Garland Science, 2002).

2. NBAC, *Ethical and Policy Issues in Research Involving Human Participants: Report and Recommendations* i (2001).

3. Alison Wichman, *Protecting Vulnerable Research Subjects: Practical Realities of Institutional Review Board Review and Approval*, 1 J Health Care Law & Policy 88, 99 (1998).

4. John Dewey, *The Ethics of Animal Experimentation*, The Atlantic (September 1926).

5. Richard Preston, *Foreword*, in Donald A. Henderson, *Smallpox: The Death of a Disease* 12 (Prometheus, 2009).

6. William D. Nordhaus, *The Health of Nations: The Contribution of Improved Health to Living Standards*, in Kevin M. Murphy & Robert H. Topel, eds., *Measuring the Gains from Medical Research: An Economic Approach* 35 (University of Chicago Press, 2003).

7. Paul Heidenreich & Mark McClellan, *Biomedical Research and Then Some: The Causes of Technological Change in Heart Attack Treatment*, in Kevin M. Murphy & Robert H. Topel, eds., *Measuring the Gains* 163–164 (University of Chicago Press, 2003).

8. William Burman & Robert Daum, *Grinding to a Halt: The Effects of the Increasing Regulatory Burden on Research and Quality Improvement Efforts*, 49 Clinical Infectious Diseases 328, 328 (2009) (doi: 10.1086/605454).

9. David J. Stewart & Razelle Kurzrock, *Cancer: The Road to Amiens*, 27 J Clinical Oncology 328 (2009) (doi: 10.1200/JCO.2008.18.9621).

10. J. L. Marsh et al., *AOA Symposium: Barriers (Threats) to Clinical Research*, 90 J Bone & Joint Surgery 1769, 1769 (2008) (doi: 10.2106/JBJS.G.01422).

11. Susan H. Wootton et al., *Unproven Therapies in Clinical Research and Practice: The Necessity to Change the Regulatory Paradigm*, 132 Pediatrics 599, 600 (2013) (doi: 10.1542/peds.2013-0778).

12. Michelle H. Biros, *Research without Consent: Exception from and Waiver of Informed Consent in Resuscitation Research*, 13 Science & Engineering Ethics 361 (2007).

13. Brian T. Bateman et al., *Conducting Stroke Research with an Exception from the Requirement for Informed Consent*, 34 Stroke 1317 (2003).

14. Norman Fost, *Waived Consent for Emergency Research*, 24 American J Law & Medicine 163, 164 (1998).

15. *Protection of Human Subjects; Informed Consent and Waiver of Informed Consent Requirements in Certain Emergency Research; Final Rules*, 61 Fed Reg 51498, 51498 (1996).

16. DHHS, *Waiver of Informed Consent Requirements in Certain Emergency Research*, 61 Fed Reg 51531–51533 (October 2, 1996). FDA promulgated nearly identical rules in 21 CFR 50.24.

17. Sandra J. Carnahan, *Promoting Medical Research without Sacrificing Patient Autonomy: Legal and Ethical Issues Raised by the Waiver of Informed Consent for Emergency Research*, 52 Oklahoma L Rev 565, 566 (1999).

18. Emily S. Dix et al., *Implementation of Community Consultation for Waiver of Informed Consent in Emergency Research: One Institutional Review Board's Experience*, 52 J Investigative Medicine 113 (2004).

19. Mark Stuart Kremers et al., *Initial Experience Using the Food and Drug Administration Guidelines for Emergency Research without Consent*, 33 Annals Emergency Medicine 224 (1999).

20. Frank W. Moler, *Resuscitation Research and the Final Rule: Is There an Impasse?*, 114 Pediatrics 859 (2004) (doi: 10.1542/peds.2004-1458).

21. Amy A. Ernst & Susan Fish, *Exception from Informed Consent: Viewpoint of Institutional Review Boards*, 12 AEM 1050 (2005).

22. Michelle Biros, *Struggling with the Rule: The Exception from Informed Consent in Resuscitation Research*, 14 AEM 344 (2007).

23. Laura J. Damschroder et al., *Patients, Privacy and Trust: Patients' Willingness to Allow Researchers to Access Their Medical Records*, 64 SSM 223, 224 (2007).

24. Stephanie K. Gonzalez & Thomas S. Helling, *Effect of the Final Rule on the Conduct of Emergency Clinical Research*, 64 Trauma 1665 (2008).

25. G. Nichol et al., *Impact of Informed Consent Requirements on Cardiac Arrest Research in the United States: Exception from Consent or from Research?*, 62 Resuscitation 3 (2004).

26. Katherine M. Hiller et al., *Impact of the Final Rule on the Rate of Clinical Cardiac Arrest Research in the United States*, 12 AEM 1091 (2005).

27. Henry Halperin et al., *Recommendations for Implementation of Community Consultation and Public Disclosure under the Food and Drug Administration's "Exception from Informed Consent Requirements for Emergency Research": A Special Report from the American Heart Association Emergency Cardiovascular Care Committee and Council on Cardiopulmonary, Perioperative and Critical Care*, 116 Circulation 1855 (2007).

28. Hiller et al., 12 AEM at 1091 (cited in note 26).

29. Joshua G. Salzman et al., *Implementing Emergency Research Requiring Exception from Informed Consent, Community Consultation, and Public Disclosure*, 50 Annals of Emergency Medicine 448 (2007) (doi:10.1016/j.annemergmed.2006.10.013).

30. Charles Contant et al., *Community Consultation in Emergency Research*, 34 Critical Care Medicine 2051 (2006).

31. Dix et al., 52 J Investigative Medicine at 115 (cited in note 18).

32. Kremers et al., 33 Annals Emergency Medicine at 224 (cited in note 19).

33. Vincent N. Mosesso, Jr. et al., *Conducting Research Using the Emergency Exception from Informed Consent: The Public Access Defibrillation (PAD) Trial Experience*, 61 Resuscitation 29 (2004).

34. Joseph A. Catania et al., *Survey of U.S. Human Research Protection Organizations: Workload and Membership*, 3 JERHRE 57 (2008) (doi: 10.1525/jer.2008.3.4.57).

35. John H. Mueller, *Ignorance Is Neither Bliss Nor Ethical*, NwS 809, 822.

36. Todd Zywicki, *Institutional Review Boards as Academic Bureaucracies: An Economic and Experiential Analysis*, NwS 861.

37. Monika Pogorzelska et al., *Changes in the Institutional Review Board Submission Process for Multicenter Research Over 6 Years*, 58 Nursing Outlook 181, 184–185 (2010) (doi: 10.1016/j.outlook.2010.04.003).

38. Jeanne L. Speckman et al., *Determining the Costs of Institutional Review Boards*, 29 BMJ 7 (2007).

39. Todd H. Wagner et al., *Costs and Benefits of the National Cancer Institute Central Institutional Review Board*, 28 J Clinical Oncology 662, 665 (2010) (doi: 10.1200/JCO.2009.23.2470).

40. James Bell et al., *Final Report: Evaluation of NIH Implementation of Section 491 of the Public Health Service Act, Mandating a Program of Protection for Research Subjects*, Office of Extramural Research, National Institutes of Health 7 (1998).

41. Ibid at 8.

42. Ibid at 41.

43. Robert L. Klitzman, *Local IRBs vs. Federal Agencies: Shifting Dynamics, Systems, and Relationships*, 7 JERHRE 50, 54–55 (2012) (doi: 10.1525/jer.2012.7.3.50).

44. Sydney Halpern, *Hybrid Design, Systematic Rigidity: Institutional Dynamics in Human Research Oversight*, 2 Regulation & Governance 85, 96 (2008).

45. See NRC, *Protecting Participants and Facilitating Social and Behavioral Sciences Research* 2–3 (NAP, 2003) 36; Philip Hamburger, *The New Censorship: Institutional Review Boards*, 2004 Supreme Court Review 271, 345.

46. Wade Rich et al., *Antenatal Consent in the SUPPORT Trial: Challenges, Costs, and Representative Enrollment*, 126 Pediatrics 215 (2010).

47. Pogorzelska et al., 58 Nursing Outlook at 183 (cited in note 37).

48. William D. Schlaff et al., *Increasing Burden of Institutional Review in Multicenter Clinical Trials of Infertility*, 96 Fertility and Sterility 1, 2 (2011) (doi: 10.1016/j.fertnstert.2011.05.069).

49. Markus Hessling, *When Dr. Mopp Tried to Get into Research*, 329 BMJ 279, 279 (2004).

50. NBAC, *Ethical and Policy Issues* at vii (cited in note 2).

51. IOM, *Responsible Research: A Systems Approach to Protecting Research Participants* 61 (NAP, 2003).

52. NBAC, *Ethical and Policy Issues* at 15 (cited in note 2).

53. Ibid at vii.

54. Bell et al., *Final Report* at 66–67 (cited in note 40).

55. Lee A. Green et al., *IRB and Methodological Issues: Impact of Institutional Review Board Practice Variation on Observational Health Services Research*, 41 HSR: Health Services Research 214, 216 (2006).

56. Bell et al., *Final Report* at 11 (cited in note 40).

57. Salim Yusuf, *Randomized Clinical Trials: Slow Death by a Thousand Unnecessary Policies?*, 171 CMAJ 889, 889 (2004).

58. Zywicki, *Institutional Review Boards Note* at 882 (cited in note 36).

59. 45 CFR 46.114.

60. Keith Humphreys et al., *The Cost of Institutional Review Board Procedures in Multicenter Observational Research*, 139 Annals of Internal Medicine 77 (2003).

61. C. C. Vick et al., *Variation in Institutional Review Processes for a Multisite Observational Study*, 190 American J Surgery 805 (2005).

62. Drawn from Fredric L. Coe, *The Costs and Benefits of a Well-Intended Parasite: A Witness and Reporter on the IRB Phenomenon*, NwS 723–734.

63. L. S. Gittner et al., *Health Service Research: The Square Peg in Human Subjects Protection Regulations*, 37 J Medical Ethics 118–122 (2011) (doi: 10.1136/jme.2010.037226).

64. Mylaina L. Sherwood et al., *Unique Challenges of Obtaining Regulatory Approval for a Multicenter Protocol to Study the Genetics of RRP and Suggested Remedies*, 135 Otolaryngology-Head & Neck Surgery 189, 190–191 (2006) (doi: 10.1016/j.otohns.2006.03.028).

65. 45 CFR 46.110(b).

66. Scott Burris & Kathryn Moss, *U.S. Health Researchers Review Their Ethics Review Boards: A Qualitative Study*, 1 JERHRE 39, 51 (2006). Expedited reviews took longer (mean, 54.8 days) than "either exempt (mean, 10.8 days) or full (mean, 47.1 days) reviews." Elaine Larson et al., *A Survey of IRB Process in 68 U.S. Hospitals*, 36 J Nursing Scholarship 260, 261 (2004). "Our finding that expedited reviews took longer than full board reviews is consistent with one other" UK study. Ibid at 262.

67. Cristina I. Cann & Kenneth J. Rothman, *IRBs and Epidemiologic Research: How Inappropriate Restrictions Hamper Studies*, 6 IRB 5, 7 (1984).

68. Penelope M. Jester et al., *Regulatory Challenges: Lessons from Recent West Nile Virus Trials in the United States*, 27 Contemporary Clinical Trials 254, 254 (2006) (doi: 10.1016/j.cct.2006.02.004).

69. Ibid at 258.

70. Samuel P. Jacobs, *Stern Lessons for Terrorism Expert*, Harvard Crimson (March 23, 2007).

71. Thomas L. Beauchamp, *Viewpoint: Why Our Conceptions of Research and Practice May Not Serve the Best Interest of Patients and Subjects*, 269 J Internal Medicine 383, 385 (2011).

72. Drawn from Sunday Clark et al., *Feasibility of a National Fatal Asthma Registry: More Evidence of IRB Variation in Evaluation of a Standard Protocol*, 43 J Asthma 19 (2006).

73. Available at http://www.aafa.org/display.cfm?sub=42&id=8.

74. Elvi Whittaker, *Adjudicating Entitlements: The Emerging Discourses of Research Ethics Boards*, 9 Health 513, 528–529 (2005).

75. Cann & Rothman, 6 IRB at 6 (cited in note 67).

76. Kathryn A. Becker-Blease & Jennifer J. Freyd, *Research Participants Telling the Truth About Their Lives: The Ethics of Asking and Not Asking About Abuse*, 61 American Psychologist 218, 219 (2006).

77. Page S. Morahan et al., *New Challenges Facing Interinstitutional Social Science and Educational Program Evaluation Research at Academic Centers: A Case Study from the ELAM Program*, 81 AM 527 (2006).

78. Jacobs, *Stern Lessons* (cited in note 70).

79. John F. Galliher et al., *Laud Humphreys: Prophet of Homosexuality and Sociology* 101–102 (University of Wisconsin Press, 2004).

80. Jack V. Tu et al., *Impracticability of Informed Consent in the Registry of the Canadian Stroke Network*, 350 NEJM 1414 (2004).

81. Michelle Ng Gong et al., *Surrogate Consent for Research Involving Adults with Impaired Decision Making: Survey of Institutional Review Board Practices*, 38 Critical Care Medicine 2146, 2153 (2010) (doi: 10.1097/CCM.0b013e3181f26fe6).

82. Sarah M. Greene et al., *Impact of IRB Requirements on a Multicenter Survey of Prophylactic Mastectomy Outcomes*, 16 Annals of Epidemiology 275 (2006).

83. William W. Lowrance, *Learning from Experience: Privacy and the Secondary Use of Data in Health Research* 4 (Nuffield Trust, 2002).

84. D. H. Brewster et al., *Cancer Information Under Threat: The Case for Legislation*, 12 Annals of Oncology 2, 145 (2001).

85. Enrique Regidor, *The Use of Personal Data from Medical Records and Biological Materials: Ethical Perspectives and the Basis for Legal Restrictions in Health Research*, 59 SSM 1975, 1979 (2004) (doi: 10.1016/j.socscimed.2004.02.032).

86. David Armstrong et al., *Potential Impact of the HIPAA Privacy Rule on Data Collection in a Registry of Patients with Acute Coronary Syndrome*, 165 Archives of Internal Medicine 1125, 1127–1128 (2005).

87. Fred H. Cate, *Principles for Protecting Privacy*, 22 Cato J 33, 53 (2002).

88. Norman Fost, Interview by Patricia C. El-Hinnawy, *OHRP: Oral History of the Belmont Report and the National Commission for the Protection of Human*

Subjects of Biomedical and Behavioral Research, Belmont Oral History Project 10 (May 13, 2004).

89. Simon N. Whitney et al., *Principal Investigator Views of the IRB System*, 5 International J Medical Sciences 68, 72 (2008).

90. Kirsten Bell & Amy Salmon, *What Women Who Use Drugs Have to Say About Ethical Research: Findings of an Exploratory Qualitative Study*, 6 JERHRE 84, 85 (2011) (doi: 10.1525/jer.2011.6.4.84).

91. NRC & IOM, *Ethical Considerations for Research on Housing-Related Health Hazards Involving Children* (NAP, 2005).

92. Caroline H. Bledsoe et al., *Regulating Creativity: Research and Survival in the IRB Iron Cage*, NwS 593, 620 (2007).

93. Stephanie S. Park & Mitchell H. Grayson, *Clinical Research: Protection of the "Vulnerable"?*, 121 J Allergy & Clinical Immunology 1103, 1105–1106 (2008) (doi: 10.1016/j.jaci.2008.01.014).

94. Rich et al., *Antenatal Consent* at 215 (cited in note 46); Simon N. Whitney, *The Python's Embrace: Clinical Research Regulation by Institutional Review Boards*, 129 Pediatrics 576 (2012) (doi:10.1542/peds.2011-3455).

95. Leslie Acoca, *Are Those Cookies for Me or My Baby? Understanding Detained and Incarcerated Teen Mothers and Their Children*, 55 Juvenile & Family Court J 65 (2004).

96. Bledsoe et al., NwS at 621 (cited in note 92).

97. Dale Carpenter, *Institutional Review Boards, Regulatory Incentives, and Some Modest Proposals for Reform*, NwS 687, 693 (2007).

98. Bledsoe et al., NwS at 604 (cited in note 92).

99. Philip Hamburger, *The New Censorship: Institutional Review Boards*, 2004 Supreme Court Review 271, 294.

100. Mark H. Ashcraft & Jeremy A. Krause, *Social and Behavioral Researchers' Experiences with Their IRBs*, 17 Ethics & Behavior 1, 15 (2007).

101. Bledsoe et al., NwS at 620 (cited in note 92).

102. Kevin D. Haggerty, *Ethics Creep: Governing Social Science Research in the Name of Ethics*, 27 Qualitative Sociology 391, 406 (2004).

103. Zachary M. Schrag, *Ethical Imperialism: Institutional Review Boards and the Social Sciences, 1965–2009* 14 (Johns Hopkins University Press, 2010).

104. Gittner et al., 37 J Medical Ethics at 118 (cited in note 63).

105. David A. Thompson et al., *Variation in Local Institutional Review Board Evaluations of a Multicenter Patient Safety Study*, 34 J Healthcare Quality 33, 37 (2012).

106. Will C. van den Hoonaard, *Seduction of Ethics: Transforming the Social Sciences* 255 (University of Toronto Press, 2011).

107. Robert J. Levine, *Ethics and Regulation of Clinical Research* 333 (Yale University Press, 1988) (2nd ed).

108. Law & Society Association, Membership & Professional Issues Committee, *The Impact of Institutional Review Boards (IRBs) on Law & Society Researchers* 7 (2007).

109. Green et al., 41 HSR at 216 (cited in note 55).

110. Ashcraft & Krause, 7 Ethics and Behavior at 12 (cited in note 100).

111. Hamburger, 2004 S Ct Rev at 335 (cited in note 45).

112. Beauchamp, 269 J Internal Medicine at 383–84 (cited in note 71) (doi: 10.1111/j.1365-2796.2001.2350.x).

113. Ibid at 385.

114. Ann R. Stark et al., *Variation Among Institutional Review Boards in Evaluating the Design of a Multicenter Randomized Trial*, 30 J Perinatology 163 (2009) (doi:10.1038/jp.2009.157).

115. Amy Flowers, *The Fantasy Factory: An Insider's View of the Phone Sex Industry* 22 (University of Pennsylvania Press, 1998).

116. Green et al., 41 HSR at 226 (cited in note 55).

117. Van den Hoonaard, *Seduction of Ethics* at 134 (cited in note 106).

118. Mitch Librett & Dina Perrone, *Apples and Oranges: Ethnography and the IRB*, 10 Qualitative Research 729, 737 (2010) (doi: 10.1177/1468794110380548).

119. Zachary Schrag, *Criminologists: IRB Demands Threatened Confidentiality*, Institutional Review Blog (November 23, 2011), http://www.institutionalreview blog.com/2011/11/criminologists-irb-demands-threatened.html.

120. Matt Bradley, *Silenced for Their Own Protection: How the IRB Marginalizes Those It Feigns to Protect*, 6 ACME 339 (2007).

121. Schrag, *Ethical Imperialism* at 2 (cited in note 103).

122. Lynne Kipnis, *Case Study: An Undergraduate's Experience with Human Subjects Review Committees*, in Murray L. Wax & Joan Cassell, eds., *Federal Regulations: Ethical Issues and Social Research* 219 (Westview, 1979).

123. Ronald F. White, *Institutional Review Board Mission Creep: The Common Rule, Social Science, and the Nanny State*, 11 Independent Review 547, 559 (2007).

124. Schrag, *Ethical Imperialism* at 166 (cited in note 103).

125. C. K. Gunsalus, *Rethinking Protections for Human Subjects*, 49 Chronicle of Higher Education B4 (2002).

126. Malcolm M. Feeley, *Legality, Social Research, and the Challenge of Institutional Review Boards*, 41 Law & Society 757, 769–770 (2007).

127. Todd Zywicki, *Institutional Review Boards as Academic Bureaucracies*, NwS 861, 867 (cited in note 36).

128. Van den Hoonaard, *Seduction of Ethics* at 232 (cited in note 106).

129. Bledsoe et al., NwS at 622 (cited in note 92).

130. Dvora Yanow & Peregrine Schwartz-Shea, *Reforming Institutional Review Board Policy: Issues in Implementation and Field Research*, 41 Political Science & Politics 483, 485 (2008).

131. Feeley, 41 Law and Society at 764 (cited in note 126).

132. Robert T. Sataloff, *HIPAA: An Impediment to Research*, 87 ENT: Ear, Nose & Throat J 182, 184 (2008).

133. Burman & Daum, Clinical Infectious Diseases at 330 (cited in note 8).

134. Ibid.

135. Van den Hoonaard, *Seduction of Ethics* at 238–239 (cited in note 106).

136. Fost, Interview at 11 (cited in note 88).

137. Sarah M. Greene et al., *Impact of the HIPAA Privacy Rule in the HMO Research Network: A Sub-study for the Institute of Medicine Committee on Health Research and the Privacy of Health Information: The HIPAA Privacy Rule*, NAS 13 (2008).

138. Coe, NwS at 724 (cited in note 62).

139. Bledsoe et al., NwS at 619 (cited in note 92).

140. Mark J. Rice, *The Institutional Review Board Is an Impediment to Human Research: The Result Is More Animal-Based Research*, 6 Philosophy, Ethics, & Humanities in Medicine 1 (2011).

141. Bledsoe et al., NwS at 622 (cited in note 92).

142. Robert Klitzman, *The Ethics Police?: IRBs' Views Concerning Their Power*, 6 PLoS One, 1, 3–4 (2011) (doi: 10/1371/journal/pone.00287730).

143. Yanow & Schwartz-Shea, 41 Political Science & Politics at 483 (cited in note 130).

144. Elmer D. Abbo, *Promoting Free Speech in Clinical Quality Improvement Research*, NwS 575, 576–578 (2007).

145. Brian E. Mavis & Rebecca C. Henry, *Being Uninformed on Informed Consent: A Pilot Survey of Medical Education Faculty*, 5 Bio Med Central Medical Education 1, 4 (2005) (doi: 10.1186/1472-6920-5-12).

146. Gail M. Sullivan, *Education Research and Human Subject Protection: Crossing the IRB Quagmire*, 3 J Graduate Medical Education 1, 2 (2011) (doi: 10.4300/JGME-D-11-00004.1).

147. John M. Tomkowiak & Anne J. Gunderson, *To IRB or Not to IRB?*, 79 Academic Medicine 628 (2004).

148. Coe, NwS at 726 (cited in note 62).

149. Paul Fussell, *Wartime: Understanding and Behavior in the Second World War* 80 (Oxford University Press, 1990).

150. Van den Hoonaard, *Seduction of Ethics* at 47 (cited in note 106).

151. Scott, quoted in Will C. van den Hoonaard, *Seduction of Ethics* at 180 (cited in note 106).

152. Yvonna S. Lincoln & William G. Tierney, *Qualitative Research and Institutional Review Boards*, 10 Qualitative Inquiry 219, 222 (2004).

153. Van den Hoonaard, *Seduction of Ethics* at 190 (cited in note 106).

154. Ibid at 243.

155. Ibid at 133.

156. Rory Collins et al., *Ethics of Clinical Trials*, in C. J. Williams, ed., *Introducing New Treatments for Cancer: Practical, Ethical, and Legal Problems*, 49 (Wiley, 1992).

157. Ibid at 54.

158. ISIS-2 (Second International Study of Infarct Survival) Collaborative Group, *Randomized Trial of Intravenous Streptokinase, Oral Aspirin, Both, or Neither Among 17 187 Cases of Suspected Acute Myocardial Infarction: ISIS-2*, 332 Lancet 349 (1988) (doi:10.1016/S0140-6736(88)92833-4).

159. P. Edwards et al., *Final Results of MRC CRASH, a Randomized Placebo-Controlled Trial of Intravenous Corticosteroid in Adults with Head Injury—Outcomes at 6 Months*, 365 Lancet 1957 (2005).

160. Iain Chalmers, *Regulation of Therapeutic Research Is Compromising the Interests of Patients*, 21 International J Pharmaceutical Medicine 395, 396–397 (2007).

PART II

1. The closest thing to an exception—OHRP's 2011 "advanced notice of proposed rulemaking" described in the Introduction—hardly does more than prove the rule. It accepts the system's essentials and would actually worsen the system in some ways, and as of this writing new rules have not emerged.

2. Frank H. Easterbrook, *What's So Special About Judges?*, 61 U Colorado L Rev 773, 778-779 (1990).

3. Eric A. Posner, *A Theory of Contract Law Under Conditions of Radical Judicial Error*, University of Chicago Law School, John M. Olin Law & Economics Working Paper No. 80 at 7 (1999).

4. Ibid at 12.

5. Neil Vidmar, *The Psychology of Trial Judging*, 20 Current Directions in Psychological Science 58 (2011) (doi: 10.1177/0963721410397283).

6. Lee Epstein et al., *The Behavior of Federal Judges: A Theoretical & Empirical Study of Rational Choice* 6 (Harvard University Press, 2013).

7. Chris Guthrie et al., *Inside the Judicial Mind*, 86 Cornell L Rev 777, 782–783 (2001).

8. Ibid at 779.

9. Ibid at 784.

10. Chris Guthrie et al., *Blinking on the Bench: How Judges Decide Cases*, 93 Cornell L Rev, 1, 27–28 (2007).

11. Birte Englich et al., *Playing Dice with Criminal Sentences: The Influence of Irrelevant Anchors on Experts' Judicial Decision Making*, 32 Personality & Social Psychology Bulletin 188 (2006).

12. Shai Danziger et al., *Extraneous Factors in Judicial Decisions*, 42 PNAS 1, 2 (2010) (doi: 10.1073/pnas.1018033108).

13. Geoffrey P. Miller, *Bad Judges*, 83 Texas L. Rev. 431, 436 (2004).

14. Ibid *passim*.

15. Gregory C. Sisk et al., *Charting the Influences on the Judicial Mind: An Empirical Study of Judicial Reasoning*, 73 NYU L. Rev. 1377, 1390–1391 (1998).

16. Ibid at 1499.

17. Chris Guthrie et al., *Blinking on the Bench: How Judges Decide Cases*, 93 Cornell L Rev 1 (2007).

CHAPTER 3

1. June Gibbs Brown, *Institutional Review Boards: A Time For Reform*, DHHS, Office of Inspector General 8 (June 1998).

2. Norman M. Goldfarb, *Greg Koski on Human Subjects Protection*, 3 J Clinical Research Best Practices 1, 2 (2007).

3. Brenda Beagan & Michael McDonald, *Evidence-Based Practice of Research Ethics Review?*, 13 Health L Rev 62, 66 (2005).

4. Ibid at 63.

5. Carl Elliott, *When Medical Muckraking Fails*, Chronicle of Higher Education (August 2, 2012), http://chronicle.com/blogs/brainstorm/when-medical-muckraking-fails/50767.

6. IOM, *Responsible Research: A Systems Approach to Protecting Research Participants 5* (NAP, 2003).

7. Ibid at 44.

8. Sydney Halpern, *Hybrid Design, Systematic Rigidity: Institutional Dynamics in Human Research Oversight*, 2 Regulation & Governance 85 (2008).

9. Beagan & McDonald, at 65 (cited in note 3).

10. Robert L. Klitzman, *Local IRBs vs. Federal Agencies: Shifting Dynamics, Systems, and Relationships*, 7 JERHRE 50, 53 (2012) (doi: 10.1525/jer.2012.7.3.50).

11. Drawn from Robert Steinbrook, *How Best to Ventilate? Trial Design and Patient Safety in Studies of the Acute Respiratory Distress Syndrome*, 348 NEJM 1393 (2003).

12. David Magnus & Arthur L. Caplan, *Risk, Consent, and SUPPORT*, 368 NEJM 1864, 1864 (2013).

13. Kathy L. Hudson et al., *In Support of SUPPORT—A View from the NIH*, 368 NEJM 2349, 2350 (2013).

14. Ibid.

15. Magnus & Caplan at 1865 (cited in note 12).

16. Hudson et al. (cited in note 13).

17. Benjamin S. Wilfond et al., *The OHRP and SUPPORT*, 368 NEJM e36(1) (2013).

18. Jeffrey M. Drazen et al., *Informed Consent and SUPPORT*, 368 NEJM 1929 (2013).

19. John D. Lantos, *Learning the Right Lessons from the SUPPORT Study Controversy*, 99 Archives of Disease in Childhood: Fetal and Neonatal Edition F1, F2 (2013) (doi: 10.1136/archdischild-2013-304916).

20. Michelle Meyer, *OHRP Suspends Compliance Action Against SUPPORT Study Sites Pending Public Hearing & Guidance*, Harvard Petrie-Flom Center, Bill of Health, June 5, 2013.

21. Adil E. Shamoo & Felix A. Khin-Maung-Gyi, *Ethics of the Use of Human Subjects in Research* 54 (Garland Science, 2002).

22. Lee A. Green et al., *IRB and Methodological Issues: Impact of Institutional Review Board Practice Variation on Observational Health Services Research*, 41 HSR: Health Services Research 214, 214 (2006).

23. Drawn from Ann R. Stark et al., *Variation Among Institutional Review Boards in Evaluating the Design of a Multicenter Randomized Trial*, 30 J Perinatology 163 (2009) (doi:10.1038/jp.2009.157); Jon E. Tyson et al., *Vitamin A Supplementation for Extremely-Low-Birth-Weight Infants*, 340 NEJM 1962 (1999); Namasivayam Ambalavanan et al., *Vitamin A Supplementation for Extremely Low Birth Weight Infants: Outcome at 18 to 22 Months*, 115 Pediatrics e249 (2005) (doi: 10.1542/peds.2004-1812).

24. Eleanor Singer & Felice J. Levine, *Protection of Human Subjects of Research: Recent Developments and Future Prospects for the Social Sciences*, 67 Public Opinion Quarterly 148, 151 (2003).

25. Jerry Goldman & Martin D. Katz, *Inconsistency and Institutional Review Boards*, 248 JAMA 197 (1982).

26. Martin D. Katz & Jerry Goldman, *Reply: Compelling Evidence for New Policies*, IRB 6–7 (1984).

27. Goldman & Katz, 248 JAMA at 197 (cited in note 25).

28. Thomas O. Stair et al., *Variation in Institutional Review Board Responses to a Standard Protocol for a Multicenter Clinical Trial*, 8 AEM 636, 637 (2001).

29. E. Chaney et al., *Human Subjects Protection Issues in QUERI Implementation Research: QUERI Series*, 3 Implementation Science 10 (doi:10.1186/1748-5908-3-10).

30. Green et al., 41 HSR at 214 (cited in note 22); Elaine Larson et al., *A Survey of IRB Process in 68 U.S. Hospitals*, 36 J Nursing Scholarship 260, 263 (2004).

31. Mona Lydon-Rochelle & Victoria L. Holt, *HIPAA Transition: Challenges of a Multisite Medical Records Validation Study of Maternally Linked Birth Records*, 8 Maternal & Child Health J 1 (2004); Jon M. Hirshon et al., *Variability in Institutional Review Board Assessment of Minimal-Risk Research*, 9 AEM 1417 (2002); Larson et al., 36 J Nursing Scholarship at 260 (cited in note 30); Rita Mc-Williams et al., *Problematic Variation in Local Institutional Review of a Multi-center Genetic Epidemiology Study*, 290 JAMA 360 (2003); Monika Pogorzelska et al., *Changes in the Institutional Review Board Submission Process for Multi-center Research Over 6 Years*, 58 Nursing Outlook 181 (2010) (doi: 10.1016/j.outlook.2010.04.003).

32. Green et al., 41 HSR at 214 (cited in note 22).

33. Brian T. Helfand et al., *Variation in Institutional Review Board Responses to a Standard Protocol for a Multicenter Randomized, Controlled Surgical Trial*, 181 J Urology 2674 (2009) (doi: 10.1016/j.juro.2009.02.032); Goldman & Katz, 248 JAMA at 197 (cited in note 25); Michelle Ng Gong et al., *Surrogate Consent for Research Involving Adults with Impaired Decision Making: Survey of Institutional Review Board Practices*, 38 Critical Care Medicine 2146 (2010) (doi: 10.1097/CCM.0b013e3181f26fe6).

34. McWilliams et al., 290 JAMA at 360 (cited in note 31); Seema Shah et al., *How Do Institutional Review Boards Apply the Federal Risk and Benefit Standards for Pediatric Research?*, 291 JAMA 476 (2004).

35. Jonathan Mansbach et al., *Variation in Institutional Review Board Responses to a Standard, Observational, Pediatric Research Protocol*, 14 AEM 377 (2007) (doi: 10.1197/j.aem.2006.11.031); Audrey S. Rogers et al., *A Case Study in Adolescent Participation in Clinical Research: Eleven Clinical Sites, One Common Protocol, and Eleven IRBs*, 21 IRB 6 (1999).

36. McWilliams et al., 290 JAMA at 360 (cited in note 31).

37. Joshua S. Crites et al., *Payment to Participants in Pediatric Research: Variation in IRB Members' Attitudes*, 35 IRB: Ethics & Human Research 9 (Sept/Oct 2013).

38. Shah et al., 291 JAMA at 476 (cited in note 34).

39. Ann R. Stark et al., *Variation Among Institutional Review Boards in Evaluating the Design of a Multicenter Randomized Trial*, 30 J Perinatology 163 (2009) (doi:10.1038/jp.2009.157).

40. Helfand et al., 181 J Urology at 2674 (cited in note 33).

41. Amy Whittle et al., *Institutional Review Board Practices Regarding Assent in Pediatric Research*, 113 Pediatrics 1747 (2004).

42. Henry S. Silverman et al., *Variability Among Institutional Review Boards' Decisions within the Context of a Multicenter Trial*, 29 Critical Care Medicine 235 (2001).

43. Sunday Clark et al., *Feasibility of a National Fatal Asthma Registry: More Evidence of IRB Variation in Evaluation of a Standard Protocol*, 43 J Asthma 19 (2006) (doi 10-.1080/00102200500446896); Kathleen Dziak et al., *IRBs and*

Multisite Studies: Variations Among Institutional Review Boards Reviews in a Multisite Health Services Research Study, 40 HSR 279 (2006).

44. Silverman et al., 29 Critical Care Medicine at 235 (cited in note 42).

45. Sarah M. Greene et al., *Impact of IRB Requirements on a Multicenter Survey of Prophylactic Mastectomy Outcomes*, 16 Annals Epidemiology 275 (2006); Goldman & Katz, 248 JAMA 197 (cited in note 25).

46. Michael B. Kimberly et al., *Variation in Standards of Research Compensation and Child Assent Practices: A Comparison of 69 Institutional Review Board-Approved Informed Permission and Assent Forms for 3 Multicenter Pediatric Clinical Trials*, 117 Pediatrics 1706 (2006).

47. Rogers et al., 21 IRB at 6 (cited in note 35).

48. Greene et al., 16 Annals of Epidemiology at 275 (cited in note 45).

49. C. C. Vick et al., *Variation in Institutional Review Processes for a Multisite Observational Study*, 190 American J Surgery 805 (2005); Greene et al., 16 Annals Epidemiology at 275 (cited in note 45).

50. Greene et al., 16 Annals Epidemiology at 275 (cited in note 45).

51. Ibid.

52. Gong et al., 38 Critical Care Medicine at 2146 (cited in note 33).

53. Ibid.

54. Ibid.

55. Hirshon et al., 9 AEM at 1417 (cited in note 31).

56. Liselotte N. Dyrbye et al., *Medical Education Research and IRB Review: An Analysis and Comparison of the IRB Review Process at Six Institutions*, 82 Academic Medicine 654 (2007); Helfand et al., 181 J Urology at 2674 (cited in note 33); McWilliams et al., 290 JAMA at 360 (cited in note 31); William D. Schlaff et al., *Increasing Burden of Institutional Review in Multicenter Clinical Trials of Infertility: The Reproductive Medicine Network Experience with the Pregnancy in Polycystic Ovary Syndrome (PPCOS) I and II Studies*, 96 Fertility & Sterility 1 (2011) (doi: 10.1016/j.fertnstert.2011.05.069); Stair et al., 8 AEM at 636 (cited in note 28).

57. Kimberly et al., 117 Pediatrics at 1706 (cited in note 46); McWilliams et al., 290 JAMA at 360 (cited in note 31); Mylaina L. Sherwood et al., *Unique Challenges of Obtaining Regulatory Approval for a Multicenter Protocol to Study the Genetics of RRP and Suggested Remedies*, 135 Otolaryngology-Head & Neck Surgery 189 (2006) (doi: 10.1016/j.otohns.2006.03.028).

58. McWilliams et al., 290 JAMA at 360 (cited in note 31).

59. Kevin P. Weinfurt et al., *Policies of Academic Medical Centers for Disclosing Financial Conflicts of Interest to Potential Research Participants*, 81 AM 113 (2006).

60. Vick et al., 190 American J Surgery at 805 (cited in note 49).

61. Elizabeth R. Woods et al., *Assessing Youth Risk Behavior in a Clinical Trial Setting: Lessons from the Infant Health and Development Program*, 46 J of Adolescent Health 1 (2010) (doi: 10.1016/j.jadohealth.2009.10.010).

62. Vincent N. Mosesso, Jr., et al., *Conducting Research Using the Emergency Exception from Informed Consent: The Public Access Defibrillation (PAD) Trial Experience*, 61 Resuscitation 29 (2004).

63. Green et al., 41 HSR at 214 (cited in note 22).

64. Greene et al., 16 Annals of Epidemiology at 275 (cited in note 45).

65. Keith Humphreys et al., *The Cost of Institutional Review Board Procedures in Multicenter Observational Research*, 139 AnIM 77 (2003).

66. Pogorzelska et al., 58 Nursing Outlook at 181 (cited in note 31).

67. Green et al., 41 HSR at 225 (cited in note 22).

68. Goldman & Katz, 248 JAMA at 197 (cited in note 25).

69. Fredric L. Coe, *The Costs and Benefits of a Well-Intended Parasite: A Witness and Reporter on the IRB Phenomenon*, NwS 723 (2007).

70. Goldman & Katz, 248 JAMA at 197 (cited in note 25).

71. Robert Klitzman, *The Myth of Community Differences as the Cause of Variations Among IRBs*, 2 AJOB Primary Research 24, 26 (2011) (doi: 10.1080/21507716.2011.601284).

72. Ibid at 26.

73. Ibid at 28.

74. Green et al., 41 HSR at 214 (cited in note 22).

75. Ibid at 223.

76. Ibid at 225–226.

77. Shah et al., 291 JAMA at 478 (cited in note 34).

78. NRC & IOM, *Ethical Considerations for Research on Housing-Related Health Hazards Involving Children* 114–115 (NAP, 2005).

79. Jan Federici Jaeger, *An Ethnographic Analysis of Institutional Review Board Decision-Making*, Dissertation UMI Number 3246171 at 52 (2006).

80. Sherwood et al., 135 Otolaryngology-Head & Neck Surgery at 192–193 (cited in note 57).

81. Ibid at 190.

82. Bernard A. Fischer & Praveen George, *The Investigator and the IRB: A Survey of Depression and Schizophrenia Researchers*, 122 Schizophrenia Research 206, 211 (2010) (doi: 10.1016/j.schres.2009.12.019).

83. Eric C. Schneider et al., *Developing a System to Assess the Quality of Cancer Care: ASCO's National Initiative on Cancer Care Quality*, 22 J Clinical Oncology 2985, 2986 (2004).

84. Schlaff et al., 96 Fertility & Sterility at 5–6 (cited in note 56).

85. Helfand et al., 181 J Urology at 2674 (cited in note 33).

86. Paul Glasziou, *Ethics Review Roulette: What Can We Learn? That Ethics Review Has Costs and One Size Doesn't Fit All*, 328 BMJ 121, 122 (2004).

87. E. Angell et al., *Consistency in Decision Making by Research Ethics Committees: A Controlled Comparison*, 32 J Medical Ethics 662, 663 (2006).

88. John Saunders, *Research Ethics Committees—Time for Change?*, 2 Clinical Medicine 534, 534–535 (2002).

89. Green et al., 41 HSR at 225 (cited in note 22).

90. Klitzman, 2 AJOB Primary Research at 24 (cited in note 71).

91. Ezekiel J. Emanuel et al., *Oversight of Human Participants Research: Identifying Problems to Evaluate Reform Proposals*, 141 AnIM 282, 283 (2004).

92. Ivor A. Pritchard, *How Do IRB Members Make Decisions? A Review and Research Agenda*, 6 JERHRE 31, 33 (2011) (doi: 10.1525/jer.2011.6.2.31).

93. Stair et al., 8 AEM at 636 (cited in note 28).

94. Dale H. Cowan, *Human Experimentation: The Review Process in Practice*, 25 Case Western Reserve L Rev 533, 547 (1974).

95. Dawn F. Underwood, *Reporting Problems in Human Subjects Research: A Comparative Study* 75–76 (2010) (Indiana State University, Ph.D. Thesis).

96. Charles L. Bosk, *The New Bureaucracies of Virtue or When Form Fails to Follow Function*, 30 Political & Legal Anthropology Review 192, 202 (2007).

97. Sherwood et al., 135 Otolaryngology-Head & Neck Surgery at 192 (cited in note 57).

98. David Hyman, *Institutional Review Boards: Is This the Least Worst We Can Do?*, NwS 749, 758 (2007).

99. Goldman & Katz, 248 JAMA at 197 (cited in note 25).

100. Klitzman, 2 AJOB Primary Research at 30 (cited in note 71).

101. Ibid at 26.

102. *Crawford v. Washington*, 541 US 36, 63 (2003).

103. Charles W. Lidz et al., *How Closely Do Institutional Review Boards Follow the Common Rule?*, 87 AM 969, 973 (2012) (doi: 10.1097/ACM.0b013e3182575e2e).

104. Clifford Winston, *The Efficacy of Information Policy*, 46 J Economic Literature 704, 713–714 (2008).

105. Omri Ben-Shahar & Carl E. Schneider, *More Than You Wanted to Know: The Failure of Mandated Disclosure* (Princeton University Press, 2014). For criticism of informed consent, see Carl E. Schneider, *The Practice of Autonomy: Patients, Doctors, and Medical Decisions* (Oxford University Press, 1998).

106. OHRP, *Guidebook*, chapter 3.

107. Mary Dixon-Woods et al., *Beyond "Misunderstanding": Written Information and Decisions About Taking Part in a Genetic Epidemiology Study*, 6 SSM 2212, 2213 (2007) (doi: 10.1016/j.socscimed.2007.08.010).

108. Marshall B. Kapp, *Patient Autonomy in the Age of Consumer-Driven Health Care: Informed Consent and Informed Choice*, II J Health & Biomedical Law 1, 10 (2006).

109. Barrie R. Cassileth et al., *Informed Consent—Why Are Its Goals Imperfectly Realized?*, 302 NEJM 896 (1980).

110. NRC, *Protecting Participants and Facilitating Social and Behavioral Sciences Research* 2–3 (NAP, 2003).

111. Charles W. Lidz, *Informed Consent: A Critical Part of Modern Medical Research*, 342 American J Medical Sciences 273 (2011).

112. Steven Joffe et al., *Quality of Informed Consent in Cancer Clinical Trials: A Cross-Sectional Survey*, 358 Lancet 1772, 1775 (2001).

113. Ibid at 1774.

114. Bruce Gordon et al., *Conflict between Research Design and Minimization of Risks in Pediatric Research*, 22 BMJ 1, 12 (2000).

115. Norman Fost & Robert J. Levine, *The Dysregulation of Human Subjects Research*, 298 JAMA 2196, 2197–2198 (2007).

116. Schlaff et al., 96 Fertility & Sterility at 3 (cited in note 56).

117. Paul S. Appelbaum, *Informed Consent: Always Full Disclosure?*, in Joan E. Sieber, ed., *NIH Readings on the Protection of Human Subjects In Behavioral and Social Science Research: Conference Proceedings and Background Papers* 33 (University Publications of America, 1984).

118. Lidz, 342 American J Medical Sciences at 275 (cited in note 111).

119. Kapp, II J Health & Biomedical Law at 13 (cited in note 108).

120. Jerry Menikoff with Edward P. Richards, *What the Doctor Didn't Say: The Hidden Truth about Medical Research* 34 (Oxford University Press, 2006).

121. S. Michael Sharp, *Consent Documents for Oncology Trials: Does Anybody Read These Things?*, 27 American J Clinical Oncology 570, 570 (2004) (doi: 10.1097/01.coc.0000135925.83221.b3).

122. OHRP, *Guidebook*, chapter 3, at 10.

123. Department of Health and Human Services, ANPRM, 45 CFR Parts 46, 160, and 164, 44512–44531 (2011).

124. NRC, *Protecting Participants* at 2–3 (cited in note 110).

125. IOM, *Responsible Research* at viii (cited in note 6).

126. OHRP, *Guidebook*, chapter 3 (emphases added).

127. Todd Zywicki, *Institutional Review Boards as Academic Bureaucracies: An Economic and Experiential Analysis*, NwS 861, 867.

128. Appelbaum, *Informed Consent* at 34 (cited in note 117).

129. Mary E. Loverde et al., *Research Consent Forms: Continued Unreadability and Increasing Length*, 4 J General Internal Medicine 410, 411 (1989).

130. Ibid at 411.

131. Ilene Albala et al., *The Evolution of Consent Forms for Research: A Quarter Century of Changes*, 32 BMJ (2010).

132. Schlaff et al., 96 Fertility & Sterility at 3 (cited in note 56).

133. O. Berger et al., *The Length of Consent Documents in Oncological Trials Is Doubled in Twenty Years*, 20 Annals Oncology 379 (2009) (doi: 10.1093/annonc/mdn623).

134. Albala et al., 32 BMJ (cited in note 131).

135. Michael K. Paasche-Orlow et al., *Readability Standards for Informed-Consent Forms as Compared with Actual Readability*, 348 NEJM 721 (2003).

136. Peter Breese et al., *The Health Insurance Portability and Accountability Act and the Informed Consent Process*, 141 AnIM 897, 897 (2004).

137. Sharp, 27 American J Clinical Oncology at 574 (cited in note 121).

138. Stuart A. Grossman et al., *Are Informed Consent Forms That Describe Clinical Oncology Research Protocols Readable by Most Patients and Their Families?*, 12 J Clinical Oncology 2211, 2212 (1994).

139. William Burman et al., *The Effects of Local Review on Informed Consent Documents from a Multicenter Clinical Trials Consortium*, 24 Controlled Clinical Trials 245 (2003) (doi: 10.1016/0197-2456(03)00003-5).

140. Robin L. Penslar, *The Institutional Review Board's Role in Editing the Consent Document*, in Bankert & Amdur at 200.

141. Ibid at 201.

142. Amdur, *Handbook* 51 (Jones & Bartlett, 2002).

143. Scott C. Burris & Jen Welsh, *Regulatory Paradox in the Protection of Human Research Subjects: A Review of OHRP Enforcement Letters*, NwS 1, 33–34 (2007).

144. Robert J. Levine, *Ethics and Regulation of Clinical Research* 326 (Yale University Press, 1988) (2nd ed.).

145. Green et al., 41 HSR at 221 (cited in note 22).

146. Ibid at 221–222.

147. Burman et al., 24 Controlled Clinical Trials at 249 (cited in note 139).

148. Page S. Morahan et al., *New Challenges Facing Interinstitutional Social Science and Educational Program Evaluation Research at Academic Centers: A Case Study from the ELAM Program*, 81 AM 527, 531 (2006).

149. McWilliams et al., 290 JAMA at 362 (cited in note 31).

150. Ibid at 363.

151. Shamoo & Khin-Maung-Gyi, *Ethics of the Use of Human Subjects* at 54 (cited in note 21).

152. "Kristina C. Borror, Ph.D., Director, Division of Compliance Oversight" (July 19, 2007, letter to Johns Hopkins on study of central-line infections).

153. William J. Burman et al., *Breaking the Camel's Back: Multicenter Clinical Trials and Local Institutional Review Boards*, 134 AnIM 152, 153 (2001).

154. Burman et al., 24 Controlled Clinical Trials at 249 (cited in note 139).

155. Ibid at 248.

156. These are from the list at 45 USC 46.115, which is too long to reprint here.

157. Fost & Levine, 298 JAMA at 2196 (cited in note 115).

158. Robert J. Amdur & Elizabeth A. Bankert, *Length, Frequency, and Time of Institutional Review Board Meetings*, in Bankert & Amdur 81.

159. IOM, *Responsible Research* at 58 (cited in note 6).

160. Ibid at 63.

161. Amdur, *Handbook* at 29–30.

162. Mazur, *Guide* at 19.

163. Mazur, *Guide* at 22–23 (emphasis in original).

164. Jeffrey A. Cooper & Pamela Turner, *Training Institutional Review Board Members*, in Bankert & Amdur 314.

165. Robert J. Amdur, *Evaluating Study Design and Quality*, in Bankert & Amdur 127.

166. Sarah T. Khan & Susan Z. Kornetsky, *Overview of Initial Protocol Review*, in Bankert & Amdur 120.

167. Ibid at 121.

168. Ibid at 122.

169. Khan & Kornetsky, *Overview* in Bankert and Amdur at 123 (cited in note 166).

170. Will C. van den Hoonaard, *Seduction of Ethics: Transforming the Social Sciences* 189 (University of Toronto Press, 2011).

171. Ibid at 85.

172. Jeffrey Spike, *Extend the Reach of Institutional Review Boards First, Then Strengthen Their Depth*, 8 AJOB 11, 11–12 (2008).

173. Adrian Bardon, *Ethics Education and Value Prioritization Among Members of U.S. Hospital Ethics Committees*, 14 Kennedy Institute of Ethics J 395, 397 (2004).

174. Dennis J. Mazur, *Evaluating the Science and Ethics of Research on Humans: A Guide for IRB Members* x (Johns Hopkins University Press, 2007).

175. Levine, *Ethics and Regulation* at 55 (cited in note 144).

176. OHRP, *Guidebook*, introduction.

177. OHRP, *Guidebook*, chapter 1, part B.

178. Ibid.

179. IOM *Responsible Research* at 46 (cited in note 6).

180. Ibid at 47.

181. Laura Jeanine Morris Stark, *Morality in Science: How Research Is Evaluated in the Age of Human Subjects Regulation* 178 (2006) (Princeton University, Ph.D. Thesis).

182. Ibid.

183. Schlaff et al., 96 Fertility & Sterility at 3 (cited in note 56).

184. Michèle Lamont, *How Professors Think: Inside the Curious World of Academic Judgment* 176–177 (Harvard University Press, 2009).

185. Steven Shapin, *Never Pure* 31 (Johns Hopkins University Press, 2010).

186. Lamont, *How Professors Think* at 9–10 (cited in note 184).

187. Ibid at 53.

188. Ibid at 9–10.

189. Ibid at 2.

190. Ibid at 11.

191. Shapin, *Never Pure* at 36 (cited in note 185).

192. Ibid at 37.

193. Ibid at 222.

194. Stephen J. Ceci & Maggie Bruck, *Do IRBs Pass the Minimal Harm Test?*, 4 Perspectives Psychological Science 29 (2009).

195. Helfand et al., 181 J Urology at 2676 (cited in note 33).

196. McWilliams et al., 290 JAMA at 364 (cited in note 31) .

197. Zachary Schrag, *Ignorance Is Strength: Pseudo-Expertise and the Regulation of Human Subjects Research*, Keynote Talk for "Outside Authority," Science and Technology in Society (STS) Conference, Virginia Tech, 2011, at 3.

198. Ibid at 7.

199. Gibbs Brown, *Institutional Review Boards* at 6 (cited in note 1).

200. Amdur, *Evaluating Study Design and Quality* at 127 (cited in note 165).

201. Robert J. Amdur & Elizabeth A. Bankert, *Committee Size, Alternates, and Consultants*, in Bankert & Amdur 78.

202. Kevin M. Hunt, *Explaining the Cost of Research Participation*, in Bankert & Amdur 239.

203. David O. Sears, *On Separating Church and Lab*, 5 Psychological Science 237, 238 (1994).

204. Morris Stark, *Morality in Science* at 180 (cited in note 181).

205. Sohini Sengupta & Bernard Lo, *The Roles and Experiences of Nonaffiliated and Non-scientist Members of Institutional Review Boards*, 78 AM 212, 216 (2003).

206. H. E. M. van Luijn et al., *Assessment of the Risk/Benefit Ratio of Phase II Cancer Clinical Trials by Institutional Review Board (IRB) Members*, 13 Annals of Oncology 1307, 1310 (2002) (doi: 10.1093/annonc/mdf209).

207. Jeanne S. Mandelblatt et al., *Effects of Mammography Screening Under Different Screening Schedules: Model Estimates of Potential Benefits and Harms*, 151 AnIM 738 (2009).

208. Mette Kalager et al., *Effect of Screening Mammography on Breast-Cancer Mortality in Norway*, 363 NEJM 1203 (2010).

209. H. Gilbert Welch, *Screening Mammography—A Long Run for a Short Slide?* 363 NEJM 1276 (2010).

210. Gina Kolata, *Mammograms' Value in Cancer Fight at Issue*, New York Times, September 22, 2010.

211. Zachary M. Schrag, *Ethical Imperialism: Institutional Review Boards and the Social Sciences, 1965–2009* 138 (Johns Hopkins University Press, 2010).

212. Ibid at 138–139 (cited in note 211).

213. Zachary Schrag, *Ignorance Is Strength: Pseudo-Expertise and the Regulation of Human Subjects Research*, Keynote Talk for "Outside Authority," Science and Technology in Society (STS) Conference, Virginia Tech, 2011, at 11.

214. Sears, 5 Psychological Science at 238 (cited in note 203).

215. Zywicki, NwS at 871 n43 (cited in note 127).

216. NBAC, *Ethical and Policy Issues in Research Involving Human Participants: Report and Recommendations* 14 (2001).

217. Joseph A. Catania et al., *Survey of U.S. Human Research Protection Organizations: Workload and Membership*, 3 JERHRE 57 (2008) (doi: 10.1525/jer.2008.3.4.57).

218. Richard S. Saver, *Medical Research Oversight from the Corporate Governance Perspective: Comparing Institutional Review Boards and Corporate Boards*, 46 William & Mary L Rev 619, 727 (2004).

219. Fost & Levine, 298 JAMA at 2197–2198 (cited in note 115).

220. *Beyond the HIPAA Privacy Rule: Enhancing Privacy, Improving Health Through Research* 13 (NAS, 2009).

221. *Grimes v. Kennedy Krieger Institute*, 782 A2d 807, 813 (Md 2001). On the court's errors, see Carl E. Schneider, *Craft and Power*, 38 HCR 9 (Jan/Feb 2008).

222. Saver, 46 William & Mary L Rev at 727 (cited in note 218).

223. *Beyond the HIPAA Privacy Rule* at 12–13 (cited in note 220).

224. Cowan, 25 Case Western Reserve L Rev at 538 (cited in note 94).

225. Fost & Levine, 298 JAMA at 2197–2198 (cited in note 115).

226. Illinois Center for Advanced Study, *Improving the System for Protecting Human Subjects: Counteracting IRB "Mission Creep"* 1, 12 (2005).

227. Norman Fost, *Fusing and Confusing Ethics and Regulations*, in Paula Knudson et al., *1974–2005 PRIM&R Through the Years: Three Decades of Protecting Human Subjects* 462 (2006).

228. Ibid at 457.

229. Sears, 5 Psychological Science at 238 (cited in note 203).

230. Lamont, *How Professors Think* at 51 (cited in note 184).

231. Ibid at 132.

232. Ibid at 16.

233. Ibid at 34.

234. Ibid at 35.

235. Ibid.

236. Ibid at 36.

237. Ibid.

238. Ibid at 45.

239. Michael J. Mahoney, *Publication Prejudices: An Experimental Study of Confirmatory Bias in the Peer Review System*, 1 Cognitive Therapy & Research 161, 173 (1977).

240. Lamont, *How Professors Think* at 8 (cited in note 184).

241. Van den Hoonaard, *Seduction of Ethics* at 162 (cited in note 170).

242. Ibid at 165.

243. Ibid at 176.

244. Maureen H. Fitzgerald et al., *The Research Ethics Review Process and Ethics Review Narratives*, 16 Ethics & Behavior 377, 387 n5 (2006).

245. Ibid at 388.

246. Ibid.

247. Ibid at 389.

248. Federici Jaeger, *An Ethnographic Analysis* at 61 (cited in note 79).

249. Philip J. Candilis et al., *The Silent Majority: Who Speaks at IRB Meetings?*, 34 IRB: Ethics & Human Research 15, 17–18 (2012).

250. Federici Jaeger, *An Ethnographic Analysis* at 92 (cited in note 79).

251. For a helpful summary, see Cass R. Sunstein, *Laws of Fear: Beyond the Precautionary Principle* (Cambridge University Press, 2005).

252. Matthew D. Adler & Eric A. Posner, *Cost–Benefit Analysis: Legal, Economic and Philosophical Perspectives* 228–229 (University of Chicago Press, 2001).

253. Francis Bacon, *Novum Organum* 58 (Peter Urbach & John Gibson, trans. & eds.) (Open Court, 1994).

254. Sunstein at 81 (cited in note 251).

255. Ibid.

256. Manish Agrawal & Ezekiel J. Emanuel, *Ethics of Phase 1 Oncology Studies: Reexamining the Arguments and Data*, 290 JAMA 1075, 1077–1078 (2003).

257. van Luijn et al., 13 Annals Oncology at 1307 (cited at note 206).

258. Ibid at 1310.

259. Murray Levine, *IRB Review as a "Cooling Out" Device*, 5 IRB: Ethics & Human Research 8, 9 (1983).

260. Charles Bosk, *The Ethnographer and the IRB: Comment on Kevin D. Haggerty, "Ethics Creep: Governing Social Science Research in the Name of Ethics,"* 27 Qualitative Sociology 417, 420 (2004).

261. Rene Lederman, *Educate Your IRB: An Experiment in Cross Disciplinary Communication*, 48 Anthropology News 33 (2007).

262. Lillian M. Range & C. Randy Cotton, *Reports of Assent and Permission in Research with Children: Illustrations and Suggestions*, 5 Ethics & Behavior 49, 55 (1995).

263. Kristen H. Perry, *Challenging the IRB: Ethics and the Politics of Representation in Literacy Research Involving Adult Refugees*, paper for the National Reading Conference Annual Meeting, December 2009, Albuquerque, New Mexico.

264. J. Grignon et al., *Ensuring Community-Level Research Protections: Proceedings of the 2007 Educational Conference Call Series on Institutional Review Boards and Ethical Issues in Research*, Community-Campus Partnerships for Health (2008).

265. Betty Ferrell, *Palliative Care Research: The Need to Construct Paradigms*, 7 J Palliative Medicine 408 (2004).

266. Margaret Olivia Little et al., *Moving Forward with Research Involving Pregnant Women: A Critical Role for Wisdom from the Field*, 2 AJOB Primary Research 15 (2011).

267. Patricia Keith-Spiegel et al., *What Scientists Want from Their Research Ethics Committee*, 1 JERHRE 67 (2006).

268. Michelle D. Hamilton et al., *A Novel Protocol for Streamlined IRB Review of Practice-Based Research Network (PBRN) Card Studies*, 24 J Am Board of Family Medicine 605 (2011).

269. Larry Forney et al., *Report of the Working Group on Genetics and Microbial Communities (Metagenomics/Microbiome)*, in Office of Research on Women's Health, NIH, *Moving Into the Future with New Dimensions and Strategies: A Vision for 2020 for Women's Health Research, Volume II: Regional Scientific Reports* (2010).

270. Crista E. Johnson et al., *Building Community-Based Participatory Research Partnerships with a Somali Refugee Community*, 37 Am J Preventive Medicine S230 (2009).

271. Sherwood et al., 135 Otolaryngology-Head & Neck Surgery at 189 (cited in note 57).

272. Judith Jarvis Thomson et al., *Regulation of Research on Human Subjects: Academic Freedom and the Institutional Review Board*, AAUP 1, 11 (2013).

273. Ibid at 13.

CHAPTER 4

1. Drawn from Scott Atran, *Research Police—How a University IRB Thwarts Understanding of Terrorism*, Monday (May 28, 2007), http://www.institutional reviewblog.com/2007_05_01_archive.html.

2. Robert J. Levine, *Reflections on 'Rethinking Research Ethics,'* 5 American J Bioethics 1, 2 (2005).

3. R. K. Lie et al., *The Standard of Care Debate: The Declaration of Helsinki versus the International Consensus Opinion*, 30 J Medical Ethics 190, 192 (2004).

4. Ibid at 190.

5. FDA, Final Rule, Human Subject Protection; Foreign Clinical Studies Not Conducted Under an Investigational New Drug Application, 73 Fed Reg 22800, 22804 (2008) (amending 21 CFR 312).

6. *Lochner v. New York*, 198 US 45, 76 (1905) (Holmes, J. dissenting).

7. Norman Fost, Interview by Patricia C. El-Hinnawy, *OHRP: Oral History of the Belmont Report and the National Commission for the Protection of Human Subjects of Biomedical and Behavioral Research*, Belmont Oral History Project 17 (May 13, 2004).

8. Joan E. Sieber, *Using Our Best Judgment in Conducting Human Research*, 14 Ethics & Behavior 297, 298 (2004).

9. Zachary M. Schrag, *Ethical Imperialism: Institutional Review Boards and the Social Sciences, 1965–2009* 78 (Johns Hopkins University Press, 2010).

10. Renée C. Fox & Judith P. Swazey, *Observing Bioethics* 140–141 (Oxford University Press, 2008).

11. Ibid at 128.

12. Amdur, *Handbook* at 24.

13. Schrag, *Ethical Imperialism* at 93 (cited in note 9).

14. Ibid at 88.

15. Carl E. Schneider, *Making Biomedical Policy through Constitutional Adjudication: The Example of Physician-Assisted Suicide*, in Carl E. Schneider, *Law at the End of Life: The Supreme Court and Assisted Suicide* at 164, 166 (University of Michigan Press, 2000).

16. *Planned Parenthood of SE PA v. Casey*, 505 US 833, 983 (1992) (dissenting).

17. David M. Walker, *The Oxford Companion to Law* 689 (Oxford University Press, 1980).

18. Oliver Wendell Holmes, Letter to John C. H. Wu, in Max Lerner, ed., *The Mind and Faith of Justice Holmes* 435 (Transaction Publishers, 1943). When a protégé said to Justice Holmes "Well, sir, goodbye. Do justice!," Holmes famously replied, "That is not my job. My job is to play the game according to the rules." Learned Hand, *A Personal Confession*, in *The Spirit of Liberty* 302, 306–307 (Irving Dilliard, ed.) (Knopf, 1960) (3rd ed.).

19. Neal W. Dickert, *Re-Examining Respect for Human Research Participants*, 19 Kennedy Institute of Ethics J 311, 326 (2010).

20. Franklin G. Miller & Alan Wertheimer, *Facing Up to Paternalism in Research Ethics*, 37 HCR 24, 32 (2007).

21. *Ancheff v. Hartford Hospital*, 799 A 2d 1067, 1079 (2002).

22. OHRP, *Guidebook*, introduction.

23. Schrag, *Ethical Imperialism* at 16 (cited in note 9).

24. Enrique Regidor, *The Use of Personal Data from Medical Records and Biological Materials: Ethical Perspectives and the Basis for Legal Restrictions in Health Research*, 59 SSM 1975, 1976 (2004) (doi: 10.1016/j.socscimed.2004.02.032).

25. Ibid.

26. David E. Winickoff & Richard N. Winickoff, *The Charitable Trust as a Model for Genomic Biobanks*, 349 NEJM 1180–1184 (2003).

27. Ibid at 1181.

28. Ibid.

29. Regidor, 59 SSM at 1977 (cited in note 24).

30. Will C. van den Hoonaard, *Seduction of Ethics: Transforming the Social Sciences* 167 (University of Toronto Press, 2011).

31. Amdur, *Handbook* at 79–80.

32. Ibid at 27.

33. Mazur, *Guide* at 41–42.

34. Kenneth Getz, *Frustration with IRB Bureaucracy & Despotism*, Applied Clinical Trials (January 1, 2011), http://www.appliedclinicaltrialsonline.com/appliedclinicaltrials/article/articleDetail.jsp?id=703033.

35. James P. Orlowski & James A. Christensen, *The Potentially Coercive Nature of Some Clinical Research Trial Acronyms*, 121 Chest 2023 (2002) (doi: 10.1378/chest.121.6.2023).

36. NBAC, *Ethical and Policy Issues in Research Involving Human Participants: Report and Recommendations* vi (2001).

37. NRC & IOM, *Ethical Considerations For Research on Housing-Related Health Hazards Involving Children* 12 (NAP, 2005) (originally in bold).

38. NBAC, *Ethical and Policy Issues* at vi (cited in note 36).

39. Schrag, *Ethical Imperialism* at 6 (cited in note 9).

40. Elizabeth Murphy & Robert Dingwall, *Informed Consent, Anticipatory Regulation and Ethnographic Practice*, 65 SSM 2223, 2225 (2007).

41. Ibid.

42. Ibid at 2226.

43. NBAC, *Ethical and Policy Issues* at 42 (cited in note 36).

44. Carl E. Schneider, *Bioethics in the Language of the Law*, 24 HCR 16, 17 (July/August 1994).

45. Greg Koski, *Changing the Paradigm: New Directions in Federal Oversight of Human Research*, 37 J Pediatric Gastroenterology & Nutrition S2, S3 (2003).

46. Jeffrey P. Kahn, *Moving from Compliance to Conscience: Why We Can and Should Improve on the Ethics of Clinical Research*, 161 ArIM 925, 925 (2001).

47. Robert Klitzman, *The Myth of Community Differences as the Cause of Variations Among IRBs*, 2 AJOB Primary Research 24, 30 (2011) (doi: 10.1080/21507716.2011.601284).

48. Ibid at 29.

49. Zachary Schrag, *Ignorance Is Strength: Pseudo-Expertise and the Regulation of Human Subjects Research*, Keynote Talk for "Outside Authority," Science and Technology in Society (STS) Conference, Virginia Tech, 2011, at 12.

50. Ibid at 13.

51. Ronald Bayer, statement before the Presidential Commission for the Study of Bioethical Issues, "Implementing Federal Standards – Ethics Issues," New York, NY, May 18, 2011, at http://bioethics.gov/node/229, accessed August 25, 2012.

52. Zachary Schrag, *The CITI Program as Mortifyingly Stupid, Marxist Doxology*, Institutional Review Blog (June 4, 2011), http://www.institutionalreview-blog.com/2011/06/citi-program-as-mortifyingly-stupid.html, accessed August 25, 2012.

53. Thomas L. Haskell, *Justifying the Rights of Academic Freedom in the Era of "Power/Knowledge*,*"* in Louis Menand, ed., *The Future of Academic Freedom* 47 (University of Chicago Press, 1996).

54. Ibid.

55. Thomas L. Haskell, *The New Aristocracy*, New York Review of Books 47, 51 (Dec. 4, 1997).

56. Carl E. Schneider, *Craft and Power*, 38 HCR 1 (Jan/Feb 2008).

57. Julian Savulescu, *Harm Ethics Committees and the Gene Therapy Death*, 27 J Medical Ethics 148, 148 (2001).

58. John H. Mueller, *Ignorance Is Neither Bliss Nor Ethical*, NwS 809, 815 (2007).

59. Ibid.

60. See the essays in R. A. Laud Humphreys, *Tearoom Trade: Impersonal Sex in Public Places* (Aldine Transaction, 2007).

61. Schrag, *Ethical Imperialism* at 23 (cited in note 9).

62. Scott Burris & Kathryn Moss, *U.S. Health Researchers Review Their Ethics Review Boards: A Qualitative Study*, 1 JERHRE 39, 40–41 (2006).

63. Eugene Bardach & Robert A. Kagan, *Going by the Book: The Problem of Regulatory Unreasonableness* 207 (Transaction Publishers, 2002).

64. Norman Fost & Robert J. Levine, *The Dysregulation of Human Subjects Research*, 298 JAMA 2196, 2196 (2007).

65. Schrag, *Ethical Imperialism* at 21 (cited in note 9).

66. Ibid at 23.

67. Ibid at 22 (cited in note 9).

68. Burris & Moss, JERHRE at 39 (cited in note 62).

69. Philip Hamburger, *The New Censorship: Institutional Review Boards*, 2004 Supreme Court Review 271, 336.

70. Jonathan Moss, *If Institutional Review Boards Were Declared Unconstitutional, They Would Have to be Reinvented*, NwS 801, 804.

71. NBAC, *Ethical and Policy Issues* at 26 (cited in note 36).

72. Greg Koski et al., *Cooperative Research Ethics Review Boards: A Win-Win Solution?*, 27 BMJ 1, 1 (2005).

73. Louis L. Jaffe, *Law as a System of Control*, 98 Daedalus 406, 406 (1969).

74. Sydney Halpern, *Hybrid Design, Systematic Rigidity: Institutional Dynamics in Human Research Oversight*, 2 Regulation & Governance 85, 93 (2008).

75. Jon M. Harkness, review of James F. Childress et al., *Belmont Revisited: Ethical Principles for Research with Human Subjects*, 355 NEJM 634, 634–635 (2006).

76. http://www.gallup.com/poll/141512/congress-ranks-last-confidence-institutions.aspx.

77. http://www.gallup.com/poll/1654/honesty-ethics-professions.aspx.

78. Association of Academic Health Centers Press Release, Association of Academic Health Centers, *HIPAA Creating Barriers to Research and Discovery: HIPAA Problems Widespread and Unresolved Since 2003* 6–7 (June 16, 2008).

79. OHRP, *OHRP Fact Sheet*, http://www.hhs.gov/OHRP/about/ohrpfactsheet.htm.

80. Jerry Menikoff, *Toward a General Theory of Research Ethics*, 37 HCR 3, 3 (May/June 2007) (doi: 10.1353/hcr.2007.0043).

81. Howard Brody, *The Healer's Power* 15 (Yale University Press, 1992).

82. NBAC, *Ethical and Policy Issues* at iii (cited in note 36).

83. Ibid.

84. Miller & Wertheimer, 37 HCR at 29–30 (cited in note 20).

85. Cary Nelson, *Can E.T. Call Home? The Brave New World of University Surveillance*, 89 Academe 30 (2003).

86. Steven Shapin, *The Scientific Life: A Moral History of a Late Modern Vocation* x (University of Chicago Press, 2008).

87. Van den Hoonaard, *Seduction of Ethics* at 142 (cited in note 30).

88. Robert J. Levine, *Ethics and Regulation of Clinical Research* 47 (Yale University Press, 1988) (2nd ed.).

89. *Canterbury v. Spence*, 464 F2d 772 (DC Cir 1972).

90. OHRP, *Guidebook*, chapter 3.

91. Robert M. Sade, *Research on Stored Biological Samples Is Still Research*, 162 ArIM 1439, 1439–1440 (2002).

92. Eleanor Singer & Felice J. Levine, *Protection of Human Subjects of Research: Recent Developments and Future Prospects for the Social Sciences*, 67 Public Opinion Quarterly 148, 163 (2003).

93. Robert L. Klitzman, *How IRBs View and Make Decisions About Social Risks*, 8 J of Empirical Research on Human Research Ethics 58, 61 (2013) (doi: 10.1525/jer.2013.8.3.58).

94. Edmund Burke, *Reflections on the Revolution in France* 51 (Bobbs-Merrill, 1955).

95. Edward Gibbon, *The Autobiography of Edward Gibbon* 73 (Meridian, 1961).

96. Michelle Ng Gong et al., *Surrogate Consent for Research Involving Adults with Impaired Decision Making: Survey of Institutional Review*

Board Practices, 38 Critical Care Medicine 2146, 2150 (2010) (doi: 10.1097/CCM.0b013e3181f26fe6).

97. C. K. Gunsalus, *The Nanny State Meets the Inner Lawyer: Overregulating While Underprotecting Human Participants in Research*, 15 Ethics & Behavior 369, 375 (2004).

98. Drawn from Helene Cummins, *A Funny Thing Happened on the Way to the Ethics Board: Studying the Meaning of Farm Life for Farm Children*, 4 J Academic Ethics 175 (2006) (doi: 10.1007/s10805-006-9015-3).

99. Carol Levine et al., *The Limitations of "Vulnerability" as a Protection for Human Research Participants*, 4 American J Bioethics 44, 44 (2004).

100. 45 CFR 46.111(b).

101. Levine, *Ethics and Regulation* at 72 (cited in note 88).

102. Levine et al., 4 American J Bioethics at 46 (cited in note 99).

103. NBAC, *Ethical and Policy Issues in Research Involving Human Participants: Report and Recommendations* 85 (2001).

104. Lee Murray et al., *Reflections on the Ethics-Approval Process*, 18 Qualitative Inquiry 43, 54 (2011) (doi:10.1177/1077800411427845).

105. Kathryn A. Becker-Blease & Jennifer J. Freyd, *Research Participants Telling the Truth About Their Lives: The Ethics of Asking and Not Asking About Abuse*, 61 American Psychologist 218, 219 (2006).

106. Ibid at 224.

107. Kirsten Bell & Amy Salmon, *Good Intentions and Dangerous Assumptions: Research Ethics Committees and Illicit Drug Use Research*, 8 Research Ethics 191, 192 (2012) (doi: 10.1177/1747016112461731).

108. Stephanie S. Park & Mitchell H. Grayson, *Clinical Research: Protection of the "Vulnerable"?*, 121 J Allergy & Clinical Immunology 1103, 1105 (2008) (doi: 10.1016/j.jaci.2008.01.014).

109. Levine et al., 4 American J Bioethics at 47 (cited in note 99).

110. John C. McDonald, *Why Prisoners Volunteer to Be Experimental Subjects*, 202 JAMA 175, 176 (1967).

111. Ibid.

112. Ibid.

113. Heith Copes et al., *Inmates' Perceptions of the Benefits and Harm of Prison Interviews*, Field Methods 1 (2012) (doi: 10.1177/1525822X12465798).

114. Robert H. Gilman & Hector H. Garcia, *Ethics Review Procedures for Research in Developing Countries: A Basic Presumption of Guilt*, 3 Canadian Medical Association J 248, 248 (2004).

115. Jonathan Baron, *Against Bioethics* 4 (MIT Press, 2006).

116. Fox & Swazey, *Observing Bioethics* at 163 (cited in note 10).

117. Beth J. Seelig & William H. Dobelle, *Altruism and the Volunteer: Psychological Benefits from Participating as a Research Subject*, 47 American Society Artificial Internal Organs J 3, 3 (2001).

118. Samuel Hellman & Deborah S. Hellman, *Of Mice but Not Men: Problems of the Randomized Clinical Trial*, 324 NEJM 1585, 1587 (1991).

119. Ibid at 3.

120. Ibid at 5.

121. Alexis de Tocqueville, *Democracy in America* 299 (Knopf, 1994).

122. Francis Fukuyama, *Trust: The Social Virtues and the Creation of Prosperity* 351 (Free Press, 1995).

123. Amy L. Fairchild & David Merritt Johns, *Beyond Bioethics: Reckoning with the Public Health Paradigm*, 102 Am J Public Health 1447, 1447 (2012).

124. David A. Hyman, *Rescue without Law: An Empirical Perspective on the Duty to Rescue*, University of Illinois Legal Working Paper Series. University of Illinois Law and Economics Working Papers. Working Paper 32, 3 (2005).

125. Hans-Martin Sass, *Ethical Decision Making in Committee: A View from Germany*, 18 Notizie di Politeia 65, 72 (2002) (emphasis in original).

126. David Orentlicher, *Making Research a Requirement of Treatment*, 35 HCR 20, 24 (2005).

127. Ibid at 25.

128. Barbara P. Yawn et al., *The Impact of Requiring Patient Authorization for Use of Data in Medical Records Research*, 47 J Family Practice 361, 363 (1998).

129. David Wendler et al., *Research on Stored Biological Samples: The Views of Ugandans*, 27 BMJ 1, 1 (2005).

130. Mary Brydon-Miller & Davydd Greenwood, *A Re-Examination of the Relationship Between Action Research and Human Subjects Review Processes*, 4 Action Research 117, 119–120 (2006) (doi: 10.1177/1476750306060582). On the ethical foundations of action research, see Anne Inga Hilsen, *And They Shall Be Known by Their Deeds*, 4 Action Research 23 (2006) (doi: 10.1177/1476750306006539).

131. See Carl E. Schneider, *The Practice of Autonomy: Patients, Doctors, and Medical Decisions* (Oxford University Press, 1998).

132. Ibid at 27.

133. Carl E. Schneider & Lee E. Teitelbaum, *Life's Golden Tree: Empirical Scholarship and American Law*, 2006 Utah L Rev 53, 106.

134. Charles L. Bosk, *What Would You Do?: Juggling Bioethics and Ethnography* (University of Chicago Press, 2008).

CHAPTER 5

1. Jerry L. Mashaw, *Dignitary Process: A Political Psychology of Liberal Democratic Citizenship*, 39 U Florida L Rev 433, 437 (1987).

2. *Marbury v. Madison*, 5 US 137 (1803).

3. Alfred C. Aman & William T. Mayton, *Administrative Law* 4, 33 (West, 2001).

4. Mazur, *Guide* at 8.

5. Jan Federici Jaeger, *An Ethnographic Analysis of Institutional Review Board Decision-Making*, Dissertation UMI Number 3246171 (2006).

6. John Locke, *Second Treatise of Government* 17 (Hackett, 1980).

7. *Grayned v. City of Rockford*, 408 US 104, 108–109 (1971).

8. Lon L. Fuller, *The Morality of Law* 39 (Yale University Press, 1969).

9. Stephen J. Ceci & Maggie Bruck, *Do IRBs Pass the Minimal Harm Test?*, Perspectives on Psychological Science 28, 28 (2009). (doi: 10.1111/j.1745-6924.2009.01084.x 4).

10. *Connally v. General Construction Co.*, 269 US 385, 391 (1926).

11. Susan M. Labott & Timothy P. Johnson, *Psychological and Social Risks of Behavioral Research*, 26 BMJ 11, 12 (May–June 2004).

12. Charles Weijer & Paul B. Miller, *When Are Research Risks Reasonable in Relationship to Anticipated Benefits?* in Bankert & Amdur 147.

13. Learned Hand, *Lectures on Legal Topics: 1921–1922: Subject: The Deficiencies of Trials to Reach the Heart of the Matter* 91–92 (MacMillan, 1926).

14. Thomas L. Beauchamp, *Why Our Conceptions of Research and Practice May Not Serve the Best Interest of Patients and Subjects*, 269 Internal Medicine 383, 384 (2011) (doi: 10.1111/j.1365-2796.2001.2350.x).

15. Robert L. Klitzman, *Local IRBs vs. Federal Agencies: Shifting Dynamics, Systems, and Relationships*, 7 JERHRE 50, 53–54 (2012) (doi: 10.1525/jer.2012.7.3.50).

16. 45 CFR 46.111(b).

17. 45 CFR 46.109(b).

18. 21 CFR 50.24(a)(7).

19. Carol Rambo, *Handing IRB an Unloaded Gun*, 13 Qualitative Inquiry 353, 362 (2007).

20. Michele Russell-Einhorn & Thomas Puglisi, *Requiring a Witness Signature on the Consent Form*, in Bankert & Amdur 208.

21. Daniel R. Vasgird, *Research-Related Injuries*, in Bankert & Amdur 230–231.

22. Jeffrey Cohen, HRPP Blog, http://hrpp.blogspot.com/.

23. Sohini Sengupta & Bernard Lo, *The Roles and Experiences of Nonaffiliated and Non-scientist Members of Institutional Review Boards*, 78 AM 212, 216 (2003).

24. Zachary M. Schrag, *Ignorance Is Strength: Pseudo-Expertise and the Regulation of Human Subjects Research*, Keynote Talk for "Outside Authority," Science and Technology in Society Conference, Virginia Tech, 2011, at 12.

25. Rambo, 13 Qualitative Inquiry at 362 (cited in note 19).

26. Jonathan Moss, *If Institutional Review Boards Were Declared Unconstitutional, They Would Have to Be Reinvented*, NwS 801, 802–803 (2007).

27. Dean R. Gallant & Alan Bliss, *Qualitative Social Science Research*, in Bankert & Amdur 400.

28. Elisabeth Smith Parrott, *Ethnographic Research*, in Bankert & Amdur 403.

29. Zachary M. Schrag, *Ethical Imperialism: Institutional Review Boards and the Social Sciences, 1965–2009* 7 (Johns Hopkins University Press, 2010).

30. OHRP, *Guidebook*, chapter 3.

31. NRC & IOM, *Ethical Considerations for Research on Housing-Related Health Hazards Involving Children* 11 (NAP, 2005).

32. Association of Academic Health Centers Press Release, *HIPAA Creating Barriers to Research and Discovery: HIPAA Problems Widespread and Unresolved Since 2003*, Association of Academic Health Centers 1, 2 (June 16, 2008).

33. IOM, *Beyond the HIPAA Privacy Rule: Enhancing Privacy, Improving Health Through Research* 36 (NAS, 2009).

34. Ibid at 53–54.

35. Schrag, *Ethical Imperialism* at 171–172 (cited in note 29).

36. Robert L. Klitzman, *Local IRBs vs. Federal Agencies: Shifting Dynamics, Systems, and Relationships*, 7 JERHRE 50, 51–52 (2012) (doi: 10.1525/jer.2012.7.3.50).

37. Ibid at 57 (emphasis in original).

38. Schrag, *Ethical Imperialism* at 134 (cited in note 29).

39. Robert Klitzman, *The Myth of Community Differences as the Cause of Variations Among IRBs*, 2 AJOB Primary Research 24, 29 (2011) (doi: 10.1080/21507716.2011.601284).

40. Thomas G. Keens, *Informing Subjects About Research Results*, in Bankert & Amdur 234.

41. J. H. U. Brown et al., *The Costs of an Institutional Review Board*, 54 J Medical Education 294, 297 (1979).

42. *Holmes v. New York City Housing Authority*, 398 F2d 262, 265 (2d Cir 1968).

43. Jeffrey Cohen, HRPP Blog, http://hrpp.blogspot.com.

44. Henry J. Friendly, *Some Kind of Hearing*, 123 U Penn L Rev 1267 (1975).

45. Drawn from Stefan Timmermans, *Cui Bono? Institutional Review Board Ethics and Ethnographic Research*, 19 Studies Symbolic Interaction 153 (1995).

46. Daniel K. Nelson, *Conflict of Interest: Institutional Review Boards*, in Bankert & Amdur 179.

47. Elvi Whittaker, *Adjudicating Entitlements: The Emerging Discourses of Research Ethics Boards*, 9 Health: An Interdisciplinary J for the Social Study of Health, Illness and Medicine 513, 524 (2005).

48. Moss, NwS at 803–804 (cited in note 26).

49. Rambo, 13 Qualitative Inquiry at 361 (cited in note 19).

50. Klitzman, 2 AJOB Primary Research at 29 (cited in note 39).

51. Simon N. Whitney et al., *Principal Investigator Views of the IRB System*, 5 International J Medical Sciences 68–72 (2008).

52. Will C. van den Hoonaard, *Seduction of Ethics: Transforming the Social Sciences* 173 (University of Toronto Press, 2011).

53. Michael Bakunin, *Marxism, Freedom and the State* 28 (Freedom Press, 1950).

54. ABA Standards Relating to the Administration of Criminal Justice Standard 6–3.4.

55. Robert Klitzman, *The Ethics Police?: IRBs' Views Concerning Their Power*, 6 PloS One 1, 3 (2011).

56. Amdur, *Handbook* at 37.

57. Rambo, 13 Qualitative Inquiry at 353 (cited in note 19).

58. *Armstrong v. Manzo*, 380 US 552 (1965).

59. Maureen H. Fitzgerald et al., *The Research Ethics Review Process and Ethics Review Narratives*, 16 Ethics & Behavior 377, 383 (2006).

60. Ibid at 391 (emphasis in original).

61. Ibid at 385.

62. *In re Oliver*, 333 US 257 (1948).

63. Jerry Menikoff, *Making Research Consent Transparent*, 304 JAMA 1713, 1714 (2010).

64. Klitzman, 6 PLoS One at 6 (cited in note 55).

65. Carl Elliott, *When Medical Muckraking Fails*, Chronicle of Higher Education (August 2, 2012), http://chronicle.com/blogs/brainstorm/when-medical-muckraking-fails/50767, accessed August 25, 2012.

66. Van den Hoonaard, *Seduction of Ethics* at 90 (cited in note 52).

67. Klitzman, 6 PLoS One at 6 (cited in note 55).

68. Zachary M. Schrag, *The Case Against Ethics Review in the Social Sciences*, 7 Research Ethics 120, 125 (2011).

69. Marvin E. Frankel, *Lawlessness in Sentencing*, U Cincinnati L Rev 1, 15–16 n54 (1972).

70. Ibid at 9–10.

71. Mazur, *Guide* at 8.

72. Frankel, *Lawlessness in Sentencing* at 9 (cited in note 69).

73. Ibid at 16.

74. Ibid at 13–14.

75. Van den Hoonaard, *Seduction of Ethics* at 13 (cited in note 52).

76. Frankel, *Lawlessness in Sentencing* at 7 (cited in note 69).

77. Edmund Burke, *On Conciliation with the American Colonies*.

78. Klitzman, 7 JERHRE at 55 (2012) (cited in note 36).

79. *Morrissey v. Brewer*, 408 US 471 (1971).

80. Neil Vidmar, *The Psychology of Trial Judging*, 20 Current Directions in Psychological Science 58, 60 (2011) (doi: 10.1177/0963721410397283).

81. Tom R. Tyler & Lindsay Rankin, *The Mystique of Instrumentalism*, in Jon Hanson, ed., *Ideology, Psychology, and Law*, 545–546 (Oxford University Press, 2012).

82. Tom R. Tyler, *Self-Regulatory Approaches to White-Collar Crime: The Importance of Legitimacy and Procedural Justice*, in S. S. Simpson & D. Weisburd, *The Criminology of White-Collar Crime* 195, 206 (Springer Science & Business Media, LLC, 2009).

83. Ibid at 200.

84. Tyler & Rankin, *Mystique of Instrumentalism* at 542 (cited in note 81).

85. Bruno S. Frey, *A Constitution for Knaves Crowds Out Civic Virtues*, 107 The Economic J 1043, 1048 (1997).

86. Tom R. Tyler, *Legitimacy and Criminal Justice: The Benefits of Self-Regulation*, 7 Ohio State J Criminal Law 307, 319 (2009); Tom R. Tyler, *Compliance with Intellectual Property Laws: A Psychological Perspective*, 29 NYU J Int'l L & Politics 219, 232–233 (1997).

87. NBAC, *Ethical and Policy Issues in Research Involving Human Participants: Report and Recommendations* 21–22 (2001).

88. Cary Nelson, *Can E.T. Call Home? The Brave New World of University Surveillance*, 89 Academe 30 (2003).

89. Angela R. Holder & Robert J. Levine, *Informed Consent for Research on Specimens Obtained at Autopsy or Surgery: A Case Study in the Overprotection of Human Subjects*, 24 Clinical Research 68, 76 (1976).

90. Whitney et al., 5 International J Medical Sciences at 68 (cited in note 51).

91. Brenda Beagan & Michael McDonald, *Evidence-Based Practice of Research Ethics Review?*, 13 Health L R 62, 67 (2005). REBs are Canadian IRBs.

92. Schrag, *Ethical Imperialism* at 134 (cited in note 29).

93. Patricia Keith-Spiegel & Gerald P. Koocher, *The IRB Paradox: Could the Protectors Also Encourage Deceit?*, 15 Ethics & Behavior 339, 341 (2005).

94. Charles L. Bosk, *The New Bureaucracies of Virtue or When Form Fails to Follow Function*, 30 Political & Legal Anthropology R 192, 194 (2007).

95. Herbert Kaufman, *Red Tape: Its Origins, Uses, and Abuses* 18–19 (Brookings, 1977) (quoting "one congressional witness").

96. Van den Hoonaard, *Seduction of Ethics* at 206 (cited in note 52).

97. Ryan Spellecy & Thomas May, *More than Cheating: Deception, IRB Shopping, and the Normative Legitimacy of IRBs*, 40 JLME 990, 991 (2012).

98. C. K. Gunsalus, *The Nanny State Meets the Inner Lawyer: Overregulating While Underprotecting Human Participants in Research*, 15 Ethics & Behavior 369, 379 (2004).

99. Caroline H. Bledsoe et al., *Regulating Creativity: Research and Survival in the IRB Iron Cage*, NwS 593, 594 & 623–624 (2007).

100. Office of Inspector General, Department of Health & Human Services, *Institutional Review Boards: A Time For Reform* 7 (1998).

101. Bledsoe et al., NwS at 637–638 (cited in note 99).

102. Christopher Shea, *Don't Talk to the Humans: The Crackdown on Social Science Research*, Lingua Franca 27, 32 (Sept. 2000).

103. Mark H. Ashcraft & Jeremy A. Krause, *Social and Behavioral Researchers' Experiences with Their IRBs*, 17 Ethics & Behavior 1, 12 (2007).

104. Keith-Spiegel & Koocher, 15 Ethics & Behavior at 347 (cited in note 93).

105. Van den Hoonaard, *Seduction of Ethics* at 219 (cited in note 52).

106. Jack Katz, *Ethical Escape Routes for Underground Ethnographers*, 33 American Ethnologist 499, 499 (2006).

107. Ibid.

108. Ibid.

109. Joanna Kempner, *The Chilling Effect: How Do Researchers React to Controversy?*, 5 PloS Medicine 1571, 1575 (2008) (doi: 10.1371/journal.pmed.0050222).

110. Shea, Lingua Franca at 32 (cited in note 102).

111. Geoffrey R. Stone, *Free Speech in the Age of McCarthy: A Cautionary Tale*, 93 California L Rev 1387, 1392–93 (2005).

112. Mashaw, *Dignitary Process* at 437 (cited in note 1).

CHAPTER 6

1. Because my subject is policy, I do not analyze the doctrinal argument that IRB censorship violates the first amendment. Philip Hamburger has ably done so in *The New Censorship: Institutional Review Boards*, 2004 Supreme Court Review 271, and *Getting Permission*, NwS 405 (2007).

2. *Watchtower Bible & Tract Society v. Stratton*, 536 US 150, 166 (2001).

3. Thomas I. Emerson, *The System of Freedom of Expression* 619–620 (Random House, 1971).

4. Drawn from Stephen J. Ceci et al., *Human Subjects Review, Personal Values, and the Regulation of Social Science Research*, 40 American Psychologist 994 (1985).

5. Emerson, *System of Freedom* at 3 & 6 (cited in note 3).

6. Steven Peckman, *A Shared Responsibility for Protecting Human Subjects*, in Bankert & Amdur 17.

7. J. Michael Oakes, *Risks and Wrongs in Social Science Research: An Evaluator's Guide to the IRB*, 26 Evaluation Review 443, 454 (2002) (doi: 10.1177/0193841102236520).

8. Thomas Eissenberg et al., *IRBs and Psychological Science: Ensuring a Collaborative Relationship* 1, 7 (2008), www.apa.org/research/responsible/irbs-psych-science.aspx.

9. Jonathan Moss, *If Institutional Review Boards Were Declared Unconstitutional, They Would Have to Be Reinvented*, NwS 801, 803–804 & 807 (2007).

10. Oakes, 26 Evaluation Review at 461 (cited in note 7).

11. Dean R. Gallant & Alan Bliss, *Qualitative Social Science Research*, in Bankert & Amdur 397 .

12. Oakes, 26 Evaluation Review at 463 (cited in note 7).

13. Roy G. Spece & Jennifer Weinzierl, *First Amendment Protection of Experimentation: A Critical Review and Tentative Synthesis/Reconstruction of the Literature*, 8 Southern California Interdisciplinary Law J 185, 214 (1998).

14. Mazur, *Guide* at ix–x.

15. Drawn from Matt Bradley, *Silenced for Their Own Protection: How the IRB Marginalizes Those It Feigns to Protect*, 6 ACME: An International E-Journal for Critical Geographies 339 (2007).

16. Vincent Blasi, *The Checking Value in First Amendment Theory*, 2 L & Social Inquiry 521, 527 (1977).

17. Ibid at 558.

18. Geoffrey R. Stone, *Autonomy and Distrust*, 64 U Colorado L Rev 1171, 1171 (1993).

19. Daniel P. Tokaji, *First Amendment Equal Protection: On Discretion, Inequality, and Participation*, 101 Michigan L Rev 2409, 2411 (2003).

20. *Police Department of Chicago v. Mosley*, 408 US 98, 95 (1972).

21. *Cox v. Louisiana*, 379 US 536, 557–558 (1964).

22. *Forsyth County v. Nationalist Movement*, 505 US 123, 133 (1991).

23. Vincent Blasi, *A Theory of Prior Restraint: The Central Linkage*, 66 Minnesota L Rev 11 50 (1981).

24. *Freedman v. Maryland*, 380 US 51, 57–58 (1964).

25. Henry P. Monaghan, *First Amendment "Due Process,"* 83 Harvard L Rev 518, 520 (1970).

26. *Bantam Books, Inc. v. Sullivan*, 372 US 58, 66 (1963).

27. Tokaji, 101 Michigan L Rev at 2446 (cited in note 19).

28. Ibid at 2447.

29. Ibid.

30. *Lakewood v. Plain Dealer Publishing*, 486 US 750, 760 (1987).

31. *Bantam*, 372 US at 70 (cited in note 26).

32. *Cox*, 379 US at 557 (cited in note 21).

33. *Near v. Minnesota*, 283 US 697, 713 (1930).

34. Philip Hamburger, *Getting Permission*, NwS 405, 429 (2007).

35. William Blackstone, 4 Commentaries 151–152 (1769).

36. Emerson, *System of Freedom* at 506 (cited in note 3).

37. *Freedman*, 380 US at 57–58 (cited in note 24).

38. Monaghan, 83 Harvard L Rev at 543 (cited in note 25).

39. *Bantam*, 372 US at 69–70 (cited in note 26).

40. Emerson, *System of Freedom* at 506 (cited in note 3).

41. Laurence H. Tribe, *American Constitutional Law* 1059–1061 (Foundation Press, 1988).

42. *United States v. Harriss*, 347 US 612, 617 (1954).

43. *Forsyth*, 505 US at 131 (cited in note 22).

44. *Grayned v. City of Rockford*, 408 US 104, 108–109 (1971).

45. *Lakewood*, 486 US at 757 (cited in note 30).

46. *Keyishian v. Board of Regents*, 385 US 589, 601 (1966).

47. Nathan W. Kellum, *Permit Schemes: Under Current Jurisprudence, What Permits Are Permitted?*, 56 Drake L Rev 381, 390–391 (2008).

48. *Bantam*, 372 US at 66 (cited in note 26).

49. Monaghan, 83 Harvard L Rev at 518–519 (cited in note 25).

50. *Speiser v. Randall*, 357 US 513, 521 (1958).

51. *Schenck v. United States*, 249 US 47, 52 (1919).

52. *Brandenburg v. Ohio*, 395 US 444, 444 (1969).

53. Philip Hamburger, *The New Censorship: Institutional Review Boards*, 2004 Supreme Court Review 271, 312 (2005).

54. Drawn from Joan E. Sieber, *On Studying the Powerful (or Fearing to Do So): A Vital Role for IRBs*, 11 IRB: A Review of Human Subjects Research 1 (1989).

55. David O. Sears, *On Separating Church and Lab*, 5 Psychological Science 237, 239 (1994).

56. Yvonna S. Lincoln & William G. Tierney, *Qualitative Research and Institutional Review Boards*, 10 Qualitative Inquiry 219, 220 (2004).

57. Ibid at 222.

58. *Abrams v. US*, 250 US 616, 630 (dissenting).

59. Alan R. Fleischman et al., *Dealing with the Long Term Social Implications of Research*, Consortium to Examine Clinical Research Ethics 1, 6 (2011).

60. Robert L. Klitzman, *How IRBs View and Make Decisions About Social Risks*, 8 JERHRE 58, 62 (2013) (doi: 10.1525/jer.2013.8.3.58).

61. Gallant & Bliss, *Qualitative Social Science Research* in Bankert and Amdur at 399 (cited in note 11).

62. Ibid at 398.

63. Elisabeth Smith Parrott, *Ethnographic Research* in Bankert & Amdur 404.

64. Robert J. Levine, *Ethics and Regulation of Clinical Research* 53–54 (Yale University Press, 1988) (2nd ed.).

65. Robert J. Amdur, *Evaluating Study Design and Quality*, in Bankert & Amdur 127.

66. John van Maanen, *Tales of the Field: On Writing Ethnography* 11 (University of Chicago Press, 1988).

67. AAUP, *Research on Human Subjects: Academic Freedom and the Institutional Review Board* 1, 2 (2006).

68. Kendra Hamilton, *Finding the 'Right' Research Mix*, Diverse Issues in Higher Education (May 8, 2003), http://diverseeducation.com/article/2941/.

69. Laura Jeanine Morris Stark, *Morality in Science: How Research Is Evaluated in the Age of Human Subjects Regulation* 3 (2006) (Princeton University, Ph.D. Thesis).

70. Patricia A. Adler & Peter Adler, *Do University Lawyers and the Police Define Research Values?*, quoted in Will C. van den Hoonaard, ed., *Walking the Tightrope: Ethical Issues for Qualitative Research* 40 (University of Toronto Press, 2002).

71. Louis Sahagun, *Panel Rejects Study of Casino Benefits*, Los Angeles Times (August 24, 2003).

72. Elizabeth Murphy & Robert Dingwall, *Informed Consent, Anticipatory Regulation and Ethnographic Practice*, 65 SSM 2223, 2229 (2007).

73. Malcolm M. Feeley, *Legality, Social Research, and the Challenge of Institutional Review Boards*, 41 L & Society 757, 765–766 (2007).

74. Ibid at 767.

75. Elvi Whittaker, *Adjudicating Entitlements: The Emerging Discourses of Research Ethics Boards*, 9 Health: An Interdisciplinary J for the Social Study of Health, Illness and Medicine 513, 524 (2005).

76. Christopher Shea, *Don't Talk to the Humans: The Crackdown on Social Science Research*, Lingua Franca 27, 29 (September 2000).

77. Simon N. Whitney et al., *Principal Investigator Views of the IRB System*, 5 Int'l J Medical Sciences 68 (2008).

78. Jeffrey M. Drazen & Julie R. Ingelfinger, *Grants, Politics, and the NIH*, 349 NEJM 2259, 2259 (2003).

79. Robert R. Kuehn, *Suppression of Environmental Science*, 30 American J L & Medicine 333, 349–350 (2004).

80. Herbert L. Needleman, *Salem Comes to the National Institutes of Health: Notes from Inside the Crucible of Scientific Integrity*, 90 Pediatrics 977, 977 (1992).

81. Bruce Rind, *Meta-Analysis, Moral Panic, Congressional Condemnation, and Science: A Personal Journal*, in Donald A. Hantula, ed., *Advances in Social and Organizational Psychology: A Tribute to Ralph Rosnow* 170 (Lawrence Erlbaum, 2006).

82. Ibid at 164.

83. Kenneth J. Sher & Nancy Eisenberg, *Publication of Rind et al. (1998): The Editor's Perspective*, 57 American Psychologist 206, 209 (2002) (doi: 10.1037//003-066X.57.3.206).

84. *Grutter v. Bollinger*, 539 US 306 (2003).

85. *Sweezy v. New Hampshire*, 354 US 234, 250 (1957).

86. Richard M. O'Brien, *The Institutional Review Board Problem: Where It Came from and What to Do About It*, 15 J Social Distress and the Homeless 23, 35 (2006).

87. Will C. van den Hoonaard, *Seduction of Ethics: Transforming the Social Sciences* 167 (University of Toronto Press, 2011).

88. Whittaker, 9 Health at 521–522 (cited in note 75).

89. Moss, *Institutional Review Boards,* at 801(cited in note 9).

90. Ibid at 803.

91. AAUP, *1940 Statement of Principles on Academic Freedom and Tenure.*

92. AAUP, *Appendix A: General Report of the Committee on Academic Freedom and Academic Tenure (1915), General Declarations of Principles*, 53 L & Contemporary Problems 393, 397 (1990).

93. William J. Curran, *Governmental Regulation of the Use of Human Subjects in Medical Research*, 98 Daedalus 542, 574 (1969).

94. IRB *Guidebook*, chapter 1.

95. Levine, *Ethics and Regulation* at 349 (cited in note 64).

96. Cary Nelson, *Can E.T. Call Home? The Brave New World of University Surveillance*, 89 Academe 30 (2003).

97. Whitney et al., 5 International J Medical Sciences at 70 (cited in note 77).

98. Dale Carpenter, *Institutional Review Boards, Regulatory Incentives, and Some Modest Proposals for Reform*, NwS 687, 693 (2007).

99. Amdur, *Handbook* at 37.

100. *Rust v. Sullivan*, 500 US 173, 200 (1991).

101. Feeley, 41 L & Society at 765–766 (cited in note 73).

102. OHRP, *Guidebook*, chapter 3A.

103. NRC & IOM, *Ethical Considerations for Research on Housing-Related Health Hazards Involving Children* 10 (NAP, 2005).

104. Gallant & Bliss, *Qualitative Social Science Research* in Bankert and Amdur at 399 (cited in note 11).

105. *Forsyth*, 505 US at 134–135 (cited in note 22).

106. Howard S. Becker, *Sociological Work* 113 (Transaction, 1976).

107. NRC & IOM, *Ethical Considerations* at 85 (cited in note 103).

108. Ibid at 84.

109. Ibid at 78.

CONCLUSION

1. Edmund Burke, *On Conciliation with the Colonies*.

2. Zachary M. Schrag, *Ethical Imperialism: Institutional Review Boards and the Social Sciences, 1965–2009* 9 (Johns Hopkins University Press, 2010).

3. Ithiel de Sola Pool, *The New Censorship of Social Research*, 59 Public Interest 57, 57 (1980).

4. Todd J. Zywicki, *Institutional Review Boards as Academic Bureaucracies: An Economic and Experiential Analysis*, NwS 861, 881 (2007).

5. David Hyman, *Institutional Review Boards: Is This the Least Worst We Can Do?*, NwS 749, 761 n67 (2007).

6. Julianne B. Bochinski, *The Complete Workbook for Science Fair Projects* 53–54 (John Wiley, 2005).

7. See, e.g., Benjamin Ginsberg, *The Fall of the Faculty: The Rise of the All-Administrative University and Why It Matters* (Oxford University Press, 2011); Mary Burgan, *What Ever Happened to the Faculty?: Drift and Decision in Higher Education* (Johns Hopkins University Press, 2006).

8. Schrag, *Ethical Imperialism* at 139 (cited in note 2).

9. Nancy M. P. King & Ana S. Iltis, Comments on ANPRM Human Subjects Research Protections. HHS-OPHS-2011–0005–0257.

10. Will C. van den Hoonaard, *Seduction of Ethics: Transforming the Social Sciences* 47 (University of Toronto Press, 2011).

11. Ibid at 8.

12. Elmer D. Abbo, *Promoting Free Speech in Clinical Quality Improvement Research*, NwS 575, 578 (2007).

13. John H. Mueller, *Best Practices: What Perspective, What Evidence?*, 15 J Social Distress & Homeless 13, 17 (2006).

14. Monika Pogorzelska et al., *Changes in the Institutional Review Board Submission Process for Multicenter Research Over 6 Years*, 58 Nursing Outlook 181, 183 (2010) (doi: 10.1016/j.outlook.2010.04.003).

15. NRC & IOM, *Ethical Considerations for Research on Housing-Related Health Hazards Involving Children* 10 (NAP, 2005).

16. Van den Hoonaard, *Seduction of Ethics* at 110 (cited in note 10).

17. Dale H. Cowan, *Human Experimentation: The Review Process in Practice*, 25 Case Western Reserve L Rev 533, 550 (1974).

18. Illinois Center for Advanced Study, *Improving the System for Protecting Human Subjects: Counteracting IRB "Mission Creep"* 1, 4 (2005).

19. Scott Burris, *Regulatory Innovation in the Governance of Human Subjects Research: A Cautionary Tale and Some Modest Proposals*, 2 Regulation & Governance 65, 69 (2008).

20. Elvi Whittaker, *Adjudicating Entitlements: The Emerging Discourses of Research Ethics Boards*, 9 Health 513, 519 (2005).

21. Mazur, *Guide* at 174.

22. Cowan, 25 Case Western Reserve L Rev at 554 (cited in note 17).

23. Ibid at 561.

24. Norman Fost & Robert J. Levine, *The Dysregulation of Human Subjects Research*, 298 JAMA 2196, 2196 (2007).

25. Helen McGough, *Support Staff*, in Bankert & Amdur 48.

26. IOM, *Responsible Research: A Systems Approach to Protecting Research Participants* 47 (NAP, 2003) (footnotes omitted).

27. NBAC, *Ethical and Policy Issues in Research Involving Human Participants: Report and Recommendations* vi (2001).

28. Department of Health & Human Services, ANPRM, 45 CFR Parts 46, 160, and 164, 44512–44531 (2011).

29. Whittaker, 9 Health at 519 (cited in note 20).

30. Sheelagh McGuinness, *Research Ethics Committees: The Role of Ethics in a Regulatory Authority*, 34 J Medical Ethics 695, 696 (2007) (doi: 10.1136/jme.2007.021089).

31. Stacy W. Gray et al., *Attitudes Toward Research Participation and Investigator Conflicts of Interest Among Advanced Cancer Patients Participating in Early Phase Clinical Trials*, 25 J Clinical Oncology 3488, 3492 (2007) (doi: 10.1200/JCO.2007.11.7283).

32. Van den Hoonaard, *Seduction of Ethics* at 137 (cited in note 10).

33. Nancy Shore et al., *Understanding Community-Based Processes for Research Ethics Review: A National Study*, 101 American J Public Health e1, e5 (2010).

34. Carol A. Heimer & JuLeigh Petty, *Bureaucratic Ethics: IRBs and the Legal Regulation of Human Subjects Research*, 6 Annual Review of Law & Social Science 601, 605 (2010) (doi: 10.1146/annurev.lawsocsci.annual reviews.org).

35. Zachary M. Schrag, *How Talking Became Human Subjects Research: The Federal Regulation of the Social Sciences, 1965–1991*, 21 J Policy History 3, 29 (2009).

36. Ibid at 38.

37. Ibid at 12.

38. Ibid at 76.

39. Ibid at 77.

40. Ibid at 79.

41. Ibid at 85–86.

42. Ibid at 20.

43. Ibid at 20.

44. Ibid at 21.

45. Howard S. Becker, *Comment on Kevin D. Haggerty, "Ethics Creep: Governing Social Science Research in the Name of Ethics,"* 7 Qualitative Sociology 415, 415 (2004).

46. Zywicki, NwS at 882 (cited in note 4).

47. Heimer & Petty, 6 Annual Review of Law & Social Science at 620 (cited in note 34).

48. McGough, *Support Staff*, in Bankert & Amdur at 48 (cited in note 25).

49. Susan J. Delano et al., *Certification of Institutional Review Board Professionals*, in Bankert & Amdur 322.

50. Van den Hoonaard, *Seduction of Ethics* at 285 (cited in note 10).

51. Carl Elliott, *When Medical Muckraking Fails*, Chronicle of Higher Education, August 2, 2012.

52. Upton Sinclair, Jr., *I, Candidate for Governor: And How I Got Licked* 109 (1935, reprinted University of California Press, 1994).

53. Howard S. Becker, *Moral Entrepreneurs: The Creation and Enforcement of Deviant Categories*, in Delos H. Kelly, *Deviant Behavior: Readings in the Sociology of Deviance* 13 (St. Martin's, 1979).

54. Will C. van den Hoonaard, *Is Research-Ethics Review a Moral Panic?*, 38 Canadian Review of Sociology & Anthropology 19, 25 (2001).

55. Ibid at 32.

56. Daniel Kahneman, *Thinking, Fast and Slow* 215–217 (Farrar, Straus & Giroux, 2011).

57. Daniel R. Vasgird, *Resisting Power and Influence: A Case Study in Virtue Ethics*, 1 JERHRE 19, 21 (2006).

58. Burris, 2 Regulation & Governance at 68 (cited in note 19).

59. Carol A. Heimer et al., *Risk and Rules: The 'Legalization' of Medicine*, in Bridget Hutter & Michael Power, eds., *Organizational Encounters with Risk* 120–121 (Cambridge University Press, 2005).

60. Schrag, *Ethical Imperialism* at 2 (cited in note 2).

61. See, e.g., *Diaz v. Hillsboro County Hospital Authority*, 2000 U.S. Dist. LEXIS 14061 (August 7, 2000).

62. 782 A2d 807 (Md 2001).

63. See Carl E. Schneider, *Craft and Power*, 28 HCR 9 (Jan/Feb 1998).

64. See Margaret H. Lemos, *Special Incentives to Sue*, 95 Minnesota L Rev 782 (2011).

65. David P. McCaffrey & David W. Hart, *Wall Street Polices Itself: How Securities Firms Manage the Legal Hazards of Competitive Pressures* 58 (Oxford University Press, 1998).

66. Jeneen Interlandi, *Unwelcome Discovery*, New York Times Magazine (October 22, 2006).

67. Walter Lippmann, *A Preface to Morals* 276–277 (The Macmillan Company, 1929).

68. Tom Tyler & Lindsay Rankin, *The Mystique of Instrumentalism*, in Jon Hanson, *Ideology, Psychology, and Law* 537 (Oxford U Press, 2012).

69. Tom R. Tyler, *Legitimacy and Criminal Justice: The Benefits of Self-Regulation*, 7 Ohio State J Criminal Law 307, 326 (2009).

70. Ibid.

71. Ibid at 319.

72. Richard B. Stewart, *Administrative Law in the Twenty-First Century*, 78 NYU L Rev 437, 446 (2003).

73. Ibid at 450.

74. Tom R. Tyler, *Self-Regulatory Approaches to White-Collar Crime: The Importance of Legitimacy and Procedural Justice*, in S.S Simpson & D. Weisburd, *The Criminology of White-Collar Crime* 205 (Springer Science & Business Media, LLC, 2009).]

75. Zachary M. Schrag, *Ethical Imperialism: Institutional Review Boards and the Social Sciences, 1965-2009*, 23 (John Hopkins University Press, 2010).

76. Ibid at 20.

77. Ibid at 25.

78. Ibid at 31.

79. NRC & IOM, *Ethical Considerations* at 8 (cited in note 15).

80. Philip Pettit, *Rules, Reasons, and Norms: Selected Essays* 396 (Clarendon, 2003). See my discussion in the due process section.

81. Sydney A. Halpern, *Lesser Harms: The Morality of Risk in Medical Research* 132 (University of Chicago Press, 2004).

82. Ibid at 139.

83. Richard S. Saver, *Medical Research Oversight from the Corporate Governance Perspective: Comparing Institutional Review Boards and Corporate Boards*, 46 William & Mary L Rev 619, 720 (2004).

84. Halpern, *Lesser Harms* at 42–43 (cited in note 81).

85. Thomas L. Haskell, *The New Aristocracy*, New York Review of Books 47, 52 (December 4, 1997).

86. Thorstein Veblen, *The Theory of the Leisure Class* 30 (Modern Library, 1899).

87. Halpern, *Lesser Harms* at 42 (cited in note 81).

88. Ibid at 91.

89. See, e.g., H. Gil Rushton, *Institutional Review Board Approval—More Red Tape or a Step in the Right Direction?*, 180 J Urology 804 (2008).

90. E.g., S. Schroter et al., *Reporting Ethics Committee Approval and Patient Consent to Study Design in Five General Medical Journals*, 32 J Medical Ethics 718 (2006).

91. Joan E. Sieber, *Using Our Best Judgment in Conducting Human Research*, 14 Ethics & Behavior 297, 298 (2004).

92. Halpern, *Lesser Harms* at 3 (cited in note 81).

93. Schrag, *Ethical Imperialism* at 6 (cited in note 2).

94. Heimer et al., *Risk and Rules* at 120 (cited in note 59).

95. Philip Hamburger, *The New Censorship: Institutional Review Boards*, 2004 Supreme Court Rev 271, 338–339 (2005).

96. Scott Burris & Kathryn Moss, *U.S. Health Researchers Review Their Ethics Review Boards: A Qualitative Study*, 1 JERHRE 39, 50 (2006).

97. Robert J. Levine, *Ethics and Regulation of Clinical Research* 40 (Yale University Press, 1988).

98. Heimer et al., *Risk and Rules* at 120 (cited in note 59).

Index

Basic Bioethics
Arthur Caplan, editor

BOOKS ACQUIRED UNDER THE EDITORSHIP OF GLENN
MCGEE AND ARTHUR CAPLAN

Peter A. Ubel, *Pricing Life: Why It's Time for Health Care Rationing*

Mark G. Kuczewski and Ronald Polansky, eds., *Bioethics: Ancient Themes in Contemporary Issues*

Suzanne Holland, Karen Lebacqz, and Laurie Zoloth, eds., *The Human Embryonic Stem Cell Debate: Science, Ethics, and Public Policy*

Gita Sen, Asha George, and Piroska Östlin, eds., *Engendering International Health: The Challenge of Equity*

Carolyn McLeod, *Self-Trust and Reproductive Autonomy*

Lenny Moss, *What Genes Can't Do*

Jonathan D. Moreno, ed., *In the Wake of Terror: Medicine and Morality in a Time of Crisis*

Glenn McGee, ed., *Pragmatic Bioethics, second edition*

Timothy F. Murphy, *Case Studies in Biomedical Research Ethics*

Mark A. Rothstein, ed., *Genetics and Life Insurance: Medical Underwriting and Social Policy*

Kenneth A. Richman, *Ethics and the Metaphysics of Medicine: Reflections on Health and Beneficence*

David Lazer, ed., *DNA and the Criminal Justice System: The Technology of Justice*

Harold W. Baillie and Timothy K. Casey, eds., *Is Human Nature Obsolete? Genetics, Bioengineering, and the Future of the Human Condition*

Robert H. Blank and Janna C. Merrick, eds., *End-of-Life Decision Making: A Cross-National Study*

Norman L. Cantor, *Making Medical Decisions for the Profoundly Mentally Disabled*

Margrit Shildrick and Roxanne Mykitiuk, eds., *Ethics of the Body: Post-Conventional Challenges*

Alfred I. Tauber, *Patient Autonomy and the Ethics of Responsibility*

David H. Brendel, *Healing Psychiatry: Bridging the Science/Humanism Divide*

Jonathan Baron, *Against Bioethics*

Michael L. Gross, *Bioethics and Armed Conflict: Moral Dilemmas of Medicine and War*

Karen F. Greif and Jon F. Merz, *Current Controversies in the Biological Sciences: Case Studies of Policy Challenges from New Technologies*

Deborah Blizzard, *Looking Within: A Sociocultural Examination of Fetoscopy*

Ronald Cole-Turner, ed., *Design and Destiny: Jewish and Christian Perspectives on Human Germline Modification*

Holly Fernandez Lynch, *Conflicts of Conscience in Health Care: An Institutional Compromise*

Mark A. Bedau and Emily C. Parke, eds., *The Ethics of Protocells: Moral and Social Implications of Creating Life in the Laboratory*

Jonathan D. Moreno and Sam Berger, eds., *Progress in Bioethics: Science, Policy, and Politics*

Eric Racine, *Pragmatic Neuroethics: Improving Understanding and Treatment of the Mind-Brain*

Martha J. Farah, ed., *Neuroethics: An Introduction with Readings*

Jeremy R. Garrett, ed., *The Ethics of Animal Research: Exploring the Controversy*

BOOKS ACQUIRED UNDER THE EDITORSHIP OF ARTHUR CAPLAN

Sheila Jasanoff, ed., *Reframing Rights: Bioconstitutionalism in the Genetic Age*

Christine Overall, *Why Have Children? The Ethical Debate*

Yechiel Michael Barilan, *Human Dignity, Human Rights, and Responsibility: The New Language of Global Bioethics and Bio-Law*

Tom Koch, *Thieves of Virtue: When Bioethics Stole Medicine*

Timothy F. Murphy, *Ethics, Sexual Orientation, and Choices about Children*

Daniel Callahan, *In Search of the Good: A Life in Bioethics*

Robert Blank, *Intervention in the Brain: Politics, Policy, and Ethics*

Gregory E. Kaebnick and Thomas H. Murray, eds.,

Synthetic Biology and Morality: Artificial Life and the Bounds of Nature

Dominic A. Sisti, Arthur L. Caplan, and Hila Rimon-Greenspan, eds., *Applied Ethics in Mental Healthcare: An Interdisciplinary Reader*

Barbara K. Redman, *Research Misconduct Policy in Biomedicine: Beyond the Bad-Apple Approach*

Russell Blackford, *Humanity Enhanced: Genetic Choice and the Challenge for Liberal Democracies*

Nicholas Agar, *Truly Human Enhancement: A Philosophical Defense of Limits*

Bruno Perreau, *The Politics of Adoption: Gender and the Making of French Citizenship*

Carl E. Schneider, *The Censor's Hand: The Misregulation of Human-Subject Research*